Understanding
the
HOLOCAUST

Understanding the HOLOCAUST

VOLUME 1

GEORGE FELDMAN

DETROIT • LONDON

Understanding the
HOLOCAUST

by George Feldman

Staff

Julie L. Carnagie, *U·X·L Developmental Editor*
Sonia Benson, Senior *U·X·L Developmental Editor*
Carol DeKane Nagel, *U·X·L Managing Editor*
Thomas L. Romig, *U·X·L Publisher*

Mary Beth Trimper, *Production Director*
Evi Seoud, *Production Manager*
Shanna P. Heilveil, *Production Associate*

Cynthia Baldwin, *Product Design Manager*
Barbara J. Yarrow, *Graphic Services Supervisor*
Tracey Rowens, *Art Director*

Margaret A. Chamberlain, *Permissions Specialist*

Library of Congress Cataloging-in-Publication Data

Feldman, George.
    Understanding the Holocaust / Feorge Feldman
       p.   cm.
    Includes bibliographical references and index.
    ISBN 0-7876-1740-7 (set). — 0-7876-1741-5 (v. 1.) — 0-7876-1742-3 (v. 2)
    1. Holocaust, Jewish (1939-1945)--Causes. 2. Germany—Politics and government—
1933-1945. 3. Germany—History—1933-1945. 4. National socialism.   I. Title.

    D804.3.F46 1998
    940.53'18—dc21

                                     97-26864
                                       CIP AC

Printed in the United States of America
10 9 8 7 6 5 4 3 2 1

To my father, Benjamin, who fought in the French Army against the Nazis and escaped to hide,

To my mother, Sonia, who lived in hiding in Limoges,

To my sister, Renée, who was born in hiding, and who looks, in old pictures, like the children who disappeared,

To my uncle Boris, who fought in the French Army against the Nazis, was captured, and spent five years as a prisoner of war,

To my aunt Lisa, his wife, who was arrested by the French police and sent to Bergen-Belsen, and came back,

To their sons, my cousins Toli and Mara, who went with her and came back,

And to my daughter, Nina, who will never have to go.

"And you shall not oppress an outsider, for you know the heart of an outsider because you were outsiders in the land of Egypt."

Exodus, Ch. 23, 9.

Contents

Advisory Board ix

Reader's Guide xi

Author's Note:
Jewish Victims of the Holocaust
by Country of Origin xiii

Timeline xix

Words to Know xxvii

Volume 1

CHAPTER 1:
GERMANY AND THE JEWISH PEOPLE
BEFORE THE HOLOCAUST 1

CHAPTER 2:
THE RISE OF THE NAZI PARTY 24

CHAPTER 3:
THE NAZI ATTACK ON THE JEWS 60

CHAPTER 4:
THE NAZI GOVERNMENT AND
THE ROAD TO WAR 89

CHAPTER 5:
THE JEWS OF POLAND: SETTING THE
STAGE FOR DESTRUCTION 115

CHAPTER 6:
THE WARSAW GHETTO 143

CHAPTER 7: THE BEGINNING OF GENOCIDE:
THE INVASION OF RUSSIA 177

Where to Learn More xxxvii

Picture Credits lvii

Index lxi

Volume 2

CHAPTER 8:
THE DEATH CAMPS 213

CHAPTER 9:
AUSCHWITZ 239

CHAPTER 10:
LIFE AND DEATH IN NAZI-DOMINATED
EUROPE: DENMARK AND
THE NETHERLANDS 284

CHAPTER 11:
LIFE AND DEATH IN NAZI-DOMINATED
EUROPE: FRANCE 310

CHAPTER 12:
GERMANY'S ALLIES AND THE JEWS:
ITALY AND HUNGARY 334

CHAPTER 13:
JUDGMENTS 350

CHAPTER 14:
REMEMBERING THE HOLOCAUST 381

Where to Learn More xxxvii

Picture Credits lvii

Index lxi

Advisory Board

HOLOCAUST

S pecial thanks are due for the invaluable comments and suggestions provided by U•X•L's Holocaust Reference Library advisors:

Jonathan Betz-Zall, Children's Librarian, Sno-Isle Regional Library Systems, Edmonds, Washington

Sydney Bolkosky, Professor of History, University of Michigan-Dearborn, Dearborn, Michigan

Linda Hurwitz, Director, The Holocaust Center of Greater Pittsburgh, Pennsylvania

Debra Lyman Gniewek, Library Services Coordinator, Office of Information Technology, School District of Philadelphia, Pennsylvania

Max Weitz, Director, Holocaust Resource Center of Minneapolis, Minnesota

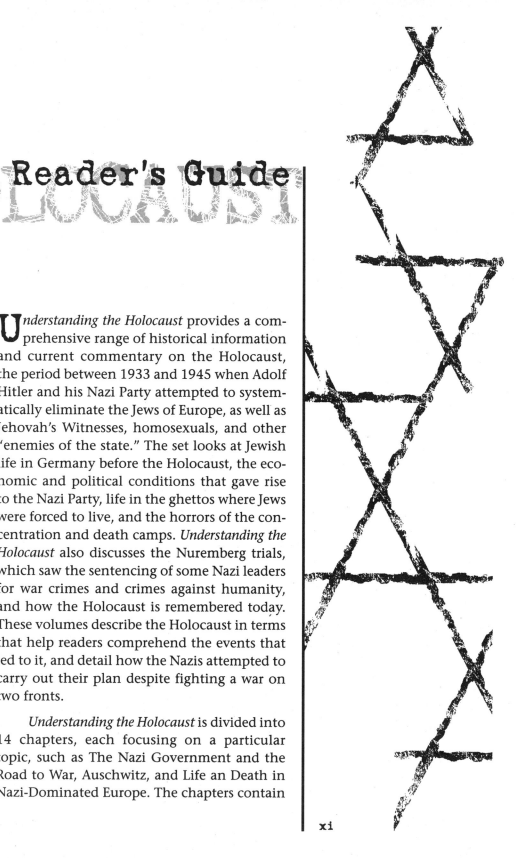

Reader's Guide

Understanding the Holocaust provides a comprehensive range of historical information and current commentary on the Holocaust, the period between 1933 and 1945 when Adolf Hitler and his Nazi Party attempted to systematically eliminate the Jews of Europe, as well as Jehovah's Witnesses, homosexuals, and other "enemies of the state." The set looks at Jewish life in Germany before the Holocaust, the economic and political conditions that gave rise to the Nazi Party, life in the ghettos where Jews were forced to live, and the horrors of the concentration and death camps. Understanding the Holocaust also discusses the Nuremberg trials, which saw the sentencing of some Nazi leaders for war crimes and crimes against humanity, and how the Holocaust is remembered today. These volumes describe the Holocaust in terms that help readers comprehend the events that led to it, and detail how the Nazis attempted to carry out their plan despite fighting a war on two fronts.

Understanding the Holocaust is divided into 14 chapters, each focusing on a particular topic, such as The Nazi Government and the Road to War, Auschwitz, and Life an Death in Nazi-Dominated Europe. The chapters contain numerous sidebar boxes, some focusing on people associated with the Holocaust, others taking a closer look at pivotal events. More than 120 black-and-white illustrations help to explain the text. Each volume also contains a timeline, a glossary of terms used throughout the text, an annotated bibliography of sources for further reading, and a cumulative subject index of the names, places, subjects, and terms discussed throughout *Understanding the Holocaust.*

Comments and Suggestions

We welcome your comments on *Understanding the Holocaust* and suggestions for other topics in history to consider. Please write: Editors, *Understanding the Holocaust*, U•X•L, 835 Penobscot Bldg., Detroit, Michigan 48226-4094; call toll free: 1-800-877-4253; or fax: 313-961-6347.

Author's Note:
Jewish Victims of the Holocaust by Country of Origin

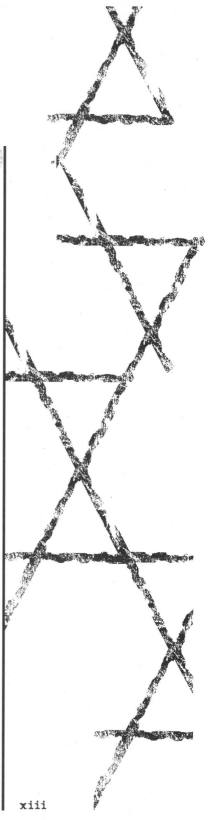

The number of Jews killed in the Holocaust is usually given as approximately 6,000,000. Although this figure was based on estimates made soon after World War II (1939–45), it has turned out to be quite accurate.

As early as April 1946, the Anglo-American Committee of Inquiry Regarding the Problems of European Jewry and Palestine reached the conclusion that 5,721,500 Jews were killed by the Nazis and their accomplices. The historian Raoul Hilberg, in his 1961 book *The Destruction of the European Jews,* gave the figures of 5,397,500 based on an estimate of the number of survivors, and of 5,100,000 based on estimates of the number of victims. Lucy S. Dawidowicz, in her 1975 book *The War Against the Jews, 1933–1945,* comes to a total of 5,933,900. In his 1982 study, *A History of the Holocaust,* Yehuda Bauer cites a figure of 5,820,960. This is very close to the total given in the chart on p. xvii, although Bauer's numbers for various countries are different than the ones used in *Understanding the Holocaust.*

There are several reasons why it is impossible to give exact figures for the number of Jews killed in the Holocaust from each country. In some countries, especially in eastern

Europe, it is not certain how many Jews there were before World War II. Many of these countries had incomplete and inaccurate records of population figures in general, not just of Jews. In addition, there is a problem in these statistics with who was considered a Jew. The Nazis defined Jews according to "race," considering anyone with Jewish ancestors to be Jewish. But Jews who had converted to Christianity, or whose parents had converted (for example in Hungary), did not consider themselves Jews. Jews who did not practice any religion (for example in urban areas of the Soviet Union) may also not have considered themselves Jews.

A second big problem with trying to determine correct figures is that statistics on the number of people killed is not accurate. Again, this is especially true in eastern Europe, specifically the Soviet Union (Russia). Relatively few Jews in western Europe were killed in their home countries. Most were arrested and deported. Because of this, there are usually records of their arrests and arrivals at transit camps, transportation by trains, and sometimes their arrivals at the place where they were killed, such as Auschwitz.

But in the Soviet Union, including areas that had been part of Poland, hundreds of thousands of people were shot within a few miles of their homes. Although the *Einsatzgruppen,* the mobile death squads that were responsible for most of these shootings, sent reports of their activities, these records are obviously not always accurate. In addition, other units—German police, army, and Waffen-SS troops, Romanian and Hungarian police and soldiers—also played a major role in these killings. So did auxiliary troops of the local population, such as in Lithuania and Ukraine. Many of the murders in the Soviet Union took place in the first weeks after the German invasion, when conditions were chaotic. It is often impossible to know, in each town, how many Jews fled eastward with the retreating Soviet army and how many stayed behind and were killed by the Nazis. Part of this difficulty can be overcome by counting survivors, rather than victims, and scholars and historians have tried to do this. This is one reason why experts now agree on the approximate number of Jews killed in the Soviet-Polish area, even though the number killed in any particular place may be uncertain.

Another example of the uncertainty of the statistics is that the figure for those killed at Auschwitz was originally estimated at around 4,000,000, while scholars now believe the number was closer to a 1,500,000. But the vast number of people killed at the Treblinka, Sobibór, and Belzec death camps was not known after the war, and the scale of shootings by the *Einsatzgruppen* was underestimated.

A third major difficulty in determining the number of victims of the Holocaust involves the many border changes that occurred in Europe from 1938 through the years of the war. Hundreds of thousands of Jews who had been Polish citizens until 1939 came under Soviet jurisdiction in that year. Many of them were killed beginning in the summer of 1941, when Germany invaded the Soviet Union. Sometimes they are counted as Polish Jews, sometimes as Soviet. In some lists, some of them have probably not been counted at all, and in other lists, some of them may have been counted twice. One example of an area with a large Jewish population may illustrate these problems. Until 1939, the city of Vilna was part of Poland. Then it became part of Lithuania, which soon became part of the Soviet Union, and then, in June 1941, was invaded and occupied by Germany. In addition, Jews from other parts of Poland fled to Vilna between 1939 and 1941 to escape the Germans. It is not always clear whether these victims have been counted as Polish, Lithuanian, or Soviet Jews.

The same problems exist in other parts of Europe. Greek and Yugoslav Jews found they were now in Bulgaria. Austria became part of the German Reich as did parts of France and Poland. A section of Czechoslovakia (the Sudetenland) became part of Germany in 1938, while other areas were given to Hungary and Poland. The next year, the remaining Czech lands (Bohemia and Moravia) became a "protectorate" of Germany, and Slovakia became a separate country. Croatia became a separate country in 1941. About 150,000 Romanian Jews, and smaller numbers of Slovakian and Yugoslav Jews, lived in areas that became part of Hungary. Large numbers of Romanian Jews lived in a territory that was part of the Soviet Union between July 1940 and July 1941. Dawidowicz treats them as Romanians, and estimates the number of Romanian Jews killed as 300,000. But Bauer includes them with Soviet Jews, and his total for Romania is 40,000. Although some of these problems do not greatly affect an accurate estimate of the total number of victims, they do affect the accuracy of the number that is listed for each country.

The same is true of refugees. For example, there were over 500,000 Jews in Germany in 1933 when Adolf Hitler came to power. Several hundred thousand German Jews moved to other countries in Europe between 1933 and 1939. Most of these refugees were killed when the Nazis occupied their new countries. For example, around 30,000 were killed in the Netherlands alone. They are counted as Dutch Jews in most lists of victims, but this gives an unrealistic picture of the number of German Jewish victims. (In addition, thousands of German Jews were killed by the Nazis *before* the Holocaust. These are usually omitted from all lists.)

Keeping all these issues in mind, the following list of the number of people killed during the Holocaust cannot be perfectly accurate. However, it is based on the best recent estimates concerning each country. The numbers for Poland and the Soviet Union are the least certain. The numbers for the countries of western and northern Europe are the most exact. Except where otherwise noted, the totals refer to the September 1939 borders.

Country or Area	Number Killed
Austria	50,000

(1937 borders; does not include refugees who
resettled in other countries and were later killed.)

Belgium	29,000
Bulgaria	———

(Includes only "Old Bulgaria"; approximately
14,000 Jews killed from areas that had been part
of Greece [Thrace] and Yugoslavia [Macedonia].)

Czech lands	78,000

("Reich Protectorate of Bohemia and Moravia")

Denmark	100
Estonia	1,700
France	77,000
Germany	135,000

(1937 borders plus Sudetenland; does not include
Austria or refugees who resettled in other countries
and were later killed.)

Greece	64,000
Hungary	550,000

(Includes territory added from Czechoslovakia,
Romania, and Yugoslavia beginning in 1938.)

Italy	7,700
Latvia	70,000
Lithuania	140,000
Luxembourg	2,000
Netherlands	105,000
Norway	750
Poland	3,000,000

(August 1939 borders, includes territory
taken by Soviet Union in September 1939.)

Romania	280,000

(Does not include territory that became part of
Hungary, but includes territory that Romania ceded to
the Soviet Union from July 1940 until reoccupied by
Romanian troops the following summer.)

Slovakia	70,000
Soviet Union	1,100,000

(Does not include territory added from Poland
in 1939 or Estonia, Latvia, and Lithuania.)

Yugoslavia	60,000

Total for Nazi-controlled Europe	5,820,250

HOLOCAUST Timeline

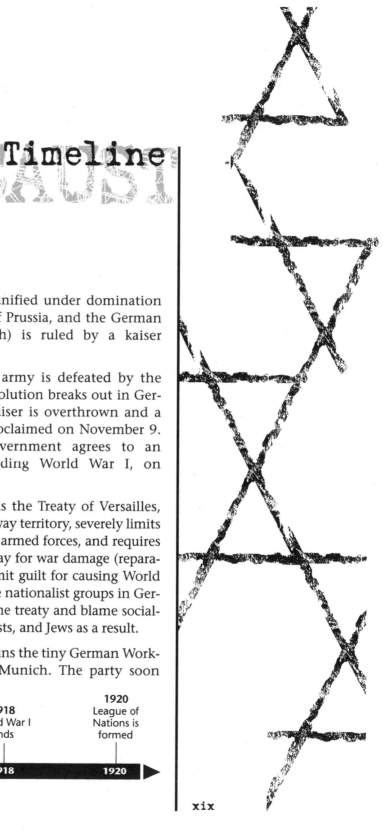

1871 Germany is unified under domination of the state of Prussia, and the German empire (Reich) is ruled by a kaiser (emperor).

1918 The German army is defeated by the Allies and revolution breaks out in Germany. The kaiser is overthrown and a republic is proclaimed on November 9. The new government agrees to an armistice, ending World War I, on November 11.

1919 Germany signs the Treaty of Versailles, which takes away territory, severely limits the size of the armed forces, and requires Germany to pay for war damage (reparations) and admit guilt for causing World War I. Extreme nationalist groups in Germany resent the treaty and blame socialists, communists, and Jews as a result.

1919 Adolf Hitler joins the tiny German Workers' Party in Munich. The party soon

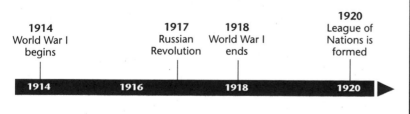

1914 World War I begins		1917 Russian Revolution	1918 World War I ends	1920 League of Nations is formed
1914	1916		1918	1920

changes its name to National Socialist German Workers' Party (NSDAP), called Nazi Party for short.

1922 Benito Mussolini and his Fascist Party march on Rome, then establish a dictatorship in Italy that becomes a model for Hitler.

1923 Adolf Hitler is in charge of the Beer Hall Putsch in Munich, the Nazis' attempt to take over the country. Police end the rebellion with gunfire, killing sixteen Nazis, injuring others, and arresting Hitler and other Nazi leaders.

1924 Hitler is sentenced to five years in prison for the Beer Hall Putsch, but serves only eight months, using the time to dictate *Mein Kampf* ("My Struggle"), which becomes the Nazi "bible."

1928 The Nazi Party receives about 800,000 votes in national elections, 2.6 percent of the total.

1930 The Nazis receive almost 6,500,000 votes in national elections and become the second-largest party in the Reichstag (German parliament.) As campaign tactics, storm troopers (SA or brownshirts), the military wing of the Nazi Party, attack opponents, break up meetings, and intimidate Jews.

1932 Although Hitler receives 11,000,000 votes in the first round of elections for German president, and over 13,000,000 million, almost 37 percent, in the second round, Paul von Hindenburg, the aged military hero of World War I, is reelected president. The Nazi storm troopers are briefly banned because of their increased violence during the campaign.

1933 Hitler becomes chancellor of Germany on January 30, but most of the government is made up of old-line conservatives who believe they can use and control the Nazis.

1925
The Scopes
"Monkey Trial"

1927
Charles Limbergh
completes first nonstop
solo transatlantic flight

1929
Great Depression
begins; it ends
in 1939

| 1925 | 1926 | 1927 | 1928 | 1929 |

1933 The Reichstag building is set on fire on February 27, and Hitler receives emergency powers from Hindenburg. Using police powers, storm troopers arrest 10,000 opponents of the Nazis, especially Communists, and send them to newly established concentration camps.

1933 The new Reichstag meets without Communist members who have been arrested or are in hiding. The Nazis and their allies win support from the Catholic parties and pass the "Enabling Act," giving Hitler dictatorial powers.

1933 The Nazis organize a national boycott of Jewish-owned businesses, and the first anti-Jewish laws are passed, removing almost all Jews from government jobs, including teaching. Further laws follow, and 53,000 Jews leave Germany during 1933.

1933 German labor unions are abolished and are replaced by the "German Labor Front," run by the Nazis. The Social Democratic Party (the largest party before the Nazi rise) is outlawed, then are all other parties. The Nazis conduct public book-burnings of works written by Jews and anti-Nazis.

1934 Hitler orders the murder of Ernst Röhm and other leaders of the SA (storm troopers), whom the German army fears as possible rivals, in what has become known as the "Night of Long Knives," June 30.

1934 Upon Hindenburg's death, Hitler combines the office of chancellor and president. Hitler is now the Führer (leader) of the Third Reich (Empire) with absolute powers.

1935 The German army enters the Rhineland, the area of western Germany that had been demilitarized by the Treaty of Versailles.

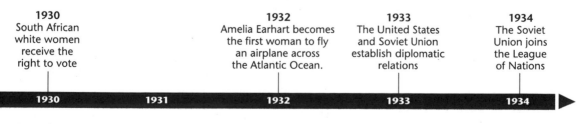

1930		1932	1933	1934
South African white women receive the right to vote		Amelia Earhart becomes the first woman to fly an airplane across the Atlantic Ocean.	The United States and Soviet Union establish diplomatic relations	The Soviet Union joins the League of Nations
1930	**1931**	**1932**	**1933**	**1934**

1935 The Nuremberg laws, followed by official decrees, define Jews in racial terms, strip them of German citizenship, and ban their marrying non-Jews.

1936 Buchenwald concentration camp is established.

1936 Hitler and the Nazis ease anti-Jewish actions as a result of the Olympic Games being held in Berlin, Germany's capital.

1936 Germany and Italy enter into agreements that develop into the "Rome-Berlin Axis," a political and military alliance of the two countries.

1938 German army moves into Austria, uniting the two countries in the *Anschluss*. Antisemitic laws are rapidly applied to Austria.

1938 An international conference is held in Evian, France, regarding the problems of Jewish refugees in Europe. Nothing is done to resolve the crisis.

1938 At a Munich conference, leaders of France and Britain agree to give Germany a section of Czechoslovakia that contains a large German minority.

1938 In Paris, Hershel Grynszpan, a young Jew, shoots and kills Ernst vom Rath, an official at the German embassy. Grynszpan's actions spark *Kristallnacht* ("Crystal Night"), the organized Nazi attacks throughout Germany in which Jews are beaten, synagogues are burned, Jewish businesses are destroyed, and 30,000 Jewish men are arrested and sent to concentration camps.

1939 Hitler violates the Munich agreement by destroying the remainder of Czechoslovakia and implements anti-Jewish measures.

1939 Nazi Germany and the Soviet Union sign the Nazi-Soviet Pact, in which the two countries promise not to attack each other and secretly agree to divide Poland.

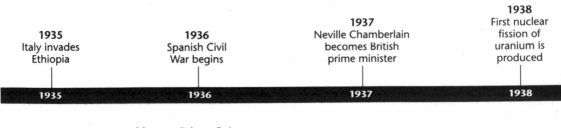

1935
Italy invades
Ethiopia

1936
Spanish Civil
War begins

1937
Neville Chamberlain
becomes British
prime minister

1938
First nuclear
fission of
uranium is
produced

| 1935 | 1936 | 1937 | 1938 |

1939 World War II begins when Germany invades Poland on September 1, and Britain and France retaliate by declaring war on Germany two days later.

1939 Beginning of the Nazi "euthanasia" ("mercy killing") program, in which 70,000 mentally and physically handicapped Germans, including children, are murdered.

1939 Reinhard Heydrich, second in command of the SS, the Nazi Party' military wing, issues an order for the concentration of all Polish Jews into large ghettos as the first step towards the unnamed "final aim."

1939 Jews in German-occupied Poland are ordered to wear a yellow star (the Star of David) at all times.

1940 Heinrich Himmler, head of the SS, orders the building of a concentration camp at Auschwitz in occupied Poland.

1940 French troops evacuate Paris on June 13, and German forces enter the city the next day. France signs an armistice with Germany, and German troops occupy northern France, while a government friendly to Germany (Vichy France) has some independence in the south. Anti-Jewish measures soon begin in western European countries controlled by Germany.

1940 The Warsaw ghetto in Poland is sealed and about 450,000 Jews are confined within its walls.

1941 Germany invades the Soviet Union during "Operation Barbarossa." Special murder squads, called *Einsatzgruppen,* follow the Germany army into the Soviet Union.

1941 Hermann Göring, second to Hitler in Nazi hierarchy, gives Reinhard Heydrich the authority "to carry out all necessary preparations . . . for a total solution of the Jewish question" throughout Nazi-controlled Europe.

1941 Six hundred Soviet prisoners of war and 250 Poles are the victims of the first gassings at Auschwitz.

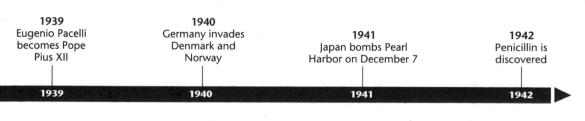

| 1939 Eugenio Pacelli becomes Pope Pius XII | 1940 Germany invades Denmark and Norway | 1941 Japan bombs Pearl Harbor on December 7 | 1942 Penicillin is discovered |

| **1939** | **1940** | **1941** | **1942** |

1941 On September 29 and 30, 33,000 Jews are machine-gunned at Babi Yar outside the city of Kiev, Ukraine.

1941 Construction begins on Birkenau (Auschwitz II) in Poland, the largest Nazi death camp.

1941 The death camp at Chelmno, in the western part of Poland that had been annexed to Germany, begins operation. Jews are gassed in sealed vans.

1942 Reinhard Heydrich calls the Wannsee Conference, where the "Final Solution" is transmitted to various branches of German government.

1942 Slovakian Jews become the first from outside of Poland to be transported to Auschwitz.

1942 Reinhard Heydrich is fatally wounded in an attack by Czech resistance fighters.

1942 The Treblinka death camp begins receiving the Jews of Warsaw. It is the last of the three camps, along with Belzec and Sobibór, that are created to exterminate the Jews of Poland. The Nazis call this "Operation Reinhard," in honor of the assassinated Heydrich.

1943 German attempts to deport Danish Jews are defeated when almost the entire Jewish population of Denmark is safely transported to Sweden.

1943 The Germans occupy Hungary and begin large-scale deportations of Hungarian Jews. By July, 400,000 Hungarian Jews have been sent to Auschwitz.

1943 A small group of German army officers wishing to end the war unsuccessfully try to assassinate Hitler. Many of them, along with their families, are tortured and executed as a result.

1943 The Soviet army enters Lublin in eastern Poland and liberates the nearby Majdanek death camp. The Soviets

1943
Allies occupy
Naples, Italy

1945
V-E Day

1947
State of Israel
is declared

1949
Israel is admitted to
the United Nations

1954
Vietnam War
begins

1943   1945   1947   1949   1951

capture much of the camp, and many documents, before they can be destroyed.

1943 The Polish underground launches a full-scale uprising against the Germans in the Warsaw ghetto. Savage fighting continues in the city for two months until the resistance is finally crushed.

1945 As Soviet troops approach, the Nazis begin the evacuation of Auschwitz. Almost 60,000 surviving prisoners are forced on a death march.

1945 American troops liberate the Buchenwald and Dachau concentration camps, and British troops free the Bergen-Belsen concentration camp.

1945 Hitler commits suicide in his fortified bunker beneath Berlin, and Germany surrenders.

1946 Hermann Göring, one of the highest Nazi officials to be accused and convicted of war crimes, testifies on his behalf during the Nuremberg Trials.

1962 Former Nazi official Adolf Eichmann is executed after being found guilty of war crimes for his part in the murder of hundreds of thousands of Jews.

1985 Human remains found in Brazil are confirmed to be those of Nazi doctor Josef Mengele, who performed inhumane experiments on the prisoners of Auschwitz.

1987 Former SS soldier Klaus Barbie is found guilty of crimes against humanity and is sentenced to life in prison.

1998 The Vatican issues a letter stating that Pope Pius XII, leader of the Catholic Church during the Holocaust, did all he could to save the Jews.

1998 Maurice Papon, a former official of the Vichy government, is sentenced to ten years in prison for helping the Germans illegally arrest and deport French Jews.

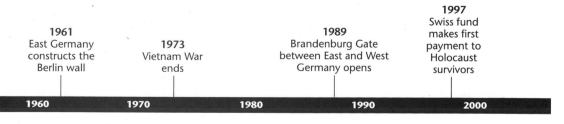

1961
East Germany constructs the Berlin wall

1973
Vietnam War ends

1989
Brandenburg Gate between East and West Germany opens

1997
Swiss fund makes first payment to Holocaust survivors

1960　　　**1970**　　　**1980**　　　**1990**　　　**2000**

Words to Know

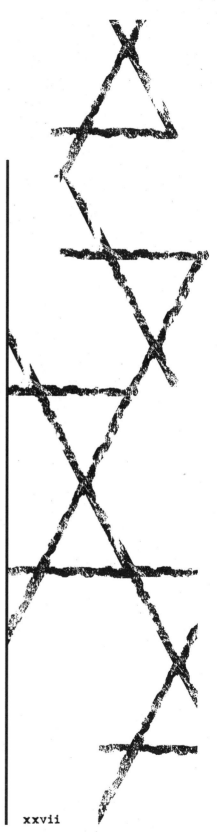

A

Aktion: The German term for the roundup and murder of Jews.

Allies: The countries of Great Britain, the United States, the Soviet Union, and France, who fought against Germany, Italy, and Japan during World War II.

Antisemetism: The hatred of Jews, who are sometimes called Semites.

Anschluss: The German invasion and annexation of Austria in 1938.

Aryans: A term originally used for the peoples speaking the languages of Europe and India. The Nazis used the term to mean anyone who was non-Jewish and of Germanic background.

Aryanization: The Nazi process of seizing the property of Jews and selling it to non-Jews.

B

Bliztkrieg: The military strategy of troops in land vehicles making quick, surprise strikes against the enemy with support from airplanes.

Bund: A Polish Jewish resistance group.

C

Chancellor: The head of the German government.

Collaborators: People who turned their own friends, families, and neighbors over to the Nazis.

Communism: An economic system that promotes the ownership of all property by the community as a whole.

Concentration camps: Places where the Nazis confined people they regarded as "enemies of the state."

Crematoriums: Buildings that held large ovens used to dispose of the bodies of dead concentration camp inmates.

Crimes against humanity: Murder, extermination, enslavement, deportation, and other acts committed against the nonmilitary population of a country.

D

D-Day: The name given to June 6, 1944, the day that British and American forces landed on the beaches of Normandy in northern France.

Death march: The process of forcing long rows of prisoners to walk great distances without the proper food or clothing.

Democracy: A system of government in which the people elect their rulers.

Deportation: The process by which Nazis forcibly removed people from their normal place of residence to a labor, concentration, or death camp.

Depression: An economic downturn.

Dictator: A person holding absolute ruling power in a country.

E

Einsatzgruppen: Special mobile units of the SS and SD that followed the German army into the Soviet Union; they shot at least 1,000,000 Jews.

Emigration: The act of leaving one's country to settle in another.

Euthanasia: The act of killing people whom the Nazis considered "unfit to live."

F

Fascism: A system of government that is marked by dictatorship, government control of the economy, and suppression of all opposition.

Final Solution: The code name given to the Nazi plan to totally eliminate the Jews of Europe.

Free Corps: Or *Freikorps;* volunteer units made up mostly of former officers and professional soldiers. Munch of the SA was made up of former Free Corps members.

Führer: The German word meaning "leader."

G

Gassing: The Nazi process of locking people in sealed rooms and then filling the rooms with poisonous gas in order to suffocate the people to death.

Genocide: The deliberate, systematic destruction of a racial, cultural, or political group.

Gentiles: Non-Jewish people.

Gestapo: An abbreviation for *Geheime Staats Politzei* or German secret police.

Ghettos: Crowded, walled sections of cities where Jews were forced to live in inferior conditions.

Gypsies: Dark-haired, dark-skinned, nomadic people who are believed to have originated in India. They are sometimes also called Roma or Sinti.

H

Holocaust: The period between 1933 and 1945 when Nazi Germany systematically persecuted and murdered millions of Jews, Gypsies, homosexuals, Jehovah's Witnesses, and other innocent people.

Home Army: A Polish secret military resistance organization.

I

Inflation: A continuing rise in prices, caused by an abnormal increase in the amount of money or credit available.

J

Jehovah's Witnesses: A religious group whose beliefs did not allow them to swear allegiance to any worldly power.

Judenrat: The German term for Jewish Council. Nazi leaders ordered the formation of Jewish Councils in the ghettos.

Junkers: Powerful German nobles.

K

Kaiser: The German word for "emperor."

Kapos: Prisoners who worked for the Nazis.

L

Lebensraum: The Nazi idea that the German people or Aryan race needed expanded living space to survive.

Liquidation: The Nazi process of destroying a ghetto by first sending prisoners to death camps and then burning the buildings.

Luftwaffe: The German air force.

N

Nationalists: People who have an intense feeling of loyalty and devotion to a nation.

Nazi: The abbreviation for the National Socialist German Worker's Party.

Neo-Nazis: People who idolize the Nazis and their policies today.

O

Occupation: Control of a country by a foreign military power.

Operation Reinhard: The name given to the Nazi plan to physically eliminate all the Jews of Europe. The name was in honor of Reinhard Heydrich, the architect of the Final Solution.

P

Partisans: Fighters who attack the enemy within occupied territory.

Passive resistance: Resistance to a government by nonviolent methods.

Pogroms: Mass attacks against a particular group of people.

Propaganda: Official government communications to the public that are designed to influence opinion. The information may be true or false.

Prussia: The largest state of the German empire from 1871 to 1918.

Putsch: An unsuccessful attempt to overthrow a government.

R

Rabbi: A Jewish religious leader.

Reds: Slang term for people who practice Communism.

Refugees: People who flee to a foreign country to escape danger and persecution.

Reich: The German word for "empire."

Reichstag: Germany's parliament or lawmaking body.

Resistance: Working against an occupying army.

Reparations: Compensation paid by a defeated nation for damage they caused to another country during a war.

Resettlement: The Nazi term for forcing Jews into ghettos and concentration camps.

S

SA: An abbreviation for *Sturmabteilungen,* or storm troopers. They were members of a special armed and uniformed branch of the Nazi Party.

Sabotage: The deliberate destruction of an enemy's property or equipment during wartime.

SD: An abbreviation for *Sicherdienst,* or Security Police. This unit served as the intelligence (spy) service of the SS.

Selection: The process by which the Nazis decided who would be spared to work and who would be killed immediately.

Socialism: A political and economic system based on government control of the production and distribution of goods.

Sonderkommando: Jewish prisoners who were forced to dispose of bodies of gassed inmates by cremation.

Soviet Union: Present day Russia; a former Communist country of eastern Europe and northern Asia that was founded in 1917 after the Russian government was overthrown. The Soviet Union, formally known as the Union of Socialist Republics, was dissolved in 1991.

SS: An abbreviation for *Shutzstaffeln,* or Security Squad. This unit provided Hitler's personal bodyguards and guards for the various concentration camps.

Storm troopers: Another name given to members of the SA.

Swastika: The Nazi symbol of a black, bent-armed cross that always appeared within a white circle and set on a red background.

Synagogue: A Jewish place of worship.

T

Third Reich: The name Hitler gave to his term as Germany's leader. It means "Third Empire."

Treaty of Versailles: The restrictive treaty that Germany was forced to sign by the Allies after World War I.

Typhus: A serious disease, usually transmitted by body lice, that is marked by a high fever, intense headache, and dark red rash.

U

Underground: Engaged in secret or illegal activity.

W

Waffen-SS: The military unit of the Nazi political police.

Wannsee Conference: The conference called by Reinhard

Heydrich in 1941 to inform branches of the German government about the "Final Solution."

War crimes: Violations of the laws or customs of war.

Weimar Republic: Democratic government imposed upon Germany at the end of World War I.

Y

Yiddish: A language spoken by Eastern European Jews.

Yom Kippur: A Jewish holy day that is accompanied by fasting and praying for the atonement of sins.

Z

Zionists: People who supported the creation of a Jewish nation in Palestine.

ZOB: The initials for *Zydowsk Organizacja Bojowa,* the military wing of the Jewish underground in the Warsaw ghetto.

Zyklon B: A highly poisonous insecticide that the Nazis used in the gas chambers to kill the victims locked inside.

Understanding the
HOLOCAUST

1

Germany and the Jewish People
Before the Holocaust

A "holocaust" is the total destruction of something, as when a terrible fire consumes everything in its path. From 1933 to 1945, the Nazi Party and its leader, Adolf Hitler, controlled Germany. During that time, now remembered as the Holocaust, the Nazis attempted to wipe out the entire Jewish population in Europe. They humiliated Jews and beat them; they fired them from their jobs; they wrecked their homes and businesses and robbed them of their property. The Nazis killed thousands of people each day, day after day. They killed the old and the sick, women and men, even children—probably 1.5 million children. Before World War II ended in 1945, the Nazis had murdered between 5.5 and 6 million Jews. Nothing in history compares with this crime in its scope or degree of brutality.

Opposite page:
An illustration of "Jewstreet"
in the Frankfurt ghetto,
1800s. Until the early
nineteenth century, European
Jews were required to live in a
special section of their town
and usually had to return
there by nightfall. The Nazis
resurrected this practice
in the 1930s.

The Jews of Germany

Although Jews had experienced antisemitism (hatred or hostility toward Jewish people) over the centuries in the German territories and in other areas of Europe, in the nineteenth century there was little indication that the new nation of Germany would be the site of an enormous crime against a people.

Jews had first arrived in Germany during the period of the Roman empire (31 B.C.–A.D. 476) and lived in the country continuously since the Middle Ages (A.D. 500–1500). Germany became one of the major centers of Jewish learning and culture, and many of the Jews of Germany later settled in eastern Europe. Most European and American Jews are Ashkenazic, which comes from the Hebrew word for "Germany." (Jews whose ancestors lived in Spain are called Sephardic Jews.) The Yiddish language, based on the German language that was spoken in the Middle Ages but written in the Hebrew alphabet, eventually became the language of Jews throughout central and eastern Europe.

Until the nineteenth century, the different countries that were later united as Germany each had special laws governing Jews. Because of their religious beliefs—Jews do not view Jesus Christ as the Messiah and son of God—and for various other reasons, Jews were not considered citizens. They could not own land, work for the government, or teach in the schools. Many were very poor. Most Jews were segregated in special sections of a town (the ghetto) and had to return to their homes there at nightfall. German laws against the Jews were gradually abolished in the different countries of Germany during the nineteenth century and, in some places, Jews became legally equal to non-Jews.

The gradual disappearance of legal discrimination (prejudice) against Jews allowed them to become part of German society. Indeed, the Jewish community produced some of the most important figures of nineteenth-century German culture, including poetic master and critic Heinrich Heine and composer Felix Mendelssohn-Bartholdy. Karl Marx, the father of modern socialism and one of the most influential writers of the century, was the grandson of a rabbi (a Jewish religious teacher and leader), though he himself had been baptized as a Christian. (Socialism is a form of government in

Jews in Germany

In 1925, Germany had about 564,000 Jews, less than 1 percent of the population. Of these, more than two-thirds lived in six large cities: Berlin, Frankfurt, Hamburg, Breslau, Leipzig, and Cologne. About 90,000, or 16 percent of the total, lived in smaller cities. Another 97,000 lived in small towns or villages.

Berlin, the German capital, was home to 180,000 Jews. Of the working population, about half were self-employed. Of the rest, about 80 percent worked in offices, 18 percent were manual workers, and 2 percent were domestic servants.

The pattern was somewhat different in other places. In Hamburg, the great port city of northern Germany, the Jewish community was among the most assimilated (absorbed into the mainstream culture), with a high rate of intermarriage. Hamburg was a center of the Reform movement in Judaism—a movement whose members did not follow many of the strict Jewish religious rules. Hamburg's Jews were also more prosperous. They were important in banking and shipping and held many prestigious university jobs.

By 1918, the great majority of German Jews had been assimilated into German society. Most German Jews could not be distinguished from other Germans in terms of daily life, and they thought of themselves as Germans.

which there is no private property and the government owns the means of production of goods.)

During the nineteenth century, large portions of the Jewish community became more prosperous. Some Jews had always been merchants and moneylenders, partly because those were the jobs they were allowed to have under German law. Historically, Jews had not been admitted into the workman's guilds (unions) and so were not represented in many trades. But around this time, many of the small merchants became owners of large companies and some of the moneylenders became bankers. Many German Jews entered the growing middle class of German society. There were still many Jews who were poor in the nineteenth century, but the

German Jews as a group were soon much better off than they had been.

As a result, the Jewish people were able to move out of Germany's ghettos. In the larger cities, they mixed into non-Jewish neighborhoods. They dressed as other Germans of their social class dressed. Many Jews began to practice their religion less strictly; they went to synagogue (a Jewish congregation's house of worship) only on special holidays rather than every Saturday, the Jewish Sabbath, and spent less of their time in prayer and strict religious study. Some converted to Christianity; others chose not to practice any religion at all. In addition, Jews began to marry outside their religion. By 1927, 54 percent of all Jews who got married in Germany married someone who was not Jewish.

German antisemitism

As in most European countries, a long history of antisemitism (anti-Jewish prejudice) existed in Germany.

Some antisemitic ideas dated back to the Middle Ages and were based on religious prejudices. By continuing to practice their own religion, Jews were seen as actively rejecting the belief that Christianity was the only true religion. Some misguided Christians even thought that the Jewish people's rejection of Christianity was a sure sign of the Jews' working with the Devil. The church had taught that the ancient Jews had rejected Jesus Christ in Roman times and were responsible for killing him. Jews were even accused of murdering Christian children and using their blood in religious ceremonies. Many Christians believed that being part of the Christian church was the only way that human beings could be saved from sin.

These feelings had serious effects. In the Middle Ages and in early modern times, there were many instances in European history of Jewish persecution, or harassment and abuse. Sometimes mobs attacked and killed Jews, burning their homes. A wave of killings swept the towns of western Germany in 1196. Repeatedly, Jews were driven out of European countries. In 1290, all Jews were ordered to leave England; the same thing happened in France in 1306 and in Spain in 1492. In sixteenth-century Germany, Martin Luther, the great religious reformer who founded the Protestant religion, preached violent hatred of the Jews.

The Origins of Antisemitism

The term antisemitism, coined in the nineteenth century, means "anti-Jewish." Also associated with the term is the idea that Jews are members of a distinct race rather than just followers of a specific religion.

The term antisemitism has its roots in linguistics (the study of language). Almost all European languages, including English, German, Russian, French, and Greek, are members of a family of languages called Indo-European. So are Iranian, Armenian, and most of the languages of India. Years ago, the word "Aryan" was sometimes used instead of "Indo-European" to describe this language family. Experts believe that all these languages come from a single language spoken thousands of years ago.

There are other major families of languages that are not connected to the Indo-European line. One of them is called Semitic. It includes Hebrew and Arabic.

In the nineteenth century, some political writers argued that modern people who spoke Indo-European languages belonged to the same race, that of the Aryans. The modern Jews—whose original Hebrew language is not Indo-European—were perceived as being of a different race, the race of the Semites. These antisemitic writers further argued that the people who spoke Indo-European languages were not only members of a different race—they were members of a superior race.

This "racial antisemitism" had a tremendous effect, especially in Germany. This new antisemitism viewed Jews not simply as people with a different religion. Instead, Jews were considered a different *race*—by their very different blood—and that could never change.

Some of these feelings continued to exist in the twentieth century, in Germany and throughout Europe.

The German nation: One nation or many?

Germany had existed as a nation for less than seventy years when the Holocaust took place. Before 1871, the territory of Germany had been divided into many different

A map showing the German states.

states, most of them monarchies with their own royal families. Some of these regions were tiny; others, like Prussia, were large and powerful. When Germany was united as one nation in 1871, the different states all had differing laws, resources, and customs. For the next seventy years, regional, social, and religious division, world war, revolution, and economic crises rocked the nation and prevented the establishment of a secure, long-term system of government.

Though the king of Prussia became the emperor (also known as the kaiser) of all of Germany in 1871, until 1918 some of the German states, such as Saxony and Bavaria, still had their own kings. For many years, the people of the various German states were convinced that they should reclaim their independence. These feelings were probably strongest in the southern state of Bavaria, which was more agricultural (more of its economy depended on farming) and more Catholic than most of Germany.

Prussia and the Junkers

The Kingdom of Prussia was the core of the German empire and in some ways, the unification of Germany was like a Prussian takeover of the other German kingdoms. The king of Prussia was automatically named emperor of Germany. The Prussian army dominated the army of united Germany and was controlled by families of the Prussian nobility, who sent their sons to be trained as military officers, generation after generation.

These powerful nobles were called Junkers (pronounced YUNK-erz). Their families lived on estates, large agricultural properties in the old lands of Prussia in eastern Germany. The Junkers lived the lives of wealthy people, even though their estates often did not make enough money to support this style of life. Believing that the most suitable occupation for a nobleman was that of a warrior, the Junkers looked down on businesspeople and workers.

The Junkers were very conservative, meaning they opposed changes to the German government. They believed in loyalty to the kaiser, honor, and obedience to authority. They resisted the formation of a democracy (government by the people). The Junkers believed in the glory of Germany and in the army that they dominated. They also wanted a government that kept crop prices high and protected their estates from being broken up into smaller farms. In terms of religion, the Junkers were Lutheran Protestants. ("Lutheran" comes from German religious reformer Martin Luther, who began the period of Reformation and founded Protestantism in protest of the corruption in the Catholic Church.) Junkers were often anti-Catholic and even more antisemitic. Up to the 1930s, they continued to have a much greater influence on Germany than their numbers or their wealth alone merited because they dominated as officers of the German army.

German industry

Large-scale manufacturing and factories arrived in Germany well after the Industrial Revolution had made first England and then France into great economic powers. (The Industrial Revolution, which began in the mid 1700s in England and eventually spread throughout Europe and to the United States, was a time of major change in industry,

The Industrial Revolution in Germany

Between 1871 and 1914, the ways in which most Germans lived and earned their livelihood changed drastically. The population grew rapidly, and more of the nation's people lived in cities. Large cities grew faster than the rest of the country. Berlin, the German capital, had about 750,000 people in 1870; by 1910 it had over 2,000,000. Cities such as Hamburg, Cologne, Frankfurt, and Leipzig all tripled in size during that period.

The great changes in Germany's demographics from 1871 to 1914 occurred because of the phenomenal growth in industry. Germany's progress can be seen from information in the following chart:

	1870	1913
Railroads (approximate miles of track):	11,000	37,000 (1910)
Coal (in millions of metric tons):	29.4 (1871)	191.5
Pig iron (crude iron for steel, in millions of metric tons):	1.6 (1871)	14.8 (1910)
Merchant marine (number of ships):	147	2,100
Merchant marine (loaded weight of all ships, in tons):	9,000	4,300,000

marked mainly by the introduction of power-driven machinery.) From around the time that Germany became a united country in 1871, it experienced tremendous and very rapid economic growth. By World War I (1914–18), Germany had great industries, steelmaking and coal mining, textiles and clothing, electrical equipment, and chemicals among them.

The speed of these economic changes in Germany had substantial effects on the nation as a whole. In other countries that had become industrialized, the power of the old nobility—the longtime landowners and military officers—had been greatly reduced or even eliminated. In Germany, however, the Junkers retained control of the Prussian government, and therefore Germany, until 1918, and they continued to control the army afterwards.

Modern antisemitism

The roots of antisemitism are deep and tangled and can be traced only in part to religious prejudice. The Prussian Junkers and other conservatives were nationalists. They believed that loyalty to Germany was more important than anything else, and that Germany should be supremely powerful, especially in the military arena. Some Junkers were extreme nationalists: they believed that the German way of doing things was always right and that any criticism of Germany was an act of treason or betrayal of one's country. Extremely nationalistic Germans disliked Jews' multinational ties. They thought Jewish loyalty to fellow Jews in many other countries crossed national boundaries. How could Jews really be loyal to Germany if there were also Jews in France and Russia, Germany's enemies? The fact that German Jews had repeatedly shown their loyalty to Germany was ignored. (This attitude toward foreign connections was also behind the Junkers' opposition to the Catholic Church.) Some also believed that Jews were responsible for bringing modern European ideas, particularly democracy and socialism (a form of government in which there is no private property and the government owns the means of production of goods), into Germany.

"The Jewish Conspiracy"

At the same time Jews were also accused of controlling the great businesses and banks that were growing in Europe. In fact, some powerful businesses had been founded by Jews. The Rothschild family, which had begun in Frankfurt, Germany, had built a great banking empire that operated from London, England, and Paris, France, as well as Germany. Later, other large German companies were established by Jews. Emil Rathenau, for example, founded the company that dominated the German electrical industry. Although most big business in Germany was run by non-Jewish Germans, many people thought that the German economy was controlled by Jews.

The most extreme anti-Semites came to believe that the Jews were behind both big business *and* socialism. Extreme

The Protocols of the Elders of Zion

When anti-Semites wanted to prove the existence of a Jewish plot to rule the world, they always pointed to a pamphlet best known as *The Protocols of the Elders of Zion*. This booklet was supposedly the record of a secret meeting held by the mysterious leaders of the twelve tribes of Israel to plan how the Jews would rule the world.

Protocols was actually written by the secret police of the czar, the Russian emperor, in the 1890s. The czar's men took the ideas from a French book written in 1864 that poked fun at French political leaders and had nothing to do with Jews. In the early 1900s, the pamphlet was repeatedly issued by the Russian government, which purposely encouraged anti-Jewish hatred to distract the Russian people from the shortcomings of their own society.

After the czar was overthrown in 1917, some Russians who fled their country brought the *Protocols* with them to western Europe.

After that, it was republished in many countries—including the United States. In 1920, Henry Ford, the founder of the Ford Motor Company, published the pamphlet as *The International Jew*; it took seven years for him to retract it.

The *Protocols* were even taken seriously, at first, by respectable newspapers. In 1920, for instance, the London *Times* treated the pamphlet's claims as if they were true. The next year, however, the *Times* published the results of its own investigation, showing beyond any doubt that the *Protocols* were a total forgery.

The German Nazis, while still a small group in the 1920s, were among the major publishers of the *Protocols*. As the Nazis grew more powerful, their newspapers never stopped referring to the pamphlet, and Adolf Hitler, who would be responsible for the killing of an estimated six million Jews, claimed it had greatly influenced him.

anti-Semites believed in the existence of an actual conspiracy or plot to undermine German strength and values. According to these extremists, the socialists and the Jewish industrialists and bankers were only pretending to be enemies with each other as part of a plot to control Germany, and the whole world, for the benefit of the Jews.

Most Germans did not accept these extremist ideas. But, as changes in German society seemed to spiral out of control, more and more Germans were increasingly willing to listen to the anti-Semites' outrageous opinions. Eventually, Adolf Hitler used these ideas to help him gain power; in time, they became the official teachings of Nazi Germany. (See Chapter 2.)

World War I

World War I brought major and drastic changes to German society. From 1914 to 1918, the countries of Europe fought the bloodiest war in the history of humanity, calling it at the time the World War or the Great War. World War I grew out of a struggle for power and territory in Europe. The German effort to expand their empire split the nations of Europe into two camps: Austria, Germany, Turkey, and Bulgaria fought against the combined powers of Serbia, Russia, France, Britain, Japan, Italy, and, later, the United States.

Like most other Europeans involved in World War I, the Germans went to battle in 1914 believing that the war would be short, that the soldiers would soon be home, and that Germany would be victorious. But four years later, in the fall of 1918, the German armies were still fighting. Almost 2 million German soldiers had been killed; another 4 million had been wounded. In the east, Germany had defeated its enemy, Russia, where a revolution had overthrown the emperor, or czar, and a Communist government had taken power. (Communism is a political and economic theory advocating the formation of a classless society through the communal, or group, ownership of all property.)

But to the west, the German armies in France were not winning their fight against the British and French forces. For almost the entire war, the two sides had faced each other across fields of barbed wire. Each army had dug hundreds of miles of trenches; the soldiers ate there, slept there, and fought from there month after month. Cannons rained shells down on them. Not a tree or a building was left standing between the front lines of the two armies. This region of intensive combat in France came to be known as the Western Front.

On the Western Front, the battles all went about the same way. Every once in a while, the generals on either side would decide to attack in one section of the front or another. The attacking army would gain some territory, perhaps a few miles, advancing across the open ground against machine-gun fire and artillery shells. Sometimes poison gas was used on the enemy. Then, the other side would try to drive them back. At the end of a week or a month, the two sides were usually about where they had started—except that thousands more soldiers, sometimes hundreds of thousands, had been killed.

This terrible slaughter became a war of attrition: the two sides attempted to kill as many of the enemy as possible and hoped that the enemy ran out of soldiers before they did. The United States joined the Allies—mainly Britain and France—in the war against Germany in 1917. With hundreds of thousands of fresh American troops arriving on the Western Front, it was clear that the German side would run out of soldiers before the Allies.

Like most of their countrypeople, German Jews were strong supporters of Germany in World War I. In 1918, there

A wounded soldier is carried off a World War I battlefield.

were about 600,000 Jews in Germany. About 100,000 of them served in the German army during the war, and about 12,000 were killed. Some Jews played vital roles during the war; for instance, Walter Rathenau, the son of a great Jewish industrialist, organized Germany's scarce supplies of raw materials, thereby allowing the country to fight as long as it did.

Revolution

At home in Germany, by 1917 food was becoming scarce. The British fleet prevented all ships, including those carrying food, from reaching German ports. Germany's allies, the Austrian empire and Turkey, were collapsing. The German generals knew that the war was lost, and they told the German emperor (or kaiser) that Germany had to surrender. But the Allies—Britain, France, and the United States—would end the war only if the kaiser gave up his throne. When he refused, the war and the deaths continued.

At the end of October 1918, Germany's admirals decided to send their ships out to fight the British navy. The German ships, except for submarines, had spent most of the war in port because the more powerful British fleet was impossible to beat. Although they knew the war was lost, German naval commanders forged ahead with plans to fight one great battle with the British. But German sailors refused to obey orders, knowing that they would be the ones to die. Their mutiny soon spread to the German army soldiers stationed in the ports.

By now, a revolution was brewing in Germany. Workers and soldiers formed councils and took over the governments of their towns. On November 9, 1918, the Spartacus League, a small Communist group, declared Germany a socialist republic and stated that the new councils of workers and soldiers should run the country and the war should end immediately.

On the same day, one of the leaders of the much larger German Social Democratic Party announced a "free German republic." The Social Democrats also considered themselves a socialist party, but they were more moderate than the Spartacus League. They wanted gradual, peaceful change in Germany—not a revolution. Fearing a loss of their supporters (especially factory workers and soldiers) to the Spartacus League, the Social Democrats felt they had no choice but to call for the end of the monarchy as well.

The end of a war; the beginning of a myth

In the face of the growing disorder throughout the country, the kaiser finally gave up the throne and left his country the next day, November 10, 1918. Then, on November 11 in France, Germany signed an armistice (pronounced ARM-iss-tuss; a truce or agreement to suspend hostilities) with the Allies, ending the Great War.

Because the war ended while Germany was in a state of revolution, and because the Allies did not require any of Germany's top generals to sign the armistice, some Germans claimed that their armies had never been defeated. Germany had lost the war, they reasoned, because the army had been "stabbed in the back." The Communists, the Social Democrats, or the politicians in general, according to this myth, were criminals who had betrayed Germany. And some Germans even held that the Jews were chiefly responsible for this treason.

A military cemetery in Verdun, France, where French and German World War I soldiers were laid to rest.

The Free Corps

The Free Corps (*Freikorps* in German) were volunteer units made up mostly of former officers and professional soldiers. They were organized by the army soon after the armistice. At their height, there were probably around 200 Free Corps units with 400,000 soldiers—four times the official size of the regular German army. Their members were extremely hostile not only to Communists but also to Social Democrats and to democracy itself. They hated unions, they hated Jews, and they glorified war and Germany's military past.

Officially, the Free Corps were supposed to guard Germany's borders and maintain order. In fact, they were used for the bloodiest work, including actions that were illegal. For example, many of those killed in the Berlin uprising of 1919 were shot after they had surrendered. Karl Liebknecht and Rosa Luxemburg, the two most important Communist Party leaders, were brutally murdered three days after the end of the uprising.

The Free Corps soldiers seemed to enjoy fighting and killing their opponents. They were a perfect tool for crushing the government's enemies. Most of the first Nazi storm troopers (members of a private army of Nazis known for their violence and brutality) were members of the Free Corps.

Years of disorder

Germany faced one crisis after another from the end of World War I to 1925. The war left millions dead and millions of others permanently disabled. Germany's loss of soldiers was made even worse by the nation's defeat and the feeling that their deaths had served no purpose.

Some historians believe that in the wake of these four years of slaughter in Europe, the world became generally less sensitive to people's suffering. The unbelievable butchery that occurred during World War I seemed to leave people feeling cold, detached, and indifferent. According to this theory, the terrible suffering experienced during World War I was one

of the things that made the killing of mullions during the Holocaust possible.

After the war, the citizens of many countries tried to return to their normal prewar lives. But in Germany, the end of the war was accompanied by revolution. Just as the new German government was born, the German army was collapsing. Over the next few years, repeated attempts were made by various factions (groups with a common goal) in different parts of Germany to overthrow this new government.

Restoring order

At the war's end, the leader of the Social Democratic Party, Friedrich Ebert, was chancellor of Germany (the head of the government). Ebert viewed restoring order as his most important job—so important, in fact, that he was willing to eliminate the rebellious councils of workers and soldiers by force if necessary.

A group of Free Corps troops, volunteers who were used to put down popular uprisings, posing with their weapons in 1919.

Throughout the first half of 1919, Ebert's government acted to abolish the councils, disarm workers' organizations, and get strikers back to work throughout Germany. In January 1919, a series of strikes took place in Berlin. The Communist Party called on the workers to overthrow the government and seized several buildings. The attempted revolution—already violent—was put down with greater bloodshed by the army's use of artillery and by the extremely aggressive units of the Free Corps. The Free Corps were units of volunteer soldiers used to restore order during popular uprisings. (See box on p. 16.)

The same story of rebellion and defeat was played out in other areas of Germany. When workers participated in strikes and building takeovers, they often proclaimed a Soviet Republic in the area. (*Soviet* is the Russian word for "council." The German revolutionaries, or "reds," used the term "Soviet Republic" to mean that the government would be composed of the council of workers and soldiers.) Then troops, usually the Free Corps, were sent in by the central government in Berlin. The result was a bloody defeat of the revolutionaries, followed by shootings and beatings of those suspected of sympathizing with the "reds."

Munich

The most important of these uprisings took place in Munich, the capital of Bavaria, a large state in southern Germany. There, the Soviet Republic lasted a little over three weeks. When the Free Corps entered the city on May 1, 1919, they were at their bloodiest: they killed more than one thousand people and executed many after they had already given up. Many of the victims had nothing to do with the revolution.

For those people who had opposed it, the chaos and violence of the short-lived Soviet Republic in Munich were long remembered. The new government of the state of Bavaria wanted to keep the Communists down, and it welcomed and protected every opponent of the hated "reds." Many of these opponents, like the members of the Free Corps, were also against democracy (government by the people) and wanted the reins of government to be held by a single ruler, either a monarch or a dictator. Munich became a center for extreme nationalists, those who wanted a powerful German army and who expressed an intense hatred for the new republic. Extreme nationalists blamed the Jews for the revolution, for Germany's defeat in the war, and for all that was wrong in the world and in their own lives. One such nationalist was Adolf Hitler.

The new German Republic

Germany held its first elections since before the Great War in January 1919. Even though the voting was held in a period of turmoil (the Communist rebellion in Berlin had just been crushed), it was fair. For the first time, everyone over the age of 20, including women, could vote. More than 80 percent of all eligible voters cast a ballot.

The Social Democrats won the most votes, about 38 percent, but they did not get a majority. The Center Party, supported by the Catholic Church, received about 20 percent, and the Democratic Party, a moderate group, did almost as well. Although they differed about many things, these three parties all supported the new government in Germany, which was soon called the Weimar Republic, after the city where the National Assembly met and the new constitution was being written. More than 75 percent of the voters supported parties that were in favor of the Weimar Republic.

The parties that were hostile to democracy—those that wanted either a return of the monarchy or some form of dictatorship (a government in which absolute power is held by a single ruler)—got about 16 percent of the vote between them. The two most important of these parties were the Nationalists and the German People's Party. The rest of the voters, about 7 percent, supported the Independent Social Democrats, a group that fell between the regular Social Democrats and the Communists in its philosophy. The Communists did not run in the election.

The three parties that had gotten the most votes now formed a government. These parties—the Social Democrats, the Center, and the Democrats—became known as the Weimar Coalition.

The Treaty of Versailles

One of the new government's first tasks was to negotiate a permanent peace treaty with the Allies. The terms of

Areas that Germany lost as a result of the Treaty of Versailles, reluctantly agreed to by the German government on June 23, 1919.

the agreement, the Treaty of Versailles, named after the city near Paris where the Peace Conference met, were quite harsh: (1) The German armed forces were strictly limited. The army would have only 100,000 men; the navy would have 15,000. They would have no planes, tanks, or submarines; (2) Germany would lose all of its colonies, which would be taken over mainly by France and Britain; and (3) Germany would also lose some of its own territory.

Alsace and Lorraine, two regions the Germans had taken from France after a war in 1870, went back to France. A section of western Germany near France, called the Rhineland, would be controlled by Allied troops for a number of years. Large sections of eastern Germany went to the newly independent country of Poland.

War guilt and reparations

The Allies made two other demands that angered Germans more than anything else. They wanted Germany to admit that it was responsible for starting the war and to make payments or reparations over many years to the Allies, especially to France, for the enormous destruction it caused. When the Allies revealed how much money, coal, lumber, and other products they wanted from Germany, the amount was staggering.

The terms of the Treaty of Versailles seemed intended to make Germany permanently poor and weak. No one in Germany approved of the treaty.

Many of the representatives in the German National Assembly wanted to reject the treaty, but the Allied armies waited on the borders, ready to continue fighting, and Germany could not beat them. German prisoners of war (POWs) were still waiting to be released. Perhaps most important, the British fleet was prepared to blockade Germany's ports once more, and this action would lead to hunger throughout the country. On June 23, 1919, the National Assembly accepted the Allied terms by a vote of 237 to 138. The assembly made it clear that it did not consider this a vote on a treaty negotiated between Germany and the Allies. Instead, it was a vote to accept a dictated peace.

Economic disaster

The German economy was already weakened by the war and by the disorder that continued around the country. The government was short of cash and temporarily "solved" this problem by simply printing more money. But because people had no confidence in this money, its value declined quickly in a process called inflation. In July 1919, it took about 14 marks (the German unit of money) to buy 1 American dollar. By July 1922, it took about 490. Because the mark was losing its value so fast, people rushed to spend their money as soon as they were paid, before prices went up again. This only made things worse: prices raced up, wages and salaries were increased to try to keep up, and prices jumped again.

By the middle of August 1923, 1 American dollar was worth almost 3 million German marks. Two weeks later it was worth 13 million, then 98 million, then 345 million. By

November 15, 1 American dollar was worth 2.5 trillion German marks.

Passive resistance against France

In the early 1920s, Germany had fallen behind on its scheduled reparation shipments of coal and lumber to France. In January 1923, the French government used this as an excuse to send troops to take over the Ruhr region of Germany. The Ruhr was the most important center of German industry, with huge steel mills and coal mines. Officially, the French army was there only to insure that Germany met its reparation duties. However, many Germans believed that France wanted to weaken them further by permanently separating the Ruhr—and its industry—from Germany.

By the summer of 1923, 100,000 French troops controlled the Ruhr. This was the size of the entire German army, so it was obvious that military resistance would not work. The German government instead called for passive resistance (nonviolent forms of rebellion). Consequently, the people of the Ruhr would not cooperate with the French. Workers refused to load coal bound for France, and the railroad crews would not transport it. Local officials ignored French instructions.

The French retaliated by jailing some German workers for refusing to obey their orders and expelling many others. The expelled people were welcomed in other areas of Germany, but they now had no jobs and had to be supported by an already strained German nation.

Not all Ruhr residents were passive in resisting the French troops; some dynamited railroad lines and bridges. If they were caught, the French executed them. During a strike at the massive Krupp factories in the city of Essen, French troops fired on the workers, killing thirteen and wounding thirty. And when the French took over the coal mines, the miners refused to work and the mines were shut down. Tens of thousands of miners lost their jobs and depended on money sent by the German government.

The end of passive resistance

When the French banned the transport of coal from the Ruhr to the rest of Germany, the German government severed all railroad traffic to the Ruhr. Most goods were shipped by rail, so the richest area of the country was now economically cut off, marking another economic disaster for the country. About 180,000 Germans had been expelled from the Ruhr. A hundred had been killed, and more were imprisoned. Hundreds of millions of gold marks (not the worthless paper marks) were being spent by the government every week to support the people who had lost their homes or their jobs.

In September 1923, the German government asked the people of the Ruhr to end passive resistance and to go back to work. Although the government probably had little choice, the decision angered nationalist Germans. To them, the failure to drive out the French was another betrayal of the country by the same "criminals" who had agreed to the Treaty of Versailles in the first place.

Five years after the end of the fighting in World War I, Germany was still experiencing very deep divisions among its people. Conservatives and industrialists vied for power against workers' groups; hostilities continued among Catholics and Protestants; the different states within Germany fought against the rule of the national government in their lands. The extremes of the economy with its high inflation had severely shaken many Germans. Losing the war and then submitting to France's military intervention were humiliating events that caused hardship within the nation. People were angry and distrustful of their government and looking for places to lay blame.

Extremist groups, which exist in every society, found the time ripe for taking action. One such group, the Nazis, succeeded in the struggle for control in a way that no one had foreseen. Their program of viciously stamping out their political opponents while promoting hatred and nationalism set the literate and educated German nation on the track of fear and violence that would end in the killing of millions of Jewish people.

2

The Rise of the Nazi Party

As a group, German nationalists in the 1920s opposed democracy (government by the people) and supported the German military. They wanted the reins of government to be held by a single ruler, either a monarch or a dictator. Their main goal was to sustain a strong Germany. They had opposed the 1918 revolution that led to the overthrow of the kaiser (the emperor of Germany). They also opposed the establishment of the Weimar Republic (the German government established after World War I) that followed. In addition, the nationalists were almost always antisemitic (anti-Jewish)—but they displayed this antisemitism in mostly nonviolent ways.

Nationalism was not unique to Germany. After the Russian Revolution of 1917 in which Communist forces took over the government to form the Union of Soviet Socialist Republics (the USSR), there were frequent attempts by

The German *Volk*

The word *volk* means "people" or "nation" in German, but when extreme nationalists used it, it meant more than that. They were referring to the Germans as a special "race" of people that shared the same "blood." Often, the word was meant to conjure up images of ancient, pre-Christian Germanic tribes, their religion, and their mythology. The *volk* supposedly had a special, almost magical, connection to the forests, streams, and mountains.

The idea of the *volk* is different from the modern idea of a nation. A member of the German *volk* was a German regardless of where that person lived or of what country that person was a citizen. However, people could not be "real Germans" if they weren't members of the German *volk,* even if their ancestors had lived in Germany for hundreds of years, even if they spoke only German, and even if they thought of themselves as German.

According to extreme nationalists, Jews could not be "real Germans." They were outsiders—dangerous outsiders—who lived among the "real Germans" in order to weaken and enslave them.

Communists to seize power in other parts of Europe, especially in Germany, Italy, and Hungary. (Communism is a political and economic theory advocating the formation of a classless society through the communal, or group, ownership of all property.) For people who opposed communism, particularly wealthy landowners and industrialists, there was strong appeal to the idea of a powerful government that would stomp out the forces of change that were sweeping Europe in the forms of both democracy (rule by the people) and communism.

In Italy, Benito Mussolini had been dictator since 1922. In many ways, Mussolini and his Fascist Party were a model for certain nationalist groups. Fascism is a system of government dominated by a single, all-powerful leader. Fascist philosophy is very nationalistic and authoritarian, glorifying the state and giving it supreme powers over its people. Fascism generally offers a promise of law and order and preserves class systems that have traditionally ruled, while intentionally eliminating individual freedoms, particularly the freedom to question or disagree with the government. With a secret police and strong military, fascist governments such as Mussolini's used strong-arm tactics to maintain absolute power. Mussolini's militia, the "Black Shirts," were thugs who beat up opponents of the Fascists. Later, the Nazis with their similar "Brownshirts" or storm troopers, were often called "Fascists."

The extreme nationalist groups in Germany believed that any criticism of the nation was treason. They were willing to use force to silence their opponents, particularly communists and socialists. Their hatred of Jews was intense. Many of these groups had military units, often manned by veterans of the Free Corps, the volunteer military units of ex-officers and soldiers who had brutally put down the workers' uprisings after the end of World War I.

These extreme nationalists believed in the superiority of the German "race." (See box on p. 25.) To them, Germany was the defender of civilization against "inferior races," especially the people of eastern Europe such as Russians and Poles. They wanted all Germans, including those in Austria, to be part of a single country. The unity of Germany and Austria was specifically banned by the Treaty of Versailles, the peace treaty Germany had been forced to sign after losing World War I. The extreme nationalists spoke against the treaty and sought revenge against Germany's enemies, especially France.

Hitler in Munich

Extreme nationalist opponents of the German government were very strong in Munich, the capital city of the state of Bavaria. During a Communist revolt in Munich in May 1919, turmoil and violence wracked the city for three weeks. Afterwards, when the Free Corps arrived to put down the Communists, the violence had been extreme. The people who had opposed the takeover of the city blamed the suffering on the Communists. The new government of the state of Bavaria wanted to keep the Communists down, and it welcomed every opponent of the hated "reds." The state of Bavaria had acted almost like an independent country since World War I

Adolf Hitler's Early Life

Adolf Hitler was born in the Austrian empire in 1889, the son of a low-level customs official. Hitler was therefore not a German citizen. He was a poor student, which led to conflicts with his father, who wanted him to train for a career as a minor official. But by the time he was fourteen and his father had died, Hitler knew he did not want a regular job. In fact, he never had one in his entire life.

Hitler's ambition was to be an artist, but he was rejected by the local art school. When he was eighteen, he went to Vienna, the capital of the Austrian empire. He lived there, sometimes in great poverty, often in men's hotels that were nothing more than dormitories for people who would otherwise be homeless. He supported himself with odd jobs, including painting picture postcards that were sold on the streets. Sometimes he begged. At that time, Hitler was little more than a bum.

Just before World War I, Vienna was one of the great capitals of Europe. It was also a center of anti-Jewish feelings and political movements. The longtime mayor of Vienna, Karl Lüger, had built his career by denouncing (condemning, criticizing) Jews. It was probably at this point that Hitler's dislike of Jews grew into a burning hatred. At the same time, Hitler learned that anti-Jewish speeches could lead to political success.

Hitler moved to Munich in 1913. The next year, when World War I started, he avoided the Austrian army and instead joined a Bavarian unit of the German Imperial Army. He served throughout the war, was wounded, won several medals, and was promoted to corporal (a military rank just above private). Despite the dangers and horrors of the war, for the first time in his life Hitler felt successful.

After the armistice, the German army sent Hitler back to Munich. The defeat of Germany and the end of the war were terrible blows to him. Hitler blamed the Jews for Germany's losses. In 1919, his hatred of Jews and Communists—he thought they were one and the same—became even more intense during the short-lived Soviet Republic (government by the workers) in Munich. He rejoiced at the bloody defeat of the "reds."

Soon Hitler came to the attention of the officers who were in charge of hunting down supporters of the Soviet Republic. The officers discovered that Hitler had a certain type of charisma, or charm—and a talent for transmitting his extreme nationalist views to crowds of dissatisfied Germans. They made him an "education officer" to help spread their shared ideas. It was at this time that Hitler was sent to investigate the German Workers' Party.

and was hostile to the Weimar Republic. Its government protected the extreme nationalists and their organizations.

Looking for allies against Communists, army officers in Munich were interested in supporting extreme nationalist groups. At this time the army decided to send a German soldier waiting to be discharged from the army to investigate

Hitler delivering a speech in 1923, at the time the Nazi Party was established.

one of these groups—the German Workers' Party. The soldier was Adolf Hitler.

Hitler becomes the "führer"

The German Workers' Party was very small, with only 40 members, when Hitler joined it in June 1919. The party was led by Anton Drexler, a locksmith. Despite its name, it did not have any support from workers. Soon Hitler became one of the party's leaders and its most effective public speaker.

A few months later, the party changed its name to the National Socialist German Workers' Party. From the German words for "National Socialists," the party soon became known as the Nazis. It was not long before Hitler took over the leadership of the party. But he was not known as the party's chairman or president. Instead, he called himself the "führer," the leader.

Storm troopers

Hitler created a military wing to the party, the SA (an abbreviation for *Sturmabteilung*) or "storm troopers." The SA men were often called "Brownshirts" because of their uniforms. Their job was supposedly to secure Nazi meetings and protect party leaders, but they were also used to physically beat opponents and to impress and frighten the public. Most of the storm troopers were former Free Corps members, who were experienced and brutal fighters.

By 1923, the Nazis had gained strength, with 15,000 members and over 5,000 storm troopers. They paraded through the towns of Bavaria and broke up political meetings of Socialists and Communists. Although still relatively small, the Nazi Party had some powerful allies. The Bavarian government, including important police officials, protected them, and Hitler still had some strong connections with the army. One of the Nazis' most important allies was Erich

A group of SA men, storm troopers, in 1923.

Die Angeklagten des Hitler-Prozesses.

Pernet   Weber   Frick   Kriebel   Ludendorff   Hitler   Brückner   Wagner
                                                              Röhm

Defendants at the trial of the Munich Beer Hall Putsch. Adolf Hitler is fourth from the right.

Ludendorff, who as a general had practically run Germany in the last years of World War I.

The Beer Hall Putsch

In the fall of 1923, as Germany yielded to the control of French soldiers in the industrial Ruhr and the economic situation in Germany hit rock bottom (see Chapter 1), the Nazis in Munich thought the time was ripe to overthrow the Weimar Republic. They chose November 9, 1923—the fifth anniversary of the revolution that had overthrown the kaiser—to make their move.

On the night of November 8, the leader of the Bavarian state government was making a speech in a Munich beer hall. The local army commander and the Munich chief of police were present, and all three had been friendly with the Nazis. Suddenly, Nazi storm troopers surrounded the hall. Hitler rushed to the stage and announced that the "national revolution" had begun. The Bavarian leaders refused to join the Nazis in a march on Berlin, Germany's capital, however, and Hitler threatened them with a gun. Ludendorff arrived to help convince them.

As soon as the Nazis released them, however, the Bavarian state government leaders ordered the army and the police to stop the Nazis. The next day the Nazis, led by Hitler and Ludendorff, marched to the center of town. There, a special unit of police blocked the way, and gunfire erupted. Sixteen storm troopers and three police officers were killed. There were many wounded, including high-ranking Nazis. Other Nazi leaders, including Hitler, escaped from the scene and went into hiding. Hitler was captured a few days later. These events are referred to as the Beer Hall Putsch. (*Putsch* is the German word for an unsuccessful rebellion.)

Unequal justice

Hitler was put on trial along with Ludendorff in February 1924. It was obvious that they were guilty of treason (betrayal of one's country) and armed rebellion. But the judges treated the defendants, especially Ludendorff, with great respect, almost with awe, and they allowed Hitler to make speech after speech in court, in which he freely admitted that he wanted to overthrow the government by force. The same courts had handed out harsh sentences, including the death penalty, to the Communists who had tried to do the same thing in 1919.

Despite the evidence, Ludendorff was acquitted. Hitler was convicted of high treason and given the minimum possible sentence—five years. He actually served only a little over eight months, and his living conditions while in prison were quite easy. He spent his time dictating a book to a private secretary. The book, *Mein Kampf* ("My Struggle"), became the bible of the Nazi movement.

When Hitler was released, he went right back to trying to build up the Nazi Party. He was not thrown out of Germany, even though he was not a German citizen but an Austrian, and according to the law he should have been expelled. Although it failed as a revolution, the Beer Hall Putsch increased the visibility of Hitler and the Nazis and motivated Hitler to expand the party.

Hitler becomes famous

Many hate groups throughout Germany first heard of Hitler and the Nazis because of the Beer Hall Putsch trial. It was a high-profile case because Erich Ludendorff was a very

Hitler's comfortable cell in Landsberg prison, where he dictated Mein Kampf.

well-known German general. But it was Hitler's speaking ability that thrilled many people who watched the trial.

Recordings of Hitler's speeches seem far from impressive when listened to today. He often rants and raves, he screams, he seems almost out of control. But people who actually heard him speak in person, even his enemies, thought he had an incredible ability to sweep away his listeners. His supporters often spoke of his piercing look as he addressed them. Crowds were spellbound, caught up in his every word, cheering. In a way, Hitler was like a modern performer, a rock star, and his speeches were like powerful concerts. But Hitler's speeches were not entertainment. They were expressions of hate, and their main purpose was to win support for the Nazis.

A new strategy

The failure of Hitler's revolution in Munich convinced him that he could never take over Germany with just a few thousand supporters, even if they were armed. His storm troopers could not successfully fight the German army. From this point on, Hitler was determined to make the Nazis into a large party. "The [Nazi] movement must avoid everything which may lessen or weaken its power of influencing the masses," he wrote in *Mein Kampf*. The Nazis would run in elections to gain publicity for themselves and their views. When their candidates were elected to the state or national parliament (the legislature), they would use the parliament to repeat the Nazi message over and over, just as Hitler had done at his trial. They would also hold large street rallies and publish newspapers that would repeat the same themes again and again. They would draw in the masses by holding great demonstrations and parades, with marchers carrying flags and slogans and feeling great loyalty to their party as they participated in the event.

Mein Kampf

In *Mein Kampf,* the book he dictated while in prison, Hitler tells his version of his life story and explains his ideas on Germany and the world, on Jews, and on how the Nazi Party should be run. People who try to read *Mein Kampf* today are often surprised that anyone could have taken Hitler seriously. The book is quite long and poorly written. It jumps from one idea to another and constantly repeats itself. Hitler writes about himself as a brilliant political genius whose ideas are completely original: he claims that only he, Adolf Hitler, understands the cause of Germany's problems, and only he can solve them.

Hitler rages against many things in *Mein Kampf*. At the same time that he attacks the injustice of the Treaty of Versailles, he blames the Jews for Germany's defeat in the war and for controlling Britain and France, the two main powers that forced Germany to agree to the treaty. He denounces democracy, socialism, and communism because, he feels, they are all inventions of the Jews. Hitler expresses his goals for Germany—mainly that the nation establishes a strong army, assumes control of more land, and regains its colonies—but, in his opinion, the Jews stand in the way of making these goals a reality.

The Nazi Party Program

Another document besides Hitler's *Mein Kampf* ("My Struggle") set out to explain the Nazis' philosophy. This was the Nazi Party program, which Hitler had helped write back in 1920. A program is a statement of a political party's beliefs and the goals it seeks to achieve.

The Nazi program is very different from *Mein Kampf*. It is quite short, containing only 25 points, most of which are quite clear. The program does not reflect the ways the Nazis actually behaved when they took power. The document also does not represent what Hitler truly believed. It does show how the Nazis *wanted* people to see them.

Many of the program's 25 points cover the usual ideas of extreme nationalism. They call for invalidating the Treaty of Versailles and for uniting all Germans into a single country. (This would include Austrians and the German minority living in the new country of Czechoslovakia.)

Similarly, the program is strongly anti-semitic (anti-Jewish). Only pure-blooded Germans could be citizens of the new Germany or hold political office. Other people, including Jews, would only be "guests." Jews who had immigrated to Germany after the beginning of World War I would be expelled from the country.

However, there are other parts of the program that reflect the "socialist" side of the Nazis. These points emphasize the party's desire to gain the support of the lower middle class. The program calls for "the creation and preservation of a healthy middle class" and "a most benevolent attitude" towards small businesses. It also says that the government should take over the big monopolies (single companies that controlled a whole industry), claim a share of the profits of other large industries, and seize all war profits. The program further proposes that unearned income, such as interest, should be abolished. Land needed by the nation should be taken by the government without payment. And department stores should be broken up and rented to small shopkeepers. (Some of the largest department stores in Germany were owned by Jews.)

If these points were carried out, they would threaten the owners of large industries, bankers, and great landowners. Small business people and farmers would benefit. The program also contains two demands meant to appeal especially to factory workers. It calls for the abolition of child labor and for workers to share in the profits of their companies. Although this was not enough to gain much support from workers, it did pose another threat to the owners of large industries.

In 1926, the Nazis declared that their program was not subject to change. Even before issuing this statement, however, Hitler was explaining that the "socialist" part of the program did not really mean what it seemed to say. The Nazis had no intention of taking over monopolies, said Hitler; the point about monopolies was aimed only at "Jewish international" bankers. Similarly, Hitler asserted two years later, the point about taking over land without payment was really "directed primarily against Jewish land-speculation companies."

While the Nazi program promised the lower middle class all sorts of advantages at the expense of big business, Hitler was assuring the big business elite that they had nothing to worry about.

Terror—psychological and physical

Mein Kampf is full of contempt for the people who later became Hitler's supporters. Hitler talks a great deal about the superiority of the German "race." But it is clear in his book that he does not think highly of the actual people who make up this "race." The "masses," he writes, have very little ability to grasp ideas, and "their understanding is feeble. On the other hand, they quickly forget."

Most people, can't think about political problems clearly, Hitler went on to write in *Mein Kampf*. In fact, they really don't think at all and their opinions are based on their emotions. They must be told what to think—or really, how to feel, he claims. They don't want to be given information because they don't want to make their own decisions. They want to be *told* what to think; indeed, they want to be "terrorized" into what to think. The same simple ideas must be repeated to them over and over until they accept them. And, they don't even *realize*, Hitler writes, that by sacrificing their power to think for themselves, they're allowing "their freedom as human beings" to be taken away.

Physical intimidation—not just verbal—is also useful in convincing supporters that a cause is a righteous one, Hitler continues in *Mein Kampf*. Violence (or the threat of violence) makes a victim believe that further resistance is useless.

"The Big Lie"

Hitler openly says that the way to convince people to support the Nazis is to tell big lies. (He claims that this is what the Jews have done.) People are more willing to believe big lies, he reasons, because "they themselves often tell little lies in little matters, but would be ashamed to resort to large-scale falsehoods." Therefore, because of the "primitive simplicity" of their minds, they cannot believe that someone would tell a big lie about an important matter.

In order to convince people, Hitler writes in *Mein Kampf,* every argument should be completely one-sided. Nothing should be partly true or mostly true—it must be absolutely true. No opponent or enemy has any good points; they are absolutely wrong. The more extreme one's position, the better, because the "masses always respond" to their speaker's

Alfred Rosenberg

Alfred Rosenberg was born in Estonia, then part of the Russian empire, where many people of German ancestry lived at that time. He was trained as an architect and attended school in Moscow. After the 1917 Russian Revolution, when the Communists took over Russia, he fled to Germany. His hatred of communism and of Jews was very similar to Hitler's.

Rosenberg became the main "philosopher" of the Nazi Party. He believed that "race" and racial differences were the most important forces of history. The Germans, according to his theory, were the superior race, and the Jews made up the lowest of the races on Earth.

Rosenberg also stressed anti-Christian themes. He believed that the Jews had used Christianity to gain control of Europe because Jews viewed Christianity as a religion of weakness. Rosenberg wanted Germans to return to the ancient myths and gods they had worshiped before Germany became Christian.

Rosenberg became the Nazi "expert" on Jews and was heavily involved in the mass murders of Jews in eastern Europe during World War II. He was tried, sentenced to death, and hanged after the war ended.

"absolute faith in the ideas put forward." The people cannot be given "free choice."

Setting the Nazis apart

Many other extreme nationalist groups viewed the world the way the Nazis did, but, unlike the Nazis, these groups thought of themselves mainly in military terms. They liked uniforms and weapons, not running in elections. They were more like gangs, not like political parties. They were street fighters, not organizers. But, similar to the Nazis, they looked down on ordinary Germans who were trying to live normal lives.

The Nazi storm troopers were also like street gangs, but the Nazi Party was comprised of more than just the storm troopers. Hitler was full of contempt for ordinary people but, despite these feelings of disdain, he realized that he had to win the support of ordinary Germans for the Nazi Party. He wanted to build a "mass" party.

Hitler's problems

Hitler faced a major challenge in building a "mass" party however, because many of the "masses" were hostile to his ideas. Most German workers had no use for the Nazi's goals, and they had no interest in ruling others as the superior race. Although he believed that Germans should rule over other nations, Hitler found most Germans generally lacking in the German greatness he idealized.

Hitler resolved this conflict between his vision of a superior German race and his disdain for the actual German masses by theorizing that the leaders of the Social Democratic Party were purposely poisoning the minds of the workers. He stated that the Social Democrats used the problems of the workers, such as their low pay and poor conditions, to advance their own goals. Most importantly, he concluded that the ideas of the Social Democrats really came from the Jews: "Knowledge of the Jews is the only key whereby one may understand the inner nature and the real aims of Social Democracy." According to Hitler, German workers were hostile to his extreme nationalist ideas because they had been fooled by the Jews.

Behind every problem, behind every opponent of the Nazis—whether a socialist worker or an antisocialist banker—there were the Jews, Hitler told his audiences. He believed that the ability to focus people's attention against one single opponent is the mark of a true leader: "The leader of genius must have the ability to make different opponents appear as if they belonged to one category." Hitler's targeted category of opponents were the Jewish people

"National Socialism"

As a party, the Nazis combined their belief in military strength with their appeals to lower-middle-class Germans— Germans who were frightened and confused by what was happening in Germany.

The Swastika and the Red Flag

The Nazi symbol was the swastika, the hooked or twisted cross. It is an ancient symbol found in many civilizations. The swastika was common in India but was also used by the early Christians and appears often in the art of Native Americans. Extreme nationalists in Germany thought the swastika was connected with the ancient Aryans or Indo-Europeans. (See box titled "The Origins of Antisemitism" on p. 6.) Some extreme nationalist groups used it on their newspapers or on the helmets of their uniforms.

The Nazis took the swastika as their emblem and put it on their flag. Hitler personally designed the party's flag. The black swastika was inside a white circle, and the rest of the flag was red.

Hitler chose the color red for the Nazi flag and its posters for good reason. Red symbolized the workers' parties and a workers' revolution. It was associated with both the German Social Democratic Party and the Communist Party. By using the red flag, the Nazis were trying to show that they were a revolutionary party, that they wanted to change society in a new way and not just go back to the old days of the kaiser. The Nazis always referred to their goal as a "national revolution." Like the official name of the Nazi Party—the National Socialist German Workers' Party—the Nazi flag was supposed to show that they were both socialists and nationalists.

To reach these people, the Nazis had to use tactics that differed from those of the extreme German nationalists. The Nazis appealed to the economic problems of the lower middle class. They wanted the lower-middle-class people of Germany to believe that the Nazi Party was "revolutionary"—that they wanted to change Germany into something new, not just go back to the old days before World War I, when their circumstances weren't any better than they were now. This was the "socialist" aspect of the Nazis.

At the same time, the Nazis wanted to be a semimilitary fighting group like the other extreme nationalists. They wore uniforms, had military-style ranks, and marched in the

The SS

In addition to the storm troopers of the SA (the Brownshirts), Hitler had created a second Nazi military organization in 1925. It was called the SS (from the German initials for *Schutzstaffel,* meaning "defense corps"). Its members wore black uniforms and were considered the elite of the Nazi Party—the best and most honored. All its members had to prove they were "pure Germans," with no Jewish ancestors. The SS looked down on the SA. Eventually, the SS became the organization that was directly responsible for carrying out the Holocaust (the period between 1933 and 1945 when the Nazi Party tried to physically eliminate the entire European Jewish population). In the mid-1920s, however, it was much smaller than the SA and not as well known to outsiders.

streets with their swastika flags. (A swastika is a cross whose arms end in right angles; see box on p. 38.) They threatened their opponents, broke up their meetings, and beat them into submission. They demanded a strong army for Germany and the cancellation of the terms of the Treaty of Versailles. The Nazis wanted Germany to regain the territory it had lost in World War I and to conquer new land in eastern Europe. This was the "nationalist" aspect of the party.

Antisemitism was the connection between these two elements of the Nazi movement. It was the key element in Hitler's strategy to make the Nazi movement grow and eventually take over Germany.

When Hitler was released from prison in the fall of 1924, he devoted himself to building up the ranks of the Nazi Party. But the success of this plan depended on other events—events that the Nazis could not control. If things improved in Germany, if people had jobs and were more confident about the future, then few would need or want to support the Nazis. Only a frightened, angry nation would look to Hitler for solutions to their problems.

Germany's short period of prosperity

For several years in the late 1920s things did get better in Germany. The country became prosperous. And the Nazis remained a small group that most Germans thought was full of crazed extremists. From 1925 to 1929, the German economy expanded rapidly. The country's industries managed to double their production from 1923 to 1928. In 1923, Germany produced about 8 percent of all the world's industrial goods; in 1928 it produced 12 percent. Production of steel increased a whopping 255 percent in only six years. Much of Germany's new prosperity depended on exporting manufactured products to other countries. Unemployment decreased and housing and other conditions improved for many people.

In addition, Germany experienced a burst of artistic and creative energy in the mid-1920s. Berlin, the nation's capital, became a great center for writers and artists from all over Europe. The German film industry created movies that film students still study today. Modern architecture and furniture design flourished.

The Nazis as a party on the fringe

As the German economy grew and people became more prosperous, the political situation calmed down considerably, and more Germans supported the political parties that were loyal to the Weimar Republic. Nonetheless, the Nazi Party continued to grow. By 1928, it was still small in comparison to other political parties, but it had acquired a membership of 175,000, including some 60,000 brownshirted storm troopers. This large private army gave the Nazis ample power to stir up trouble in Germany.

The Nazi Party did not attract large numbers of voters, however. In the elections of 1928, the party received just over 800,000 votes—about 2.6 percent of the total—and won 12 seats out of 491 in the Reichstag (the national legislature). In comparison, Germany's largest political party, the Social Democrats, received over 9 million votes and won 152 seats in the legislature. A majority of the people's representatives were from parties that favored the Weimar Republic. It looked for a time as if the new German government had survived its difficult beginnings.

The Elections of 1924 and 1928

Party	Seats Won (1924)	Seats Won (1928)
Social Democratic Party (moderate socialist)	131	152
Nationalist Party	103	78
Center Party (Catholic)	69	61
Communist Party	45	54
German People's Party (moderate nationalists)	51	45
Democratic Party (middle class)	32	25
Economic Party (conservatives)	17	23
Bavarian People's Party (Catholic)	19	17
Nazi Party	14	12

The Great Depression

The autumn of 1929 marked the beginning of an economic crisis that shook the whole world. It started in the United States (where it came to be called the Great Depression) with the shocking October crash of the U.S. stock market. A depression is a time of decreased business activity and output, falling prices, and increased unemployment. Depressions happen periodically, but the depression of 1929 devastated many nations. Companies could not sell their products, so they cut the number of their employees and, in some cases, even closed their factories. As a result, fewer people had jobs, leaving them with no money to buy goods. That meant that companies sold even fewer products, which led to more factory closures. The United States' economy, the strongest and largest the world, was in shambles from late 1929 through the 1930s. Soon after the crash in 1929, the drastic economic decline spread rapidly to the industrial countries of

A soup kitchen in 1930 Berlin, Germany.

Europe. The economies of all these countries were connected: they bought and sold each other's products.

Germany was hit harder by the depression than any other major European country, mainly because German companies depended so heavily on exporting their products to other countries. In July 1931, one of Germany's largest banks went out of business because it was unable to pay people the money they had deposited. Within hours, hundreds of thousands of Germans rushed to their own banks to try to get their money out before it was too late. Every bank in Germany was forced to close, and most could not reopen for weeks. Many people lost their entire savings.

At the same time, industrial production fell rapidly. In 1930, Germany produced only about 82 percent as much as it had in 1929. In 1931, it produced only 69 percent as much. By the beginning of 1933, 6 million Germans were unemployed, leaving only about 12 million with jobs. In other words, 1 out of every 3 Germans was out of work.

Unemployment in Germany

The unemployment figures below are probably much lower than the actual number of people who were out of work in Germany from 1929 to 1933. The numbers include only those unemployed individuals who were registered with the German government. In addition, they do not count those people who were employed in part-time positions but were looking for full-time work.

September 1929	1,320,000
September 1930	3,000,000
September 1931	4,350,000
September 1932	5,102,000
January/February 1933	6,000,000+

The unemployed and their families were becoming desperate as the German government seemed unable—or unwilling—to solve the nation's economic problems.

Economic crisis and political deadlock

As unemployment grew in Germany, so did support for those political parties that opposed the Weimar Republic. The Nazis, who had been a party on the fringe of German politics, suddenly became a major force. The storm troopers—uniformed Nazi thugs—multiplied into a huge army. In 1928, there were 60,000 of them. In 1931, there were 170,000, and a year later over 400,000. At the time, the official Germany army was limited to 100,000 soldiers.

With the depression shaking the economy, the German government was almost out of money. It was not collecting sufficient taxes because people were earning less money; it was also paying large amounts in benefits to the unemployed. The conservative parties in the Reichstag, with the support of big business and many middle-class Germans, wanted the government to cut payments to the unemployed, reduce the pay of government employees, and raise taxes on

Nazi officials Wilhelm Frick and Gregor Strasser arrive at the Reichstag building in Berlin after the Nazi Party became the second largest political party in Germany by winning 107 seats in the Reichstag.

the people who still had jobs. The Social Democrats, on the other hand, proposed that necessary funds for the government be raised by hiking taxes on those Germans who made the most money.

Neither the conservatives nor the Social Democrats could get a majority of votes in the Reichstag. The conservative chancellor (prime minister) called new elections for September 1930. He hoped that the voters would elect enough representatives who agreed with him to break the deadlock.

The Nazis stun Germany

The results of the election stunned everyone. The Nazis received almost 6.5 million votes and won 107 seats in the Reichstag. Two years earlier, they had won only 809,000 votes and 12 seats. They were now the second largest party in Germany. The Communists also did much better than they ever had. They received 4.6 million votes and won 77 seats to

Paul von Hindenburg

Conservative candidate Paul von Hindenburg was elected president of Germany in 1925, after the nation's first president, Friedrich Ebert, had died. Hindenburg had been the commander of the German armies in World War I. He was a highly respected national hero, but he was a very old man—83 years old in 1930.

Hindenburg was not a man open to new ideas. His political philosophy was rooted in the nineteenth century and he was basically a monarchist who believed in supporting the kaiser.

Hindenburg was a Junker, the Prussian nobility of eastern Germany, who feared the Communists. Their belief in communal—or group—ownership of land conflicted with his noble upbringing. He was afraid that the party would take over the land of the Junkers.

Hindenburg (a Lutheran) also stood firmly against the Social Democrats and the Catholics. On the other hand, Hindenburg was not pro-Nazi. He disliked Hitler personally, reportedly calling him a "gutter snipe." He felt that Hitler was crude, disrespectful, and low-born—a mere corporal, while Hindenburg was a field marshal in command of all German armies.

Hindenburg had also taken an oath of loyalty to the Weimar Republic. He took this promise very seriously, even though he was personally a monarchist. He believed his personal honor required him to defend the republic against its enemies if they tried to overthrow it illegally. Hitler knew that the officers of the army would obey the old field marshal and fight the storm troopers if the Nazis tried to take power by force.

become Germany's third largest party. The Social Democrats, still the largest political party in the nation with over 8.5 million votes and 143 seats, were down a half a million votes from the last election. This was not just a shift of support from one party to another. Both the Nazis and Communists were opposed to the very existence of the Weimar Republic. Almost a third of the voters had chosen parties that wanted to destroy the government.

When the new Reichstag met in October, the 107 Nazi members marched in wearing the brown uniforms of the storm troopers. At the same time, gangs of Nazis attacked Jews in the streets of Berlin.

Ruling by decree

The divisions within the Reichstag crippled the new government's power. The parties that had supported the

Weimar Republic could not form a majority because of internal disagreements on how to deal with the depression. Without the Nazis, the conservatives alone could not form a majority. It was not even possible to get a majority to agree on who should be the chancellor (the prime minister).

Although in normal times the German president was in most ways a symbolic figurehead similar to the English monarchy today, the president did have some important powers according to the German constitution. One of these powers—designed for temporary, emergency use (such as during a state of civil war)—was to issue laws himself, even though the Reichstag had not agreed to them. This power was called ruling by decree. The president, Paul von Hindenburg, appointed a conservative chancellor, but the man he appointed could not get a majority of votes in the Reichstag. For some time Hindenburg ruled Germany by issuing decrees to carry out the chancellor's policies. (See box discussing Hindenburg's politics on p. 45.)

The presidential elections

Hindenburg's term as president expired early in 1932. Although he was at this time 85 years old, he ran for reelection—not as a conservative but as a candidate who had the support of the Social Democrats and the Catholic Center Party. The Communists ran their own candidate, as did the Nationalist Party. The fourth candidate was Adolf Hitler.

The Nazis crusaded furiously for a win. Hitler made speeches in dozens of cities, crisscrossing Germany by plane, the first time a political candidate had ever done this. In every town where he spoke, Nazi posters were plastered on the walls, uniformed storm troopers stood guard, and torchlight parades lined the streets.

The storm troopers attacked opponents of the Nazis. Nazis and Communists engaged in brawls. And in every speech Hitler repeated the same things he had been saying for years. He attacked all the other parties for failing to make Germany strong. Although he failed to set forth a clear plan detailing how the Nazis would deal with the depression, he claimed that his party was Germany's last great hope: he would help Germany regain its strength, he would stand up to other countries across the world, he would end internal

Goebbels and Propaganda

The man most responsible for Hitler's election campaign strategies was Paul Josef Goebbels. Goebbels was in charge of Nazi propaganda. Propaganda is the spreading of ideas or information to further a cause or to convince a large audience of something, usually something political in nature. Today, mainly because of Goebbels's legacy, the term implies that this "information" is distorted or a complete lie.

Goebbels developed the technique of the "big lie," repeating the same accusations over and over until people believed them. He was the "orchestra leader" who made sure that the uniformed parades, the banners and posters, the speeches, and the songs all worked together to produce a powerful effect. Later, when the Nazis were in power, he controlled all radio broadcasts, films, and theatrical productions.

It was Goebbels who organized the burning of books in the first days of the Nazi government. Books written by Jews, by opponents of the Nazis, or by anyone whose ideas the Nazis hated were thrown on bonfires. At that time, Goebbels' title was Minister (Secretary) of Public Enlightenment and Propaganda.

strife and divisions within the nation. As always, he attacked the Jews, blaming them for the misery of the German people. Only now, as the depression grew worse and worse, more people were willing to listen.

When the votes were tallied, Hindenburg came in first, but over 11 million Germans had voted for Hitler to be their president. Nearly 5 million more had voted for the Communist candidate. Hindenburg had gotten just under 50 percent of the total vote. Because of this, a second round of voting was necessary to choose the president, this time between Hindenburg, Hitler, and the Communists. Again, the Nazis campaigned everywhere, and the storm troopers' violent attacks on their opponents became so outrageous that several state governments demanded the storm troopers be banned. A few days after the second round of the presidential election, the national government outlawed the SA and SS, the two Nazi

The Vote for President of Germany

Candidate	First Round	Second Round
Hindenburg	18,650,730 (49.6%)	19,359,635 (53%)
Hitler	11,339,285 (30.1%)	13,418,051 (36.8%)
Thälmann (Communists)	4,983,197 (13%)	3,706,655 (10.2%)
Dürsterberg (Nationalists)	2,558,000 (6.8%)	did not run

military organizations. The Nazis pretended to obey this law and officially disbanded the storm troopers, but the military group remained active. They simply had to stop wearing their brown uniforms and could no longer openly threaten their opponents.

Hindenburg won the second round of the election, but Hitler received almost 37 percent of the vote. Four years earlier, the Nazis had gotten less than 3 percent.

Nazi violence and Nazi success

Shortly after his reelection, Hindenburg decided to appoint a new chancellor. Franz von Papen had little support in the Reichstag and needed backing from the Nazis to stay in power. In return for their support, he agreed to two Nazi demands. First, there would be new elections to the Reichstag, scheduled for July 1932. Second, the government lifted the ban on the SA. The storm troopers quickly went back into action for the election campaign. In June and the first three weeks of July, there were 461 reported political riots in Prussia, the largest German state. Over 80 people were killed and hundreds were injured seriously.

Late in July, the Nazis marched through a suburb of Hamburg, the great seaport in northern Germany. The area was famous as a Communist stronghold. A gun battle ensued. Nineteen people were killed and almost three hundred more

were wounded. This was the atmosphere in which the German legislative elections were held.

In the elections in July 1932, the Nazi gains were again startling. They received almost 14 million votes and won 230 seats in the Reichstag—more than double their totals from 1930. This represented about 37 percent of the votes. The Nazis had become the largest political party in Germany. The Social Democrats dropped to less than 8 million votes and 133 seats. It seemed the Nazi vote would go higher and higher. In fact, although no one knew it at the time, this was the largest number of votes the Nazis would ever get in a fair election.

The Nazis lose support

Meanwhile the political, economic, and social situation in Germany continued to worsen. In November 1932 there was yet another election—the second Reichstag election in four months. The Nazi Party won less than 12 million votes and 196 seats in the Reichstag. This would have been a tremendous Nazi victory a year earlier, but it was a serious setback compared to the election held in July. They had lost nearly 2 million votes and 34 seats in the Reichstag. For the first time since the beginning of the depression, the Nazis had lost support. In addition, with the near-constant election campaigns and the running of the enormous Nazi organization, including the SA (the storm troopers), the Nazis were running out of money.

The Nazi leaders quarrel

When it looked as if the Nazis had missed their chance to take over Germany legally, disagreements arose among the Nazi leaders about what to do next. For a while, it looked as if the party might split apart. Some Nazi leaders wanted to give up Hitler's plan to come to power legally. It was becoming clear that the Nazis could never win a majority of votes in a free election. These leaders wanted the SA to take over the country by force. They held tight to the belief that the army would refuse to fight the storm troopers—some even felt that the storm troopers could defeat the army if necessary.

But Hitler did not believe the Nazis could come to power by force. The SA was very large, but the storm troopers were no match for the highly trained and well-armed troops of the army. Many army officers were friendly with the Nazis, but if the Nazis tried to take over the government illegally, Hindenburg would almost certainly order the army to resist. And if Hindenburg, only a figurehead president, but a respected war hero, gave those orders, the officers would probably obey.

Other Nazi leaders attacked Hitler for refusing to compromise with the leaders of the conservative parties. The conservatives were willing to let Hitler join the government as

Ernst Röhm

One of the most important early Nazis was Ernst Röhm. By all accounts, Röhm was an exceptionally brutal man, even compared to the other Nazis. Röhm became an officer in the German army during World War I. After the war, he stayed in the army for several years and served as a political advisor to a general.

After he left the army, Röhm had contacts with other ex-officers and with those who remained in the army—people who would not normally associate with someone like Hitler, who had only been a corporal in the army. Röhm had joined the Nazis even before Hitler, and was very important to the party because of these contacts. In addition, as a former member of the Free Corps, he became a key connection between the various Free Corps units in Bavaria and between the Free Corps and the army. (The Free Corps, or *Freikorps* in German, were brutal units of volunteers made up mostly of former officers and professional soldiers.)

Röhm was the leader of the Nazi military wing, the SA or storm troopers. He brought many of his Free Corp veterans into the SA. In later years, as the SA grew dramatically, Röhm continued to show that he was a highly effective organizer.

Because of his early membership in the Nazis, his leadership of the storm troopers, and his contacts with powerful army officers, Röhm was at one time a possible rival to Hitler to lead the Nazis. Röhm was also a homosexual, and Hitler hated homosexuals. Despite this, Röhm became one of Hitler's most important associates and probably his closest friend inside the Nazi Party.

Röhm took the "socialist" part of the Nazi program more seriously than did most of the other early Nazi leaders, including Hitler. He wanted the Nazis to lead a real revolution and completely change the way German society was run. Like all the Nazis, he hated the Jews, but he also hated the traditional leaders of Germany. Later, these views would create a problem for Hitler. Many powerful people, including big businesspeople and army generals who were willing to support Hitler, were afraid of Röhm's influence. Not long after the Nazis came to power, Hitler had Röhm murdered.

vice-chancellor but not as chancellor (prime minister). Hitler refused. He insisted on being chancellor or nothing at all.

Hitler makes a deal

Hitler bargained with various conservative leaders for months, trying to make a deal. These leaders underestimated the power—and the danger—of the Nazi Party. They felt the Nazis might actually prove useful in helping them run the country. Some conservatives even encouraged rich supporters to give money to the Nazi cause.

From his window in the Reichschancellory, Adolf Hitler addresses the public during a parade to celebrate his appointment as Chancellor of Germany on January 30, 1933.

The conservative politicians convinced Hindenburg to name Hitler as chancellor. The conservatives remained in charge of the cabinet, the army, and the national police. They were sure that Hitler would be under their control. On January 30, 1933, Hitler became the head of the German government because of a backroom deal cut between the Nazis and conservative political leaders who could not rule without Nazi support. He came to power legally, though without ever winning a majority of the votes.

The end of democracy

Hitler then decided to hold one more election. The Nazis were sure that, with the power of the government on their side, they would be able to win a majority in the Reichstag. The government controlled the radio stations. The storm troopers would not have to worry about the police. The Nazis now had plenty of money.

The Reichstag elections were scheduled for March 1933. On February 27, after Hitler had been chancellor less than a month, the Reichstag building was set on fire. The Nazis claimed this had been the work of the Communist Party. The fire was supposedly a signal for a communist revolution. The Reichstag fire and the trial that followed it became one of the major news events of the time.

The Nazi government quickly charged several people with setting the fire. One, Martinus van der Lubbe, was an ex-Communist from Holland. He was arrested at the scene and admitted setting the fire, claiming that he had acted alone. But many people thought van der Lubbe was crazy and did not believe his confession. The other accused men were leading Communists who denied having anything to do with the fire. There was no evidence to support the involvement of anyone but van der Lubbe, who was convicted and executed.

Many people at the time and in the years since have thought that the Nazis set the fire themselves so that Hitler

The Nazis and Big Business

The connection between the Nazi Party and big business has always been a subject of dispute. Some business leaders had supported the Nazis for many years. One of the most important of these leaders was Fritz Thyssen, who controlled much of the German steel industry.

However, many great industrialists preferred old-fashioned conservative parties, such as the Nationalist Party. After all, the name "Nazi" was short for "National Socialist," and some business leaders were afraid that the Nazis took the "socialist" part of that title seriously. They were worried that a Nazi-led government might interfere with the way they ran their companies, or would even take them over, as the Nazi Party program claimed they would.

In January 1932, Thyssen arranged for Hitler to speak to a meeting of German industrial leaders in Düsseldorf, the center of the steel industry. Hitler told them that the Nazi Party was totally committed to private ownership of companies and that a Nazi government would not interfere with their business dealings. In fact, the Nazis would destroy the Communists and Social Democrats, the enemies of private property.

When the speech was over, the businesspeople cheered Hitler. Financial support for the Nazis soon increased. Like many other groups in Germany, the big industrialists decided that the Nazis could be useful allies, that they were committed to a common goal.

could use emergency powers to become dictator. Historians make a case based on two main points: (1) Hitler and the Nazis reacted so quickly to the fire that they must have made their plans in advance. (2) Several witnesses later claimed that Hermann Göring bragged to them about arranging the fire. Göring, a leading Nazi, was then the chairman of the Reichstag, and his office was connected to the building. No one knows if van der Lubbe really set the fire or if he acted alone. Regardless of who actually set the fire, the Nazis were able to use the incident to destroy the Weimar Republic.

Two Nazi soldiers view the remains of the Reichstag building after the disastrous fire.

The day after the fire, Hitler issued an emergency decree signed by Hindenburg. This decree gave Hitler special powers to "protect" the nation against "Communist acts of violence." It gave the government the power to ignore almost all the rights given citizens by the constitution. Hitler could restrict freedom of speech and freedom of the press. He could ban meetings and outlaw political organizations. His police could tap telephones, open private mail, search homes without a warrant. The government could seize the property of its opponents. The decree allowed Hitler to take over each of the different German states' governments. It signaled the end of the Weimar Republic and of democracy in Germany.

The beginning of the Nazi police state

The Nazis moved quickly. The night after the Reichstag fire, the police arrested more than 10,000 people. All the leaders of the Communist Party who could be found, including

Hermann Göring

Unlike the other early Nazis, Hermann Göring was a member of the nobility. (His father had been the governor of a German colony in Africa.) Like many nobles, Göring became an officer. He was one of Germany's most famous fighter pilots during World War I.

When the war ended, Göring could not adjust to peacetime Germany. For a while he lived in Sweden, where he married a wealthy Swedish woman. When he returned to Germany, he heard Hitler speak at a nationalist demonstration and was dazzled. Göring joined the Nazi Party and was put in charge of training and drilling the storm troopers. He was badly wounded in the Beer Hall Putsch but managed to escape to Austria.

Because of his noble background and his fame as a war hero, Göring had access to many wealthy and prominent people. He was also much more skillful than most of the early Nazis in the art of socializing. Göring could be invited to a dinner party and fit right in. He could swap stories and tell jokes. He enjoyed good food and wine. He seemed much less intense and obsessed than Hitler, who apparently could never talk about anything except politics. He used his social connections to advance the Nazi cause and to introduce Hitler to prominent people in Bavaria.

Göring became one of the most powerful men in the Nazi Party and then in Germany, and he served as the commander of the German Air Force (the *Luftwaffe*). At various times, Göring was the head of Prussia, Germany's largest state; the first chief of the Gestapo (an abbreviation for *Geheime Staatspolizei,* or the secret police); and the key organizer of Hitler's economic plans for Germany. Despite his supposedly easy-going nature, he used his power ruthlessly and did not hesitate to murder opponents. But Göring never lost his taste for good living: he became immensely wealthy by robbing great works of art from all over Europe.

Göring committed suicide in his jail cell before he could be hanged as a war criminal.

---

members of the Reichstag, were jailed. The rest went into hiding. The arrested Communists were soon sent to concentration camps, prison camps that were being set up by the SA. They were the first victims of the Nazi police state.

Forty thousand members of the SA and the SS had been made special police officers. They still wore their Nazi uniforms as they beat their opponents, kidnapped them, and spread terror everywhere—only now they were acting "legally." The regular police could only stand by and watch.

The election campaign continued, but only pro-Nazi political meetings were allowed. The offices of anti-Nazi

A view of a section of the Dachau concentration camp, the first permanent camp to which the Nazis sent their enemies.

newspapers were smashed. The speeches of Hitler and other top Nazis filled the radio waves.

The last election

Almost 90 percent of the voters cast their ballots on March 5, 1933. The Nazi Party received over 17 million votes, about 44 percent. The Nationalist Party, the allies of the Nazis in the election, got another 3 million. The Social Democrats won 7 million, about the same as before, and the Communists—even though they were in jail or hiding—received almost 5 million votes.

Even in these circumstances a majority of Germans still refused to vote for the Nazis. Almost 30 percent voted for the Social Democrats or the Communists, the Nazis' strongest enemies. It was a major disappointment for the Nazis. But votes did not matter anymore. The Nazis had power—and they used it.

The Enabling Act

The new Reichstag met on March 24, 1933. The Nazis wanted to pass one more law, the Enabling Act, which would allow the government to issue laws without the approval of the Reichstag for four years. Unlike the emergency decree issued after the Reichstag fire, these laws could be issued by Hitler alone, without the approval of Hindenburg. The Enabling Act was, in effect, a law that said that from that point on, the "law" would be whatever Adolf Hitler wanted it to be. The act clearly stated that such laws could directly violate the terms of the constitution.

Because the Enabling Act would change the constitution, a two-thirds majority of the Reichstag had to vote for it. Even with their Nationalist allies, the Nazis did not have two-thirds of the vote. But they fixed this problem easily by eliminating their opposition. Of the eighty-one Communists who had been elected to the Reichstag, most were in jail, and the others knew they would be arrested if they showed up for a vote. Two dozen Social Democrats were prevented from attending, some of them by being put in prison. Finally, Hitler convinced the two Catholic parties to vote for the Enabling Act by promising them that he would not interfere with the activities of the Catholic Church.

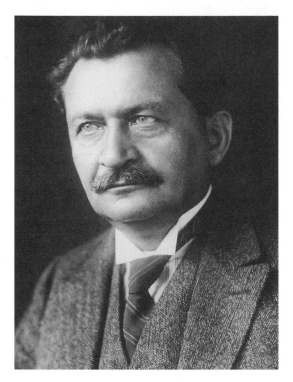

Otto Wels, a leader of the Social Democrats, courageously spoke out against the Enabling Act even though he knew his life was in danger and that the law would pass.

The building where the Reichstag met was surrounded by uniformed SS men. Inside it was filled with the storm troopers of the SA. During their speeches, the Nazis chanted that if the Enabling Act were not passed, there would be "fire and murder" throughout Germany.

The final vote was 441 in favor of the Enabling Act and 94 against it. Only the Social Democrats voted against the act.

The Nazis take control of Germany

Hitler was now "legally" allowed to do the things the Nazis had always intended to do. During the next several months, almost every organization that might oppose the Nazis was destroyed.

The various states of Germany traditionally held a great deal of power, including control of most police forces. Hitler used the Enabling Act to smash their strength. The elected governments of each state were replaced by governors who were appointed by Hitler. All were Nazis. From this point on, the state governments did exactly as they were ordered to do by the national government in Berlin—which meant they did exactly what Hitler wanted them to do.

In April 1933, the first law was issued to remove opponents of the Nazis from all government jobs. Anyone suspected of Communist or Social Democratic sympathies was fired. And, in the first of a long series of antisemitic laws, Jews were barred from holding any official positions. Soon, lawyers needed Nazi permission in order to practice their profession. Within a few months, journalists, radio broadcasters, musicians, and theatrical performers were all subject to Nazi approval.

On May 2, 1933, the SA and SS took over the offices of all the labor unions in Germany. Union leaders were beaten up and sent to concentration camps. The free labor unions were abolished and replaced by the German Labor Front, run by a Nazi official. Membership was mandatory for all workers. Later that month, the workers lost their rights to bargain with their employers and to strike.

On May 10, the Nazis took over the Social Democrats' buildings and newspapers and seized all the party's money. The next month, the Social Democratic Party was officially banned as "an enemy of the people." Similarly, on May 26, all money and property of the Communist Party was taken over. (For all practical purposes, with the bulk of its leadership imprisoned, the Communist Party had already been banned for months.)

The Nazis did not stop with their longtime enemies. The Nationalist Party, the Nazis' ally in the last election and their partner in the government, was no longer needed. The SA took over many of its offices in June. The leader of the Nationalists, who was still a member of the government, could not stop this action. Neither could Hindenburg. Soon the Nationalist Party announced that it had dissolved. The party abolished itself, knowing that it would soon be eliminated anyway.

Then the Nazis went after the other parties that had voted for the Enabling Act. In late June, they took over the offices of the Bavarian People's Party, the Catholic party of the southern state of Bavaria, and arrested the party's leaders. The Bavarian People's Party dissolved itself on July 4, 1933. Its larger ally, the Center Party—the main Catholic party that had long held the loyalty of its millions of supporters—abolished itself the next day. On July 14, 1933, Germany officially became a one-party state. On that day, a new law was published. It was very short. First it said that "the National Socialist German Workers' Party [the Nazi Party's full name] constitutes the only political party in Germany." Then it said that anyone who tried to keep another political party going, or who tried to form a new political party, could be sent to prison.

Within six months after becoming chancellor, Hitler had established himself as the dictator of Germany. His Nazi Party was the nation's only legal political party. The road to mass murder was open.

3

The Nazi Attack on the Jews

When Adolf Hitler became chancellor of Germany, the head of the German government, on January 30, 1933, he had three main goals: (1) to destroy his opponents in Germany; (2) to make Germany the strongest country in Europe; and (3) to "purify" Germany—and then Europe—of peoples he called "racial enemies" and establish Germans as the "master race." These three goals were closely connected; all hinged on Hitler's hatred of the Jews.

For the first six and a half years of the Nazi government, from early 1933 until September 1939, the Nazis took a series of steps to reach their party's objectives. At first, many of these steps were small, because the Nazis knew they would face opposition in Germany, and they also wanted to avoid outraging people and governments in the rest of the world. With the successful completion of each small step, however, the Nazi Party began to make larger

An SA member stands in front of a Jewish-owned department store. The sign next to him reads "Germans defend yourselves; don't buy from Jews!"

and more dramatic moves toward their goals. One of the most daring was Germany's September 1, 1939, invasion of Poland, which started World War II. In the years of bloody conflict that followed, the Nazis carried out the Holocaust, the attempt to physically destroy the Jewish people.

The first attack on the Jews

For years, the brown-shirted SA or storm troopers, the Nazi Party's military organization, had attacked and harassed Jews on the streets. (SA is an abbreviation for *Sturmabteilung.*)

Nazi newspapers and speeches helped to spread and reinforce this hatred. The party referred to the entire Jewish people as vermin (small pests such as lice or fleas that are difficult to control), declared them enemies of Germany, and demanded that they be thrown out of the country.

Once the Nazis gained power in 1933, these hate-filled ideas became the official policy of the German government. Almost as soon as Hitler became chancellor, the storm troopers stepped up their campaign of terror. Jews were beaten up on the streets. In one city, the storm troopers invaded the local courthouse and dragged out Jewish lawyers and judges. Jewish-owned stores were attacked. Because the Nazis ran the government, the Jews could not turn to the police for help. At this time, the person in charge of the police in Prussia, Germany's largest state, was Hermann Göring, a leading Nazi. He publicly announced that the police would not protect "Jewish department stores."

Meanwhile, Jews in some of the higher-paying professions, especially lawyers, were being forced out of their jobs. For example, the southern state of Bavaria prohibited Jews from serving as prosecutors and barred Jewish judges from presiding over criminal cases. (Prosecutors are attorneys who represent the government.) In Prussia, the new minister of justice (similar to the post of attorney-general in the United States) ordered all Jewish judges and prosecutors to "retire" by April 1, 1933, and barred Jews from serving on juries.

World protests and Nazi response

In many countries around the world, people were shocked by what was happening in Germany. Each day, newspaper stories and radio reports detailed some new outrageous action taken by the Nazis, especially in their treatment of the Jews. In several major cities worldwide, people talked of boycotting (refusing to buy) products made in Germany. In the United States, the Jewish War Veterans of America announced that its members would boycott German goods and urged others to do the same.

The Nazis accused the German Jews of causing trouble for Germany by spreading false "atrocity stories." In fact, the stories of cruelty, horror, and brutality were being spread by reliable newspaper and radio reporters—people who could

see with their own eyes what was happening to the Jews in Germany.

Hermann Göring called the leaders of German Jewish organizations to his office for a meeting on March 26, 1933, whereupon he ordered the Jewish leaders to stop spreading "atrocity stories" about the Nazis. He demanded that they convince Jewish organizations in other countries to call off their plans for a boycott. If they didn't, he threatened, massive violent action would be taken against the Jews.

Because of these threats, Germany's Jewish organizations sent telegrams to Jewish organizations in other countries warning them that anti-German stories were harming the Jews in Germany and urging Jewish groups *not* to boycott German products. Of course, most of the groups who received these messages understood that they had been written under duress (compelled by threat), but they also understood that the Nazi Party's threats were very real. For

A rally in New York to protest the enactment of anti-Jewish legislation attended by Rabbi Stephen Wise (seated left) and Bishop William T. Manning. Rallies similar to this were held around the world.

Hitler's Method: A Calm between Each Storm

Although the first anti-Jewish actions caused many problems for German Jews, very few people thought that anti-semitism would lead to the unbelievable reality of the Holocaust. Everyone understood that the Nazi government would be unfriendly to the Jews. But most Germans—Jews and non-Jews alike—believed that the physical attacks on Jews were temporary and that things would soon calm down. And, over the next few years, this is often what seemed to happened. Every time the Nazis took some major new anti-Jewish action, it was followed by a period of relative calm. Time after time, people were fooled into thinking that "the worst was over," that conditions for Jews would improve or at least level off. These periods of calm were part of Hitler's method of preventing opposition to his acts.

this reason, the boycotts of German products were never very effective.

The anti-Jewish boycott

The threat of anti-German boycotts in other countries was a perfect excuse for the Nazis to attack the German Jews with greater ferocity. On the same day as Göring's threat to the Jewish leaders, Hitler met with Josef Goebbels, the man in charge of Nazi propaganda. Propaganda is the spreading of ideas or information to further a cause or to convince a large audience of something, usually something political in nature. Today, mainly because of Goebbels's legacy, the term implies that this "information" is distorted—or even a complete lie.

Hitler instructed Goebbels to organize a large-scale boycott of all Jewish businesses in Germany. This boycott would be explained to the German people as a "defense" against the anti-German stories that the Jews were supposedly spreading. In fact, the Nazis had been trying for years to convince Germans not to shop at Jewish-owned stores. Hitler had planned

Reichminister Josef Goebbels , responsible for the spread of Nazi propaganda, speaks at a large rally in Berlin, 1933.

an anti-Jewish boycott committee even before he knew about the threat of a boycott against the Nazis. But now his plan could be disguised as a defensive measure instead of an unprovoked attack on the Jews.

The boycott was set for April 1, 1933, and Goebbels, in the meantime, tried to whip up support for the Nazi cause. The official Nazi Party paper used its entire front page on March 29 to publish a detailed order to all party members on how to organize the boycott. Every local branch of the Nazi Party was ordered to create an Action Committee. In the cities, these committees were supposed to visit factories to convince the workers to support the boycott. In the country-side, they were instructed to spread the boycott propaganda to the smallest villages.

The Nazis held mass meetings all over the country to support the boycott and demand that the government limit the number of Jews in all professions. In fact, the Nazi gov-

The Boycott: A Rehearsal for the Nazis

The boycott was the first major action taken by the new Nazi government and a real test of their methods. In this early phase of their rule, the Nazis needed to show the German people that they were firmly in control.

Even though the Nazi Party had received less than half the vote in national elections a couple of months before the boycott, they had a firm grip on the government and were already using terror tactics on their opponents. Still, the Nazis had very little support from some segments of the population, including factory workers, whose labor unions had not yet been destroyed, and farmers and other people in heavily Catholic areas of the country. The anti-Jewish boycott was partly an attempt to get these groups to support the Nazis.

In ensuing years, the Nazis used the same methods whenever they needed to rally support for *any* of their actions, not just when they were attacking the Jews. When Hitler made demands for territory from foreign countries, for instance, the newspapers and radio would repeat the official version of events over and over. Nazi Party members would be instructed on their roles. Mass meetings would be held. But alongside the propaganda campaign, there existed the constant threat of arrest and Nazi violence.

ernment had already decided to set this limit, and the "demands" were carefully arranged to look as if the Nazis were acting in response to what the German people wanted.

On the day of the boycott, uniformed storm troopers stood guard at the entrances to Jewish-owned stores. They had been given printed posters announcing the boycott. In addition, they painted anti-Jewish slogans and six-pointed Jewish stars on shop windows. The same thing happened at the offices of Jewish doctors and lawyers.

World reaction to the boycott was very negative. Within three days, the Nazis announced that the "boycott has achieved its purpose and is over."

The first anti-Jewish laws

The boycott of Jewish businesses and the Nazi-led mass meetings were supposed to show that the German people were angry at the Jews and were demanding that the government take action against them. Almost immediately after the boycott, the Nazi government began passing a series of laws and official orders targeting the Jews.

On April 7, 1933, a law removed most Jews from government jobs, including teaching in a public school or university. Any Jew hired from 1914 on was fired, except for Jews who had fought in the German army in World War I, or whose father or son had died in that war. The reason for these exceptions was a letter to Hitler from the president of Germany, Paul von Hindenburg, the old commander of the German armies in World War I. He objected to firing Jewish war veterans and their survivors. "If they were worthy to fight and bleed for Germany, then they should also be considered

Opposite page:

A reproduction of the first page of an addendum to the Reich Citizenship Law of 1935. (See p. 70 for a discussion of this, the first of the Nuremberg Laws.)

worthy to continue serving the fatherland in their professions," he wrote. He did not protest, however, over the treatment of Jews in general.

Later that month, another law removed Jewish doctors from the National Health Service. A law passed on April 25, 1933, limited the number of Jewish students in a school to 1.5 percent of the total. Other laws and official orders prevented Jews from working as pharmacists or as newspaper editors and strictly limited their access to jobs in the theater and film industries.

Although these laws did not apply to most private companies, Jews were soon being fired from these jobs as well. Many Jewish people soon found themselves unable to earn a decent living. Some moved from smaller towns and cities to larger cities, especially to Berlin, the German capital, where they hoped they could find work.

Other German Jews decided that it was no longer possible to live in their own country. In 1933, 53,000 Jews left Germany, about one out of every ten Jews in the country. Roughly 16,000 of them returned later, mainly because of the difficult conditions they faced as refugees. (Refugees are people who flee to a foreign country to escape danger or persecution. Jewish refugees are discussed at length later in this chapter, pp.79–88.)

Hitler pauses

For a while, it seemed as though the Nazi attack on the Jews would come to an end. In July 1933, Hitler announced that the Nazi "revolution" had succeeded and was officially over. The following June, the leaders of the storm troopers (the SA) were murdered on Hitler's orders. Hitler defended these murders by saying that the SA leaders had wanted Germany to continue in a state of turmoil. What Germany needed now, Hitler said, were calm and orderly procedures, not more revolution.

The storm troopers had been the most extreme and the most brutal enemies of the Jews. Their leaders had been the most "radical" of the Nazis. Many Jews, as well as other Germans, believed that Hitler's attack on the SA meant that Nazi policies against the Jews would become more moderate.

Reichsgefetzblatt

Teil I

| 1935 | Ausgegeben zu Berlin, den 14. November 1935 | Nr. 125 |

Tag	Inhalt	Seite
14. 11. 35	Erste Verordnung zum Reichsbürgergesetz.............................	1333
14. 11. 35	Erste Verordnung zur Ausführung des Gesetzes zum Schutze des deutschen Blutes und der deutschen Ehre..........................	1334

Erste Verordnung zum Reichsbürgergesetz.
Vom 14. November 1935.

Auf Grund des § 3 des Reichsbürgergesetzes vom 15. September 1935 (Reichsgesetzbl. I S. 1146) wird folgendes verordnet:

§ 1

(1) Bis zum Erlaß weiterer Vorschriften über den Reichsbürgerbrief gelten vorläufig als Reichsbürger die Staatsangehörigen deutschen oder artverwandten Blutes, die beim Inkrafttreten des Reichsbürgergesetzes das Reichstagswahlrecht besessen haben, oder denen der Reichsminister des Innern im Einvernehmen mit dem Stellvertreter des Führers das vorläufige Reichsbürgerrecht verleiht.

(2) Der Reichsminister des Innern kann im Einvernehmen mit dem Stellvertreter des Führers das vorläufige Reichsbürgerrecht entziehen.

§ 2

(1) Die Vorschriften des § 1 gelten auch für die staatsangehörigen jüdischen Mischlinge.

(2) Jüdischer Mischling ist, wer von einem oder zwei der Rasse nach volljüdischen Großelternteilen abstammt, sofern er nicht nach § 5 Abs. 2 als Jude gilt. Als volljüdisch gilt ein Großelternteil ohne weiteres, wenn er der jüdischen Religionsgemeinschaft angehört hat.

§ 3

Nur der Reichsbürger kann als Träger der vollen politischen Rechte das Stimmrecht in politischen Angelegenheiten ausüben und ein öffentliches Amt bekleiden. Der Reichsminister des Innern oder die von ihm ermächtigte Stelle kann für die Übergangszeit Ausnahmen für die Zulassung zu öffentlichen Ämtern gestatten. Die Angelegenheiten der Religionsgesellschaften werden nicht berührt.

§ 4

(1) Ein Jude kann nicht Reichsbürger sein. Ihm steht ein Stimmrecht in politischen Angelegenheiten nicht zu; er kann ein öffentliches Amt nicht bekleiden.

(2) Jüdische Beamte treten mit Ablauf des 31. Dezember 1935 in den Ruhestand. Wenn diese Beamten im Weltkrieg an der Front für das Deutsche Reich oder für seine Verbündeten gekämpft haben, erhalten sie bis zur Erreichung der Altersgrenze als Ruhegehalt die vollen zuletzt bezogenen ruhegehaltsfähigen Dienstbezüge; sie steigen jedoch nicht in Dienstaltersstufen auf. Nach Erreichung der Altersgrenze wird ihr Ruhegehalt nach den letzten ruhegehaltsfähigen Dienstbezügen neu berechnet.

(3) Die Angelegenheiten der Religionsgesellschaften werden nicht berührt.

But Hitler had the SA leaders killed for entirely different reasons, primarily to appease army officers who felt their power threatened by the SA. (The murder of the SA leaders, known as the "Night of the Long Knives," is discussed in Chapter 4.) The pause in anti-Jewish actions gave him the time he needed to get firmer control of Germany before going further and let anti-Nazi feelings around the world calm down.

The Nuremberg Laws

In 1935, anti-Jewish action returned to Germany with new vigor. Nazi newspapers increased their attacks on the Jews. In May, Jews were officially banned from the German armed forces. Then, in July, gangs of Nazis began to attack Jews in Berlin's main shopping district and destroy Jewish-owned shops.

That September, a special session of the German parliament, the Reichstag, met in the southern city of Nuremberg. The Reichstag was no longer a real legislative body; that is, its members did not really represent the majority of the people of Germany. Rather, the Reichstag was composed of faithful members of the Nazi Party.

The Reichstag passed two laws at that meeting, both written on Hitler's direct order. The first law, called the Reich Citizenship Law, stated that only a person of "German or related blood" could be a citizen of Germany, and that only a citizen could have political rights or hold office.

The second law voted by the Reichstag was called the "Law for the Protection of German Blood and German Honor." This law made it illegal for Jews and non-Jews to get married or to engage in sexual relations together. Jews were not allowed to have a non-Jewish female servant under 45 years old. In addition, Jews were forbidden to fly the German flag.

Two months later, the Nazis issued a decree to carry out these laws. It stated that anyone with three Jewish grandparents was a Jew; anyone with two Jewish grandparents was a Jew if he or she "belonged to the Jewish religious community" or if he or she were married to a Jew.

The Nuremberg Laws accomplished several things. They placed Jews in a special legal category—one that deprived

German citizens salute Hitler at the opening of the 1936 Olympic Games in Berlin.

them of basic rights. They stated that Jews were not Germans, no matter how long their families had lived in the country and no matter how loyal to the country they had been. They stated that being a German or a Jew was part of a person's "blood" and could never be changed.

A modern, supposedly civilized country had made race-hatred its law. After the Nuremberg Laws were established, the German government did not consider Jews to be citizens. The next step—a step that at this point still seemed impossible—was to consider them as being less than human.

Hitler pauses again: The Olympics

Once again, Hitler paused in his attack on the Jews. The reason this time was the opening of the 1936 Olympic Games in Berlin. Thousands of visitors from around the world would be there, and the Nazis wanted to improve their image. They erased anti-Jewish slogans from the win-

Prejudice and a Lost Opportunity

People around the world, and especially Americans, celebrated African-American track and field star Jesse Owens's medals as victories against Nazi racism. But something else happened on the American Olympic team that was much less glorious.

Two of the four Americans scheduled to run in the 400-meter relay, Marty Glickman and Sam Stoller, were Jewish. The president of the American Olympic committee, Avery Brundage, ordered them removed from the race. Many people believe that Brundage was prejudiced against Jews. Others think that he did not want to offend Hitler. Perhaps both are true. Whatever the reason, Brundage's decision prevented what might have been the most important result of the Berlin Olympics. In a complete contradiction of Nazi ideas about Jews and about the supposed weakness of racially "mixed" nations, the world would have seen four Americans, two Jewish and two non-Jewish, on the victory stand together.

dows of Jewish-owned stores. Huge processions and ceremonies took place with thousands of uniformed Nazis in attendance. The Nazis wanted everyone to see how well they had organized the games and were running Germany. The German crowds roared their approval and gave the stiff-armed Nazi salute each time Hitler appeared at the newly built Olympic Stadium.

The Nazis also wanted to use the Olympics to show the superior strength of the "Aryan race." They used the word "Aryan" to describe white Europeans, especially Germans. They thought Aryans constituted a superior "race" that should rule over the others. The Nazis expected their athletes to dominate the competitors from other countries—especially those from "racially inferior" and "weak" democratic countries.

Jesse Owens destroyed those plans. Owens was not only an American, he was an African American—a member of what the Nazis considered an "inferior race." He dominated the track and field competition, the most important part of

the games. Owens won four Olympic gold medals, including
one for the 100-meter run. That made Owens—not an
"Aryan"—the "fastest man in the world." Although Germany
won more medals than any other country, it was clearly Jesse
Owens's Olympics.

But even if they did not prove the athletic superiority of
the "Aryan race," the Nazis gained a great deal from the
Olympics. The countries of the world did not boycott them,
despite the Nuremberg Laws. Foreign visitors saw an orderly
country whose leader seemed to be very popular and whose

people seemed to be enthusiastic supporters of their government. (Of course, anyone who might oppose the Nazis had been arrested long before.) They did not see Jews being beaten up on the streets because the Nazis had ordered a temporary halt to this.

1938

What Hitler and the Nazis meant for the Jews and for Europe became clear in 1938. That year was one of great territorial expansion for Hitler. The German army marched into Austria and made it part of Germany without firing a shot. Then Hitler demanded territory from Czechoslovakia—and teetered on the brink of war with Britain and France before his demands were met—thus adding even more land to Germany.

In 1938, the campaign against the Jews, with its combination of harsh new laws and increasing violence, brought about conditions so terrible that there was no longer any future for the Jews of Germany.

New laws and new violence

A law that took effect in March 1938 stripped Jewish organizations such as synagogues, Jewish houses of worship, of the right to own property and to enter into contracts. In April, all Jewish businesses, except the very smallest, were required to register with the government. One vague portion of this law became very important a few months later. It stated that the German government could use the registered property "for the needs of the German economy." This meant that the property could be taken over.

Early in June 1938, the Great Synagogue of Munich was burned down. Later that month the police arrested all German Jews with police records—which usually meant parking tickets. Some 1,500 Jews were sent to concentration camps, brutal prison camps run by the SS, the Nazi military organization that would later be in charge of the Holocaust. (The name "SS" was taken from the German initials for *Schutzstaffel,* meaning "defense corps," a military unit made up of the Nazi elite.) During this time, the Nazis also went after the Jews of Austria, which had become part of Germany in March. By September, 4,000 Austrian Jews were in concentration camps. The arrested Jews were released only if they agreed to leave the country.

In August, the synagogue in Nuremberg was destroyed. Two months later, the Gestapo (the *Geheime Staatspolizei* or secret police) began rounding up Jewish Poles living in Germany to deport them (force them to exit) to Poland. At the time, there were over 50,000 Jewish Poles in Germany, and most had been living in Germany for many years. Nevertheless, the Gestapo arrested 18,000 Jews of Polish origin, including whole families. On the night of October 27, 1938, they were put on special trains and sent to the Polish border. The Polish government refused to allow them into their native country.

About 5,000 people were held in a dreadful camp on the Polish side of the border. Among the detainees were members of the Grynszpan family, who had lived in Germany since 1914. Zindel Grynszpan wrote a letter describing their situation to his son, who was living in Paris, France. When 17-year-old Herschel Grynszpan read his father's letter, he decided on revenge. Grynszpan went to the German embassy in Paris with a gun—intent on killing the German ambassador. When he failed to gain access to the ambassador's office, Grynszpan shot and severely wounded a lower level official, Ernst vom Rath, instead.

The Nazis used Herschel Grynszpan's shooting of a low-level official as an excuse to wreak terror during Kristallnacht.

Kristallnacht

The Nazis used this shooting as an excuse—a trick they had often used in the past. Goebbels, in charge of propaganda, attempted to stir up public outrage over the shooting of vom Rath. The Nazis declared that all Jews were responsible for the attack and that the shooting was a crime against all Germans. In the usual Nazi fashion, party meetings were held in small towns throughout Germany where local officials gave fiery speeches. Then mobs set out to destroy Jewish property, beat up Jews, and burn the local synagogue.

Germans pass by the broken shop window of a Jewish-owned business that was destroyed during Kristallnacht.

On the night of November 9, 1938, word reached Germany that vom Rath had died of his wounds. Goebbels, with Hitler's knowledge, launched a nationwide campaign of anti-Jewish mob violence. In every city in Germany, the storm troopers, wearing civilian clothing, attacked Jewish homes, stores, synagogues, and orphanages. Buildings were burned, the furniture thrown on the street. The German police did not interfere. Their orders were to make sure the fires did not spread to non-Jewish property, to prevent looting, and to protect foreigners (even if they were Jewish).

Seven thousand businesses were destroyed that night. The streets of German towns and cities were filled with shattered glass (*kristall* in German) from the broken windows of Jewish-owned stores. That gave the terrible night its name: *Kristallnacht,* or Crystal Night, the "night of broken glass."

About a hundred Jews were killed, most of them beaten to death. Thousands of others were injured. An American diplomat in the city of Leipzig described how "an eighteen-year old boy was hurled from a three-story window to land with both legs broken on a street littered with burning beds and other household furniture."

The same witness wrote that storm troopers threw terri-fied Jews into a stream after destroying their homes. Then the storm troopers ordered the spectators, ordinary Germans, to spit at the Jews and throw mud at them. The spectators, according to the American witness, were "horrified" by what was happening.

Goebbels had wanted the violence to look like the "spontaneous" anger of the German people; it was not sup-posed to look like the work of the government or the Nazi Party. But no one was fooled. The attacks were planned by Nazi officials and carried out by storm troopers. Very few other Germans took part in it. Most of them, as the American diplomat thought, were shocked and disturbed by the vio-lence. But few Germans did anything to try to stop it.

The arrests

Some Nazi leaders had not been told of Goebbels's plan in advance and were angry at what had happened. These leaders included Heinrich Himmler, the head of the SS and of the Gestapo. Himmler wanted to control anti-Jewish policies himself. In addition, he strongly opposed mob action, even if the mobs were organized by the Nazis. He liked things to be done according to orders and out of the public's sight. That was the way, within three years, that Himmler and his SS would begin the mass murder of the Jews.

Although Himmler disapproved of *Kristallnacht,* he took advantage of it. Thirty thousand Jewish men were arrested and sent to the concentration camps that the SS ran. Himm-ler's plan was to force these men and their families to buy their freedom, and then make them leave Germany.

The economic measures

Another Nazi leader who had not known about *Kristall-nacht* beforehand was Hermann Göring, who was in charge of Hitler's economic plan for Germany. Göring was furious at the destruction of the mob act because of the economic dam-

A group of Nazis hold hands in an attempt to prevent Jews from entering a university in 1938. The Nazis enacted a series of laws that first limited the number of Jewish students in German schools and then banned them entirely.

age it caused. But like Himmler, Göring used the events that occurred on *Kristallnacht* against the Jewish people.

Göring decided that the German government would seize any insurance money paid to Jewish property owners. In addition, Jews were to be held responsible for repairing the damage caused by the storm troopers. Jewish-owned businesses that had been forced to close because of the destruction would not be allowed to reopen unless they had non-Jewish owners. Göring also announced a "fine" against the Jewish community for the death of vom Rath. The total was one billion marks (German dollars), an enormous amount.

On November 12, 1938, Göring issued an official order titled "Decree on Eliminating the Jews from German Economic Life." It prohibited Jews from selling any goods or services, from being independent craftsmen, or from being in the management position of any company. Three days later all remaining Jewish children were expelled from the nation's schools. In December, Jews were barred from many public places, including movie theaters and beaches.

Forced emigration

The Jews could no longer earn a living in Germany. Their children could not attend schools. Their property was being seized and sold by the government to non-Jews, a process the Nazis called "Aryanization." Thousands of Jewish people had already been arrested and put in concentration camps. The next step was to force them out of Germany.

The Nazis set up a Reich Central Office for Jewish Emigration. (Emigration is the process of leaving one's home country.) The job of the Central Office was to get the Jews to leave Germany "by every possible means." The official in charge of this operation was Reinhard Heydrich, Himmler's deputy. Later, Heydrich would be in direct charge of the Holocaust.

Herman Göring, who was responsible for the German economy, took advantage of the destruction of Kristallnacht to seize any insurance money paid to Jews.

Heydrich had a model to follow. Since March 1938, when Germany took over Austria, the Nazis had forced thousands of Austrian Jews to leave the country. The Austrian Jews were subjected to nonstop violence and frightening threats, and then were offered emigration as their only other choice. In this way, the Nazis hoped to "rid" Germany of its Jews.

At the same time, Heydrich made it difficult for German Jews to leave. Jews had to make large payments as "exit fees." Even well-off German Jews were left with few resources to take with them as they started a new life in another country. Those who were poor to begin with had even greater problems.

By this time, there were 30,000 Jewish men in concentration camps. They were released on the condition that they and their families had to leave Germany within 30 days. Thousands of Jewish families had only days to make all the arrangements to leave the only country they had ever known.

It was much easier for physicist Albert Einstein to escape Germany because of his fame. Most Jewish emigrants weren't as fortunate

This was the policy that Heydrich followed until September 1939, when World War II began. After that, emigration became almost impossible.

The United States and refugees

Even if the Jews could get out of Germany, there had to be countries that were willing to accept them. For a few, this was not a problem. Some German Jews would be welcomed almost anywhere. World-famous scientists such as physicist Albert Einstein and musicians such as conductor Bruno Walter went to the United States. Refugee scientists, many of them Jewish, later played a vital part in the American military effort in World War II, including the building of the atomic bomb. Actors, screenwriters, and directors, including non-Jewish anti-Nazis, went to Hollywood, where they contributed greatly to the American film industry. (Ironically, the German actors who had escaped Hitler often played Nazis in American films.) But most German Jews were ordinary people, not great scientists or famous actors.

Until the early 1920s, the United States had accepted almost any healthy immigrant from Europe who could pay for boat passage. Between 1889 and 1924, more than 2.5 million European Jews, mostly poor and almost all from eastern Europe, journeyed to the United States. But a new American immigration law was passed, and as a result the number of new arrivals fell drastically in the ensuing years.

The immigration law set limits on how many people from each foreign country could settle in the United States each year. Foreigners had to receive permission from an American official stationed in their country. These officials were even stricter than the law required in issuing permits.

Even after Hitler came to power in 1933, far fewer permits were given than the law allowed. In 1933 and 1934, American immigration law would have allowed over 25,000 Germans to enter the country, but only slightly more than 4,000 actually arrived. In the first three years after the Nazi

American Attitudes

To some extent, it was understandable that countries throughout the world did not want to accept large numbers of refugees. Many of these countries, including the United States, suffered from serious unemployment in the 1930s. They felt they could not handle an influx of immigrants, especially poor immigrants.

But part of the reason for the refusal to accept refugees involved anti-Jewish feelings. Some well-known Americans—like Henry Ford, the founder of the Ford Motor Company—had spread anti-Jewish ideas. Charles Lindbergh, who became a national hero for being the first person to fly a plane nonstop across the Atlantic, accepted a medal from Hitler and made some statements defending the Nazi government. And Roman Catholic priest Charles Coughlin, "the radio priest" who broadcast to more than 3.5 million regular listeners every Sunday, blamed unemployment in America on banks—banks that he said were controlled by Jewish Communists.

So even when it was clear that the German Jews faced a special emergency, many Americans were still opposed to allowing them into the United States.

takeover, only about 13,000 German Jews came to the United States. In the next three years the Nazi campaign against the Jews worsened. Many Americans pressured President Franklin D. Roosevelt to admit more refugees, and during that period about 50,000 more were allowed entry to the States.

In total, one-fifth of the 300,000 Jews who left Germany went to the United States. But 200,000 others never got out. At that time, there were 130 million people in the United States; the number of German Jews allowed into the States was less than one-twentieth of 1 percent of the American population.

The Evian Conference

As the Nazi threat to European Jews increased during the 1930s, a refugee crisis developed. Not a single country

was willing to accept unlimited numbers of ordinary Jews escaping from Germany. In July of 1938, 32 countries met in Evian, France, at the invitation of Roosevelt to discuss the Jewish refugee issue. Instead of sending a high-level official to the conference, Roosevelt sent a businessman, Myron C. Taylor, to represent the United States. Delegate after delegate offered sympathy for the Jews' situation, but they were unwilling to allow the Jews to emigrate to their countries.

The United States declared at the beginning that discussion of its own immigration laws was off limits. Simi-

larly, the British refused to allow discussion of Palestine. (See section beginning with "Palestine and Zionism," pp.84–87.) None of the major countries was willing to do much to deal with the problem.

The reaction to the plight of the passengers aboard the SS St. Louis spoke volumes about governments' attitudes toward accepting Jewish refugees.

The *St. Louis*

The story of the *St. Louis,* a German oceanliner that sailed from the German port of Hamburg in 1939, illustrates the plight of Jews vividly. The *St. Louis,* loaded with 908 Jewish refugees, was bound for Cuba. Cuban government officials had agreed to accept them in return for huge bribes. When the ship reached the Cuban city of Havana, the Jewish organization that had made these arrangements could not come up with the money quickly enough. The Cuban authorities forced the ship back out to sea. Appeals were made to other countries to accept the passengers.

The German government made it clear that if the Jews returned to Germany they would be sent to concentration camps. The ship sailed slowly along the coast of the United States. A U.S. Coast Guard ship was ordered to shadow it and prevent the refugees from landing in the United States. The whole world followed the story in newspapers and on radio as the ship headed back to Germany.

It was only because of the bravery of the *St. Louis*'s German captain that the Jews were not returned to Hamburg. Against orders, he purposely took as long as possible on his return voyage. The *St. Louis* was at sea for 35 days. Because of this, there was enough time to arrange for Great Britian, Belgium, France, and the Netherlands—embarrassed by the story of the ship that no one would accept and the refugees that no one would save—to take them at last.

For the Nazis, the lesson of the *St. Louis* was plain. As one of their newspapers wrote later that summer: "We say openly that we do not want the Jews, while the democracies keep claiming that they are willing to let them in—and then leave the guests out in the cold!" The Nazis believed that whatever other countries might say publicly, they would do little to actually help the Jews.

Palestine and Zionism

One place that seemed a logical destination for Jewish refugees was Palestine, a region in the Middle East bordered on the west by the Mediterranean Sea and to the east by the Dead Sea. The British captured Palestine from the Ottoman Turks in 1917 and 1918. As compensation for the Jews' help in defeating the Turks, the British promised the Jews a national homeland in Palestine.

Palestine was the original home of the Jewish people. A political movement called Zionism had developed among some Jews beginning in the 1890s. The Zionists believed that Jews should return to Palestine and build a modern Jewish country in their ancestral homeland.

Zionism gained some support among European Jews early in the twentieth century, and a fair number settled in Palestine. But most Jews wanted to stay in the countries of their birth, and those who wanted to leave their own countries preferred to go somewhere other than Palestine. Over 2 million Jews migrated to America, like so many immigrants from poor countries in Europe. Many other eastern European Jews moved to Britain, France, and other wealthy and democratic countries in western Europe. These Jews later suffered terribly when Germany conquered their new countries during World War II. The Nazis deported many thousands of Jews from France, for example, and murdered them. The Jews who had just arrived—and were not yet citizens of France—were the easiest targets of the Nazis and of the French officials who cooperated with them. But in the 1920s and early 1930s, many Jews believed that countries like France offered a better place to start a new life than Palestine.

With the rise of the Nazis, however, there was suddenly a much larger number of Jews who desperately needed to leave Germany and other countries where antisemitism was growing. They were no longer able to go to America or France. Palestine now seemed a possible refuge for these people.

David Ben-Gurion, one of the founders of the Zionist movement, would become the first prime minister of the newly created Jewish nation of Israel in 1948.

British policy

As Jewish settlement in Palestine increased, there was growing anger among the Arab population, who made up the majority of the people in the region. Great Britain controlled Palestine, and it also controlled several other Arab countries. Britain wanted to stay on good terms with these countries in case of war with Germany, so the British government chose not to incite further anger among the Arabs in Palestine.

This was one reason why Britain reduced the number of Jewish immigrants allowed into Palestine. Some historians feel that there were additional reasons, the most important being that some of the British officials who ran the colonies in the Middle East were opposed to the Zionist goal of establishing an independent Jewish country—and, in fact, were themselves antisemitic.

About 50,000 German Jews entered Palestine legally between 1933 (when the Nazis came to power) and 1938.

Map of Palestine, c. 1945.

Many others came from other parts of Europe. In 1935, over 60,000 Jews—Jews from all countries—settled in Palestine. But even as the Nazi threat to the Jewish people increased, the British kept lowering the number of Jews allowed into Palestine. In 1936, the number was fewer than 30,000. By 1937, it had fallen below 11,000.

Smuggling refugees

Zionist groups kept trying to smuggle Jewish refugees into Palestine during the 1930s. From the early part of 1938 until the outbreak of World War II in September 1939, about 40 ships with 16,000 illegal immigrants landed in Palestine's waters. Most of these came from Poland and Germany.

These efforts were encouraged by the Gestapo, the Nazi secret police, which released Jewish prisoners from concentration camps on the condition that they leave Germany immediately. The Nazis wanted the Jews out of Germany, and they also wanted to embarrass the British. In addition, many Nazi officials made deals with ship owners to get a "cut" of the money that the Jews paid for their transportation.

The British navy and air force patrolled the sea routes to Palestine to stop the refugees. In a two-month period in the summer of 1939, they captured over 3,500 illegal immigrants. British agents in Europe were assigned to find out the location of the ports from which the ships had sailed. Despite increasing pressure from British and foreign public opinion, the British government never opened Palestine as a haven for the victims of Nazi persecution.

In the late summer of 1939, the British government imprisoned 1,400 Jewish refugees when their ship, the *Tiger Hill,* reached Palestine. Their long and dangerous journey had begun a month earlier, by train, in Poland. The ship was delayed in Romania because of British pressure on the Romanian government. Having run completely out of food and almost out of water while at sea, the *Tiger Hill* was in a desperate state. A British ship had fired on it off the coast of Palestine, killing two men. Finally, the ship ran aground onto a sandbar in the hope that the refugees could reach shore in small boats or by swimming.

The date was September 2, 1939. The day before, Germany had invaded Poland. The next day, Britain, along with France, declared war on Germany. World War II had begun.

Switzerland

Another country that seemed a natural place to safeguard Jewish refugees from Germany was Switzerland. Switzerland is well known for maintaining a position of political neutrality—of not taking sides in the wars between its larger neighbors such as Germany and Austria. Switzerland also has a long tradition of welcoming political refugees.

At first, the Swiss allowed many refugees from Nazi Germany to enter Switzerland. Most of these people soon moved on to other countries. But this open-door policy did not apply to the Jews. After Austria became part of Germany in March 1938, thousands of Austrian Jews tried to get into Switzerland. The Swiss government did not want to let them in. But Austrians and Germans could enter Switzerland as tourists just by showing their passports.

The Swiss government asked the German government to put a special identifying mark on the passports of German and Austrian Jews. On November 5, 1938—just four days before *Kristallnacht*—the Nazi government ordered all Jews to hand in their passports so they could be stamped with a red "J." This stood for *Jude,* the German word for "Jew." From that point on, the Swiss border police would know whether someone seeking refuge was Jewish or not. Easy entry into Switzerland hinged on being non-Jewish.

Once World War II started, the Swiss police usually tried to stop Jews at the border and force them back into the country from which they were trying to escape. This meant capture by the Nazis and, ultimately, death for the apprehended Jews. On the other hand, the Swiss made many exceptions, especially for children and the elderly; thousands of Jewish refugees did find safety there. During World War II, though, the Swiss frequently interned refugees—placed them in guarded camps—something they had never done before.

4

The Nazi Government and the Road to War

While the Nazis were carrying out their anti-semitic—or anti-Jewish—actions, they continued to increase their hold over Germany. The party wanted to make sure that no individual or group would become powerful enough to challenge them.

By the summer of 1933, many of the forces that might have opposed the Nazis had been destroyed. All rival political parties had been abolished. The labor unions no longer existed; they had been replaced by the Nazi-run German Labor Front. Germany's various state governments were now run directly by the central government in Berlin.

The Nazis also had a stranglehold on all means of communication in Germany. They controlled all radio broadcasts and shut down production of anti-Nazi newspapers. Government workers who had supported anti-Nazi political parties were fired. In fact, the expression of any criticism of Nazi leader Adolf Hitler or the Nazi Party by government employees meant termination of their jobs. Government employees in Germany included schoolteachers and university professors, railroad administrators, postal workers, and many others. If they wanted to remain employed, these workers had to express support for the Nazis—or at least keep their anti-Nazi ideas to themselves.

The concentration camps

Losing a job was only part of the fear. The Nazi Party arrested so many people that the prisons could not hold them. Nazis then opened concentration camps, temporary prison camps that were run not by the government (like regular prisons) but by the party's military units. First they were headed by the *Sturmabteilung* or SA (the storm troopers, or brownshirts) and later by the *Schutzstaffel* or SS (the black-uniformed "defense corps" headed by Heinrich Himmler). In other words, opponents of the Nazis were put under the control of the most dedicated Nazi thugs. Some of the same storm troopers who had beaten up people on the streets were now in charge of guarding the people they had attacked.

Very soon these temporary camps became permanent. Dachau, located in a suburb of Munich, Germany, was opened in March 1933. Its first prisoners included leaders of the labor unions and officials of the Communist Party. (Communism is a political and economic theory advocating the formation of a classless society through the communal, or group, ownership of all property.) Its last prisoners were not freed until the American army reached Dachau at the end of World War II, more than 12 years later.

The reputation of the concentration camps soon spread fear among Germans who might oppose the Nazis. They became widely known as brutal places in which no laws applied. Prisoners were underfed and forced to perform hard physical labor. Beatings were common. The Gestapo (an abbreviation for *Geheime Staatspolizei*), the secret police, tortured prisoners who might have information about opponents of the Nazis. Prisoners were routinely executed without trial; the Nazis usually said they had been "shot while trying to escape."

By 1934, however, the brutal chaos of the concentration camps gave way to a new system, the so-called "Dachau Sys-

Prisoners of Dachau, one of the first German concentration camps, sit on the steps of a barrack.

tem" established by Theodore Eicke, the new commandant of Dachau, and Heinrich Himmler, head of the SS. Instead of imposing the random violence for which the SA was known, the camps became subject to the strict discipline of the SS and were the sites of highly organized terror.

Terror and deals

Although the political parties and labor unions had been destroyed, there were still some powerful groups in German society over which the Nazis did not have complete control. These included the army, the big business executives and bankers, and the Protestant and Catholic Churches.

In some cases, the Nazis tried to control members of these groups by force. Some of their leaders were murdered. Many others were arrested and sent to concentration camps. This was especially true of clergymen. But for the most part, Hitler handled these groups by making deals with them.

The army and the storm troopers

One of the most important groups in Germany was the national army. It was controlled by its officers, many of them Junkers, members of the nobility of Germany's largest state, Prussia. (See pp. 8–10.) Most of them agreed with Hitler's goal of making Germany a great military power again—one with an enlarged army and navy, a modern air force, and the latest tanks and planes. Many officers also wanted to regain the territory that Germany had lost after World War I.

But the army officers wanted to keep control of the army themselves. They feared that Hitler would combine the German army with the Nazi storm troopers, the SA, which was actually much larger than the army. They were also afraid that Ernst Röhm, the head of the storm troopers and one of Hitler's closest friends inside the Nazi Party, would become the new commander of the army.

Although Röhm was a former army officer, he and the old-guard officers disliked each other intensely. (See the box on Röhm on p. 51.) The officers thought Röhm was a gangster who had no respect for their honor or their traditions. Röhm opposed Germany's old and established leaders, including the Junker army officers. He and his allies in the Nazi Party, especially the storm troopers, wanted the Nazis to lead a "second revolution" that would completely change German society. (Hitler's rise to power was the Nazis' "first revolution.")

The "Night of the Long Knives"

The conflict between Röhm's storm troopers and the German army officials continued through the first year of Hitler's rule. Röhm kept pushing Hitler to launch the "second revolution," but Hitler did not want to risk a showdown with the army.

Finally, Hitler ended the conflict by force. On the night of June 29, 1934, members of the SS began rounding up leaders of the SA and their allies. In the early morning hours, the SS seized Röhm and brought him to a prison in Munich, Germany. They left a gun in his cell, on Hitler's orders, so that Röhm could kill himself. Röhm refused. "If I am to be killed," he is supposed to have told the SS men, "let Adolf do it himself." Two SS men then emptied their pistols into Röhm.

Executions continued all through the next day. The victims included many top SA leaders. June 29 became known as "The Night of the Long Knives." All together, about 400 people were killed during that night and the following two days.

Hitler publicly defended these murders. Röhm and the others had been plotting against the government, he said. They had been executed instead of being arrested and tried because he, Adolf Hitler, was the supreme judge of Germany. "Everyone must know for all future time," warned Hitler, that anyone who tried to oppose his government by force faced "certain death."

The first great wave of Nazi murders had occurred. Most of the victims were other Nazis. For the most part, this action met with approval throughout Germany. After the disorder in Germany's recent history, many felt that Hitler was providing an atmosphere of "law and order" that was badly needed. The army officers were satisfied. Hitler swore that the SA would never again threaten the independence of the army.

The price the army officers paid, however, was the pledge of their unwavering support for the Nazi government. Almost without exception, the officers were more interested in protecting their own positions than in what happened to Germany. They were willing to accept almost anything Hitler did, including the murder of two army generals during the Night of the Long Knives, as long they were allowed to run the army.

The German Führer

A month later, the president of Germany, Paul von Hindenburg, died. He was very old and had been seriously ill for many months; everyone knew that his death was imminent. This was one of the main reasons that Hitler wanted the support of the army. The position of president and the position of chancellor, which Hitler already held, were now combined.

Hitler was now the Führer (leader) of the German *Reich* (pronounced RIKE; German word for "empire"). He was also the commander-in-chief of the army. The army officers supported this as part of the payoff for what Hitler had done to Röhm and the SA.

On the day that Hindenburg died, every officer and soldier of the German army swore a new oath of allegiance: "I swear by God this holy oath: I will give unconditional obedience to the Führer of the German Reich and People, Adolf Hitler, the Supreme Commander of the Armed Forces, and will be ready, as a brave soldier, to lay down my life at any time for this oath." The German army did not promise loyalty to the German people, or to the law, or even to the German government. It promised to obey Adolf Hitler.

The Third Reich

The Nazis called their government the "Third Reich," or third German empire. The "First Reich" was the continuation of the Holy Roman empire, which was founded in the ninth century by the emperor Charlemagne and lasted—in a very weakened form—until the early 1800s. The "Second Reich" was the German empire under the kaiser. It was created when Germany was unified under the leadership of Prussia in 1871 and came to an end in 1918, at the conclusion of World War I.

The industrialists

Another powerful group that the Nazis sought to control were the industrialists (the businesspeople who owned the great industries) and the bankers. Hitler won their favor by destroying their main enemies—the Socialists, the Communists, and the labor unions, but industrialists feared what might happen if there were a "second revolution." Röhm and other radicals, the supporters of extreme change, in the Nazi Party wanted to destroy the power of the old rulers of Germany. This included the big business executives as well as the old-line army officers. Many Nazis wanted to take over German factories and banks. Ideas like this had been part of the official Nazi Party program almost since the very beginning of the party's existence. (A program is a statement of a political party's beliefs and the goals it seeks to achieve. The Nazi Party program stated that the German government should take over the big monopolies, single companies that controlled a whole industry, and claim a share of the profits of other large industries. See the box on the Nazi Party program on p. 34.)

For many years, Hitler had promised Germany's industrialists that the Nazi Party would not interfere with the running of their companies, despite what the party program said. Hitler assured them that this section of the program would only affect property owned by Jews.

The "Night of the Long Knives" destroyed the Nazi radicals. The lesson was clear: Hitler would run the government,

Alfred Rosenberg, the leading philosopher of the Nazi Party.

but the old rulers of Germany would continue to run the army, the factories, and the banks. As long as they supported the Nazis, the Nazis would not interfere with them.

What the "Long Knives" meant to the Jews

The army officers and the industrialists were not the only people who felt relieved by the destruction of Röhm and the SA. Röhm's storm troopers were the ones who attacked and kidnapped Jews. They were the guards at Jewish shops during the anti-Jewish boycott. They were the "wild men"—often nothing more than street fighters in uniform. German Jews were afraid of what Röhm's "second revolution" might have meant for them.

When Hitler defended his actions during the Night of the Long Knives, he argued that a country could not live in a state of constant revolution. The Nazi revolution had been accomplished, he said, and now there was a need for legality and legitimacy. Many Germans, including Jews, thought that Germany would settle down and become more like a "normal" country: a country united under a system of law and order, not chaos. They did not understand that Hitler's idea of law included mass murder.

The churches

The Christian churches posed another possible threat to the Nazis. Many Nazi ideas were anti-Christian in nature. Men such as Alfred Rosenberg, the leading Nazi philosopher, wanted Germans to return to their pre-Christian practice of worshiping ancient gods and myths. (See box on p. 36.) They viewed Christianity's central tenets—the importance of love and forgiveness—as a form of "weakness" that had no place in the kind of Germany they wanted to create. Christians held that anyone who accepted Christian beliefs was an equal member of their nation; the Nazis believed that "race" and "blood" determined who was a real German.

The Catholic Church

For years, many German Catholics had supported political parties that were organized to protect their interests, especially the freedom to provide a Catholic education for their youth. In fact, until March 1933, the church officially barred German Catholics from belonging to the Nazi Party. Germany's bishops unwisely lifted this ban when Hitler promised to respect the rights of the churches. But Hitler's next step, taken just four months later, was to destroy the Catholic parties—the last non-Nazi political parties in Germany.

The concordat

Almost at the same time, the Catholic Church signed a treaty (called a concordat) with the Nazi government. Many historians believe that the church agreed to the concordat because it was more afraid of communism than of the Nazis. The Communist government in Russia was very hostile to all religion, and the Nazis were the bitter enemies of the Communists. The church—like so many other groups—thought the value of the Nazis' anticommunist stand outweighed their brutality and their persecution of the Jews.

By agreeing to the concordat, the church seemed to be validating the Nazi government, or telling the world that the Nazis were running a legitimate government. This image of normalcy and regularity was extremely important to Hitler at that time because people around the world were increasingly shocked and angered by news reports of what the Nazis were doing. Even more importantly, the church was telling German Catholics that it was possible to support the Nazis and remain a good Catholic.

In return for Catholic support, the Nazis promised to let the Catholic Church in Germany operate without interference from the government. The church, they said, could continue to run its own schools. The Nazis soon broke this agreement. But by the time Pope Pius XI publicly protested against the violation in 1937, the Nazi government's hold on Germany had become stronger than ever before.

Despite the concordat, some important German Catholic clergymen continued to protest the Nazis' treatment of the Jews. These included Father Bernard Lichtenberg of St. Hedwig's Cathedral in Berlin. Lichtenberg preached

Martin Niemöller

As a young man, Martin Niemöller had been a famous submarine commander in World War I. He later became a clergyman. Like many Protestant pastors, he had supported the Nazis before they came to power. Unlike most, however, he soon came to oppose Hitler's policies—and from that point on he never wavered from his anti-Nazi beliefs. Niemöller was sent to a concentration camp on Hitler's personal orders. He spent many years in solitary confinement and was not freed until 1945.

Niemöller is credited with one of the most famous descriptions of how Hitler destroyed his opponents one at a time—all while most Germans watched in silence:

> First they came for the communists. I did not speak out because I was not a communist. Then they came for the labor unionists. I did not speak out because I was not a labor unionist. Then they came for the Jews. I did not speak out because I was not a Jew. Then they came for me, and there was no one left to speak for me.

that it was a Christian duty to help the Jews, even though the Nazis said that it was treason to do so. Eventually, he was arrested and died in custody.

The Protestant churches

The majority of Germans were Protestants, not Catholics. German Protestants had a long tradition of obedience to the government. Hitler wanted to appoint a Reich Bishop, who would be the head of all German Protestants. Naturally, the person he would pick would support the Nazis. The majority of German Protestant pastors agreed to Hitler's plan, and in 1938 they agreed to swear an oath to obey Hitler, just as the army did in 1934. However, a significant minority of Protestant pastors led by Martin Niemöller formed a group they called the Confessing (or Confessional) church. (See box on Niemöller above.) In March 1935, they read a protest to their congregations that attacked the Nazi "religion" of

Hitler Youth saluting the swastika during a 1935 rally.

"race" and "blood" and stated that it was not a true form of Christianity. Because of this action, 700 pastors were arrested.

Despite the arrests, a few of the leaders of the Confessing Church believed in even stronger opposition to the Nazis. They thought Christian morality required them to organize active resistance to the Nazi government. The best known of these pastors is Dietrich Bonhoeffer, who was an important religious writer and philosopher. Bonhoeffer helped smuggle Jews out of Germany and was arrested. Later, he was involved in a plan to kill Hitler. He was executed near the end of World War II.

The Hitler Youth

The Nazis were determined never to give up power in Germany and tried to control almost every aspect of the daily life of the nation's people. One especially effective way of accomplishing this was through the Hitler Youth movement,

The Factory Workers

German workers were paid less during the years of Nazi rule than they had been before the Great Depression (1929–40) started, but this was still an improvement over wages paid in the early 1930s, just before Hitler had come to power. Because of this, many people felt as if their pay had gone up. In addition, many were happy to have any job—even if the pay and the working conditions were less than ideal.

Factory workers as a group had always been opponents of the Nazis. They had voted for the Social Democrats and the Communists, the first parties the Nazis had crushed. They had fought against the storm troopers in street battles. Now, however, the improvement in the economy made it much less likely that they would actively oppose the new government. This was especially true because of the destruction of the labor unions and the political parties that the workers had supported. Fear of Nazi terror—combined with better economic conditions—meant that the laborers, for the most part, worked hard at their jobs and stayed out of politics.

an organization that taught the Nazi philosophy to German youth. At first, membership was voluntary, although there was a lot of pressure on parents to enroll their children in the program. In 1936, all other youth groups were made illegal. By 1939, membership in the Hitler Youth was required.

In some ways, the Hitler Youth served as a social organization. But its main function was to indoctrinate German youth—to introduce young Germans to Nazi ideals and military policy. The members of the Hitler Youth, in uniforms and carrying Nazi flags, marched at every Nazi rally. Even if their parents were anti-Nazi, the children of Germany were taught to hate Jews. They were told that Hitler was the "savior" of their country and that they must always obey him.

Economic recovery

Many Germans gave Hitler and the Nazis credit for ending the terrible unemployment that had devastated Germany

in the depression of the early 1930s. In fact, some people still say that Hitler achieved some economic good for Germany.

Hitler's rise to power owed a lot to incredible timing. He appeared on the German political scene at just the right moment: the depression had reached rock bottom, and there was nowhere to go but up. Many of the programs that lowered unemployment had been started before Hitler came to power, but because they took some time to show results, he was given credit for the growth in new jobs.

Hitler continued and expanded these economic programs. Many of his actions had nothing to do with the ideas that Hitler and the Nazis cared about most. They were actually very similar to what President Franklin D. Roosevelt was doing in the United States at exactly the same time. Like Roosevelt, Hitler was willing to try bold new policies to create jobs. He understood that unless conditions improved—and improved quickly—support for the Nazis would disappear.

Production lines at the Krupp steel mills. Some historians claim that Hitler helped the German economy; others believe that he reaped the benefits of programs instituted before he seized power.

The German government started huge projects to put people to work. The most famous was the building of the network of autobahns, the modern highways that replaced Germany's old country roads. In the mid-1930s, these projects helped lower unemployment. In addition, the improvement in the economies of other countries meant that German products could be sold there, creating more jobs at home.

Probably the most important factor in ending German unemployment, however, was the expansion of the military and the tremendous increase in the production of weapons. Many German men were soon in the army instead of out looking for a job. Many more were building cannons, tanks, warships, and fighter planes. Steel mills were busy supplying the material for these arms; coal mines produced the fuel for making steel. The chemical industry made explosives, and the clothing industry made uniforms.

Military power for Germany

One of Hitler's main goals was to make Germany a great military power again. He had the full support of army officers in this endeavor. But building up the German army was a violation of key terms laid down in the Treaty of Versailles, the peace treaty that Germany had been forced to sign after losing World War I. The treaty limited Germany's army to 100,000 soldiers, did not allow a military draft, banned tanks and an air force, and kept the navy very small. (See pp. 19–20.)

Hitler's goal of a strong military was meshed tightly with his desire to regain the territory Germany had lost in World War I, especially the land that had become part of Poland. Hitler also wanted to unite Germany with Austria, where most of the people were German-speaking. These goals were readily supported by German nationalists, including most army officers. (Nationalists believed that loyalty to Germany was more important than anything else and that Germany should be supremely powerful, especially in the military arena.)

Lebensraum

But Hitler also believed that Germany needed to conquer vast new territory in order to provide sufficient *Lebensraum,* or room to live. Use of this word implied that without

this room, Germany could not survive. The nation, according to Hitler, was too small for the number of people in it.

The land that Hitler wanted to annex, or add, to Germany would come from eastern Europe through (1) the reconquering of western Poland, which Germany had lost after World War I, and (2) the conquest of areas like White Russia (now the country of Belarus) and Ukraine, which had long been part of the Russian empire. (These regions were then the western part of the Soviet Union [short for the Union of Soviet Socialist Republics or USSR], the country that the Communists had set up after overthrowing the Russian empire.) Hitler's hatred of the Communists and his desire to conquer territory came together in this goal of territorial expansion.

Military conquest and Nazi racial theories

Hitler's military goals and his racial theories were closely connected. The Nazis believed that Germans were members

Hitler's sending troops, including this machine gun crew, into the Rhineland in 1935 helped spark World War II.

German Condor Legion veterans of the Spanish Civil War being honored by Hitler. The German forces volunteered for the war to learn about modern air warfare, including the tactic of bombing innocent people.

of a superior race—the "Aryan" race—and that they had the right to rule over the "inferior" people of eastern Europe. Germany was anxious to take over the land and populate it with Germans. The Poles, Russians, Ukrainians, Belarussians, and others would then be allowed to serve the German overlords as sources of cheap labor.

Poland and the western areas of the Soviet Union (Russia) were also the home of the largest Jewish communities in Europe. According to Nazi racial theories, the Jews were far below even the Poles, Russians, and others on the ladder of racial superiority. In addition, Hitler firmly believed that the Communist government of the Soviet Union was part of a Jewish plot to rule the world. Jews and Communists were the same thing to the Nazis. (This form of antisemitism [hatred of Jews] is discussed at length in Chapter 1.) Therefore, the war for new German territory, when it came, would also be a war to destroy the Jews.

Understanding the Holocaust

Steps toward war

Between 1935 and 1939, Nazi Germany took a series of steps that would lead to war. In 1935, Germany again started to draft men into the army. This violated the Treaty of Versailles, but Britain and France did nothing to stop it. The next year, Hitler sent the German army into the western area of Germany, near France, called the Rhineland. The Rhineland was still part of Germany, but according to the Treaty of Versailles it was supposed to be free of troops. Hitler's action, then, was a big gamble. The German army was too weak to fight back if France opposed the stationing of German troops there. The German generals tried to talk Hitler out of making this move, but he believed that France and Britain would do nothing more than make a verbal protest—and he was right.

Bombing civilians

From 1936 to 1939, a civil war raged in Spain. Hitler sent German planes and pilots to support the side that was

Viennese police attempt to hold back the crowd cheering the conquering Hitler entering Vienna, Austria, in March 1938.

friendly to the Nazis. Although they were supposedly "volunteers," the German air force used the Spanish Civil War as a way to develop modern air warfare. This included gaining experience in the bombing of civilian populations—something that had never been done before. The German bombing of the town of Guernica shocked millions of people around the world and inspired a famous painting by Spanish-born artist Pablo Picasso.

The Anschluss

In March 1938, the German army moved into Austria; Germany and Austria were thereafter united into one country in a process called the *Anschluss,* which means "union" or "joining" in German. The Anschluss had been prepared by Austrian Nazis working with Hitler, but it was an old dream of many Germans and Austrians. According to some historians, many, if not most, Austrians welcomed unification with Germany.

But for the 200,000 Austrian Jews, the Anschluss meant that they now faced the same persecution that Jews were suffering in Germany. In the first few months after the Anschluss, Austria, possibly the most antisemitic country in Europe, "caught up" with Germany in its harsh treatment of the Jews. Within a short time, 4,000 Austrian Jews were in concentration camps.

Czechoslovakia

Almost immediately, Hitler began to demand that a part of western Czechoslovakia, called the Sudetenland, become part of Germany. As justification he claimed that Czechoslovakia was mistreating the German-speaking population of the Sudetenland. What he had told his generals in May 1938, however, was that it was his "unchangeable intention to destroy Czechoslovakia by military force in the foreseeable future."

In September 1938, Britain and France—Czechoslovakia's allies—agreed to Hitler's demands for land, and the German army marched into the Sudetenland a few days later. The Czechoslovakian government opposed the action, but it was helpless to stop it.

Within six months, Hitler conquered Czechoslovakia. The German army marched into Prague, the Czechoslovakian capital. The provinces of Bohemia and Moravia (most of what is now the Czech Republic) became part of Germany. The Nazis set up an "independent" country of Slovakia, but it was really just a German puppet, a government controlled by an outside source—in this case, by the Nazis.

Poland and war

The next target was Poland. By now, most people understood that giving in to Hitler's demands would only lead to more and more demands. The British and French governments said they would defend their ally Poland if it were attacked by Germany. Hitler knew that Britain and France had not defended Czechoslovakia, and he thought they would back down again. On September 1, 1939, the German armies launched a full-scale attack on Poland. Britain and France declared war on Germany two days later.

German tanks rolling into Warsaw, Poland, on September 1, 1939. Britain and France declared war on Germany on September 3.

Munich and Appeasement

The crisis over the Sudetenland came very close to starting a war. But Czechoslovakia's allies, Britain and France, were not willing to defend Czechoslovakia. Instead, in September 1938, the leaders of France, Britain, and Italy met with Hitler in Munich, Germany. Italy's leader was dictator Benito Mussolini, Hitler's ally. Czechoslovakia was not allowed to attend the conference.

At Munich, Britain and France agreed to let Hitler take over the Sudetenland. Hitler told the British prime minister, Neville Chamberlain, that this was his "last territorial demand in Europe," and Chamberlain chose to believe him.

The Munich Conference has become famous as the symbol of the British and French policy of appeasement of Hitler, of giving in to Hitler's demands in order to avoid war. When Chamberlain returned to London, he waved a copy of the Munich agreement at the airport and said that he had brought home "peace in our time." Less than a year later, though, Britain and France were at war with Germany.

The first mass murders: Germany's euthanasia program

World War II, combined with Nazi ideas about race, would soon lead to an uncompromising attempt to destroy the Jews. But the first major group of people to die because of these ideas were not Jews. They were people who had severe handicaps, either mental or physical, or had incurable hereditary diseases.

Many years earlier, Hitler had written in *Mein Kampf* that the government should prevent the reproduction of "all those who are in any way visibly sick or who inherited a disease and can therefore pass it on." In 1933, just after the Nazis came to power, the government passed a law that allowed retarded people, without their consent, to be sterilized, a surgical process that would leave them unable to have any children. Later laws restricted their right to marry.

As Germany prepared for war, Hitler decided to go one ruthless step further: having these people killed to "purify" the German race. The Nazis called this "mercy killing" (euthanasia), but it was not done to relieve the suffering of the victims. It was not something that the patients themselves, or their families, agreed to or even knew about.

According to the Nazis, the mentally ill and physically disabled were "useless mouths" that had to be fed without providing anything in return. They were below the standards the Nazis had set for Germany; therefore, they were not "fit to live."

Hitler created a Committee for Scientific Research of Hereditary and Severe Constitutional Diseases. This committee had nothing to do with "research." Its job was to kill people.

The first victims were children. Forms were sent to every local health department, children's hospital and clinic, and to

Attendees at the Munich conference, September 1938: French politician Edouard Daladier, British Prime Minister Neville Chamberlain, Italian leader Benito Mussolini, and Hitler. A year before Hitler invaded Poland, beginning World War II, Chamberlain assured the world of "peace in our time."

Karl Brandt, Hitler's personal physician, was responsible for overseeing the T-4 "mercy killing" program.

doctors and midwives who delivered babies to provide the committee with information about mentally retarded and physically deformed children. Then the committee staff decided which of the children fit the standard for "mercy killing." Those chosen were transferred to a special ward set up in selected hospitals. There they were killed, usually by lethal injection. An estimated 5,000 children were killed in this way.

The T-4 program

The euthanasia program was soon expanded to include adults. The new program was code-named "T-4" because its headquarters were at number 4 Tiergarten Street. Hitler was deeply involved in the development of this plan. The two men assigned to run the program were very close to him: one was his office head, the other was his personal doctor.

The T-4 program was much larger and involved many more people than the Nazis' earlier operation to kill children. Most of the staff of T-4 were SS personnel with a medical background. The people in the program followed a very impersonal technique, and many later went on to staff the Holocaust killing centers.

T-4 set up five "observation institutions" around Germany. These were really transfer points, the first stop for the victims. They were then sent to one of six killing centers, which were disguised as hospitals or nursing homes.

The Nazis had a difficult time determining the best way to kill these "inferior" members of their race. They didn't want the victims to know what was going to happen to them, and they didn't want the victims' families to find out afterward. A committee of T-4 doctors and medical experts studied possible solutions to this "problem." Later, they would use the same method on a much larger scale to try to wipe out the Jews of Europe.

In each of T-4's six killing institutions, the Nazis equipped a chamber to look like a large shower room. When

Nazi Names

The T-4 euthanasia program, developed to "purify" the German race by ridding it of mentally and physically disabled people, included three different departments, each with a phony name designed to disguise its purpose. One of them was called the "Working Team of Asylums and Nursing Homes." It sent out questionnaires to obtain information about potential victims, then picked those who would die. Another was in charge of transporting the victims to the centers set up to kill them. It was called the "Public-Benefit Patient Transportation Society." The third, called the "General Foundation for Affairs of Insane Asylums," was the staff that ran the killing centers and did the actual killing.

the door was closed, the room was airtight. Twenty or thirty victims would be brought in for "showers" at one time. Instead of water, however, the shower heads pumped carbon monoxide gas into the room, killing all the victims. Then their bodies were burned in large furnaces called crematoria that were attached to the centers. The family of a victim was told that the body had been burned to prevent the spread of disease. In some cases, the T-4 doctors removed and preserved the victims' brains so that they could "study" the cause of mental diseases.

Protests

The existence of T-4 was supposed to be a secret, but people soon began to suspect what was happening. The families of the victims received letters saying their child or brother had suddenly died, usually from pneumonia. But the places listed on the death certificate were always the same six hospitals. The families could read the death notices in the newspapers and see that too many retarded and handicapped people were dying, all at the same time, in the same places, and all from pneumonia.

In the small towns where the six killing centers were located, people soon understood the meaning of the black SS

ADOLF HITLER

BERLIN, den 1. Sept. 1939.

Reichsleiter B o u h l e r   und

Dr. med.   B r a n d t

sind unter Verantwortung beauftragt, die Befug -

nisse namentlich zu bestimmender Ärzte so zu er -

weitern, dass nach menschlichem Ermessen unheilbar

Kranken bei kritischster Beurteilung ihres Krank -

heitszustandes der Gnadentod gewährt werden kann.

[signature]

[handwritten note]
Von Bouhler mir
übergeben am 27.8.40
Dr. Gürtner

Opposite page:
Reproduction of a letter
signed by Hitler authorizing
Karl Brandt to develop
the T-4 program.

The Protests That Never Took Place

Many historians have pointed out that although the German people were able to stop the T-4 program, they did not make similar attempts to stop the persecution of the Jews. Some say that this shows that even the Nazi dictatorship could not have continued its anti-Jewish actions—and eventually its mass murder of the Jews—if the people of Germany had objected strongly enough. In particular, the German churches seem to have protested much more about the killing of Christians, as most of the T-4 victims were, than about the killing of Jews.

Similarly, although the Nazis attempted to keep the T-4 program secret, many people found out about it. They heard the rumors, and they listened to them. They wrote letters to officials, asking for answers. They pieced together the facts and realized the truth. Still, many Germans claimed after World War II that they had no idea about what was happening to the Jews.

vans that brought the "sick" to the "hospital." In one town, Hadamar, children reportedly would shout: "There goes the murder-van." Whenever the vans came by, the people of the town knew that there would soon be smoke coming from the nearby crematorium.

Soon people refused to let their relatives be taken to mental hospitals. Protestant and Catholic leaders wrote letters of protest. Some pastors publicly attacked the program in their churches. Although there were arrests, the protests continued. In August 1941, Hitler ordered that the T-4 program be officially stopped. By that time, about 70,000 people had been killed. Over the next few years, another 20,000 died "unofficially"—many were starved to death. (This method was used most often on children.)

T-4 and the murder of the Jews

In addition to mental patients and sick people from hospitals, the T-4 program was soon expanded to include concentration camp inmates. The T-4 doctors were supposed to inspect the prisoners and select those who were "mentally ill." In fact, they began to chose those Jews who were simply too sick or weak to work. One T-4 medical expert described a visit to the Buchenwald concentration camp in a letter to his wife. "Our second batch consisted of 1,200 Jews who do not have to be examined," he wrote. A new code, "14 f 13," was written on their files. This meant they had been selected for "special treatment." They were transferred to one of the "mercy killing" centers and gassed. Later, gas chambers were installed in the concentration camps for this purpose.

The men who ran T-4 and 14 f 13 were soon transferred to new duties. They were the "experts" who helped design the death camps in Poland. The SS personnel who had gassed tens of thousands of helpless Germans were put in charge of running the camps where millions more—the great majority of them Jews—were to die. (See Chapters 8 and 9.)

5

The Jews of Poland: Setting
the Stage for Destruction

O n September 1, 1939, Adolf Hitler's armies
invaded Poland. This move marked the
beginning of World War II. The Germans greatly
outnumbered the Polish army and had far more
tanks and modern artillery on their side. Within
a short time, the German air force (the *Luftwaffe*) had taken complete control of the skies.
The Polish army was defeated quickly, and by
September 19 the German army had reached
the new border with Russia. Warsaw, the capital
of Poland, withstood constant air raids and
artillery attacks as long as it could before sur-
rendering to the Germans on September 27.

The population of Poland before the war
was about 35 million. About 3.3 million of
these people were Jews—almost one-tenth of
its citizenry. It was the largest and most important Jewish community in Europe, with a long
and rich tradition. But by the fall of 1939, the
Germans had taken control of about half the

The Nazi-Soviet Pact

On August 23, 1939, just before the invasion of Poland, Nazi Germany signed a treaty with the Soviet Union. This treaty is known as the Nazi-Soviet Pact. (The Communist government of Russia had renamed Russia and the territory it controlled the Union of Soviet Socialist Republics [USSR], often called the Soviet Union.)

The treaty shocked the world. Nazi Germany had claimed to be the greatest enemy of communism and of the Soviet government. And the Soviet Union had always considered the Nazis brutal murderers and enemies of the workers.

For Germany's leader Adolf Hitler, the treaty meant that Germany could invade Poland without having to fight Russia. Since an attack on Poland might lead to war with Britain and France (in fact, this is what did happen), Hitler did not want to worry about fighting against Russia at the same time.

The reasons why Russian dictator Joseph Stalin agreed to the treaty are more complicated. The Soviet leader later claimed that the treaty was a means of "buying time" to prepare for a war against the Nazis. Stalin suspected that Britain and France really wanted Hitler to attack the Soviet Union. There was also a secret section of the treaty that gave the Soviet Union a large part of eastern Poland. Germany also agreed to let Stalin take over other nearby countries.

On September 1, the German army invaded Poland. By mid-September, German troops overan much of western and central Poland. On September 17, as the German armies were completing the conquest of Poland, the Soviet army entered Poland from the east. Over half the country, with about one-third of its population, was made part of the Soviet Union.

territory of Poland. The rest was taken over by the Soviet Union. (The Nazis and the Soviets signed a treaty—the Nazi-Soviet pact—in 1939 that gave the Soviet Union a large section of Poland if the Soviet Union did not declare war on Germany while Germany was invading Poland. See box above.) As a result, about 22 million Polish citizens, including 2 million Jews, were ruled by the Nazis.

Approximately 350,000 Jews escaped from the German-run part of Poland to the Soviet area. Over the next several months, however, about 100,000 of them went back. Some returned to be with their families or to escape harsh treatment by the Soviet government. They did not know yet that the Nazis would treat them far worse. In the early months after the German victory in Poland, it seemed as if the Poles, and not the Jews, were the Nazis' main targets.

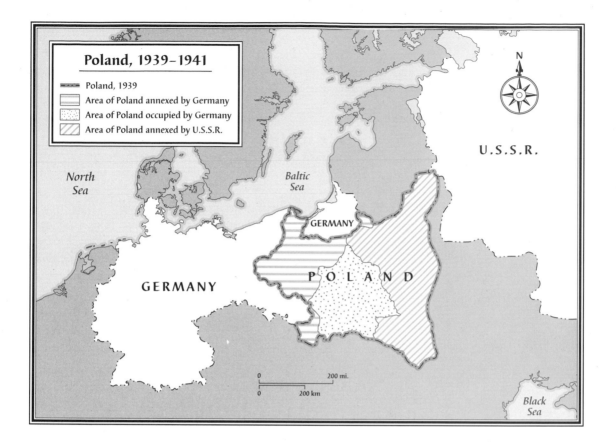

Poland, 1939–1941

- Poland, 1939
- Area of Poland annexed by Germany
- Area of Poland occupied by Germany
- Area of Poland annexed by U.S.S.R.

North Sea

Baltic Sea

GERMANY

GERMANY

P O L A N D

U.S.S.R.

Black Sea

0   200 mi.
0   200 km

The destruction of Poland

Hitler had always intended to destroy Poland as an independent country. He wanted to reclaim the land that had been part of Germany until the end of World War I, and he wanted the rest of Poland to be dominated by Germans. These goals were a natural outgrowth of the Nazis' most important ideals about race. The Nazis believed Germans were members of a superior race who needed *Lebensraum* or "space to live." According to Nazi racial ideas, the Poles—like their neighbors, the Russians, Ukrainians, and Belarussians— belonged to an inferior race.

Immediately after the German victory in Poland, a large section of western Poland was made part of Germany. The Germans called most of this area Wartheland, after the Warthe River. Many of Poland's factories and coal mines were situated in Wartheland and within the other areas of Poland that became part of Germany. Lódz, Poland's second-largest

A map of Poland showing how it was divided between Germany and the Soviet Union as a result of the Nazi-Soviet pact.

As governor-general of the section of German-controlled Poland called the General Government, Hans Frank's job was to turn Poland "into a heap of rubble."

city, was located in Wartheland. The Germans renamed this city Litzmannstadt. The rest of German-controlled Poland became the "General Government," run completely by Germans. Poland no longer existed.

Moving two million people

The Nazis intended to force all Poles, especially Jewish Poles, to leave the area that became part of Germany. There were probably around 600,000 Jews in this part of Poland. The Poles and Jews were supposed to be replaced with Germans, or *Volksdeutche* (a term meaning "ethnic Germans"; many of these were people with German ancestors who lived in the sections of Poland and neighboring countries taken over by the Soviet Union).

The German plan meant moving millions of Poles from their homes, most of them against their will. The Germans acted very quickly. People had virtually no time to pack. Able to take only small amounts of food with them, the Poles were robbed of their property as well as being forced from their homes.

Within a year of the defeat of Poland, 300,000 Jews and 1,200,000 other Poles were forced to move east into the General Government. About half a million ethnic Germans were moved into Wartheland to replace them. Many of the remaining Jews in the area were living in the city of Lódz.

In addition to relocating the Jews from western Poland, the Nazis began to send the remaining Jews of Germany into the General Government. Many Jews from both groups were sent to the city of Lublin. By February 1940, only a few months after the defeat of Poland, almost 80,000 Jews had been forced to move into the Lublin area.

Hans Frank and the Nazi plan for the General Government

The Nazis did not really want to make the General Government part of Germany. Instead, they sought to destroy

The Lublin "Reservation" and the Madagascar Plan

The large number of Jews sent to Lublin and reports that 400,000 more would arrive soon made people wonder what the Nazis were up to. There were rumors, spread by the Nazis themselves, that the Germans intended to turn the Lublin area into a "reservation" for Jews. (The Nazis got this word, and perhaps the idea, from reservations for Native Americans in the United States.) The Jews would run their own affairs and be safe there. The Nazis would have gotten rid of the Jews, thus realizing their main goal.

Later, similar stories were spread about Madagascar, a huge island off the southeast coast of Africa that was controlled by France. Supposedly, the Nazis intended to ship all the Jews of Europe there. Even some Nazis, in-cluding some fairly high-ranking officials, believed this story for a while. Some of them spent months figuring out the transportation requirements, the legal problems involved in getting the island from France, and so on. Work on the Madagascar Plan, it was said, would start when the war was over.

Neither the "Lublin Reservation" nor the "Madagascar Plan" was ever really taken seriously. Some top Nazis—including Hitler himself—may have flirted with these and other outlandish schemes as a "solution" to the "problem" of the Jews. More likely, though, they always thought of such plans as merely temporary "solutions." The Nazis would soon decide that the only real workable "Final Solution" was to kill the Jews.

Poland as a nation and run it themselves—purely for the benefit of Germany. The man Hitler picked to be governor-general was his old lawyer, Hans Frank. Hitler's instructions were simple. He told Frank his job in Poland was to turn the nation's "economic, cultural, and political structure into a heap of rubble."

On October 3, less than a week after Warsaw surrendered to Germany, Frank explained his plan for Poland to officers of the German army. He would "remove all supplies, raw materials, machines, factories, installations, etc. which are important for the German war economy." He would reduce the entire Polish economy to the absolute minimum necessary for the "bare existence of the population," he said. "The Poles shall be the slaves of the Greater German World Empire."

A few months later, Heinrich Himmler, the head of all German security forces, wrote a memo to Hitler about the situation in the General Government area and Frank's plan for the area. According to Himmler, Hitler found the memo "very good and correct. He directed however that only very few copies should be issued." Hitler wanted the report "to be treated with the utmost secrecy." Here is the part of Himmler's memo that deals with education:

> For the non-German population of the East there must be no higher school than the four-grade elementary school. The sole goal of the school is to be—

> Simple arithmetic up to 500 at the most; writing one's name; the principle that it is divine law to obey the Germans and be honest, industrious, and good. I don't think that reading is necessary.

The *Einsatzgruppen* and the murder of educated Poles

It would certainly take time to turn the Poles into slaves who could not read and who were taught that it was "divine law to obey the Germans." The first step was to remove anyone who might lead the Poles in resisting these ideas. Almost every Pole with a university education became a target of the Nazis.

The terror began as soon as the German army arrived in September 1939. The Nazis murdered 10,000 Poles. Most of the killings were committed by *Einsatzgruppen* ("special-action groups" or "special-duty groups"). These specially trained strike forces were like a combination of army troops and secret police officers. They had been used to hunt down opponents of the Nazis during the *Anschluss,* Germany's merger with Austria in March 1938. (See p. 106.)

The *Einsatzgruppen* were units of the SD (from the German initials for *Sicherheitsdienst,* meaning "security service"). The SD was the intelligence service of the *Schutzstaffel,* or SS, the Nazi Party's military wing whose members were supposed to be the most dedicated Nazis and the most "racially pure" Germans. The head of the SD was Reinhard Heydrich. He was the chief assistant to Heinrich Himmler, head of the entire SS and of the *Geheime Staatspolizei,* or Gestapo, the secret police.

In Poland, the *Einsatzgruppen* followed closely behind the regular German army, arriving in a town immediately after the army entered it. They killed every Polish political leader they could find—even those who shared some of the Nazis' own ideas. They killed members of the Polish nobility. They killed professors, high school teachers, and people with technical training. And they killed many priests—important leaders of the community in Poland, a heavily Catholic country. They also arrested thousands of other Poles and sent them to concentration camps, the brutal prison camps run by the SS.

A huge anti-Nazi underground soon developed. The Polish network of organizations working secretly to undermine the Germans' efforts was probably the largest in any country the Nazis conquered. (The Polish and Jewish undergrounds are discussed at length in Chapter 6.)

The first attacks on the Jews of Poland

A very large number of Jews, probably 120,000, were killed during and immediately after the German invasion of Poland. Jews in the Polish army, like all Polish soldiers, suffered heavy losses. Many Jewish civilians, like other Poles, died in German air raids. But many other Poles were killed for no other reason than because they were Jewish.

Nazi brutality towards the Jews began at the very beginning of the German occupation, once the German military stationed forces in the defeated Poland. Many of the worst acts of violence were committed by the *Waffen*-SS ("armed SS"), military units of the SS that fought as part of the regular army. And even though the main job of the *Einsatzgruppen* was originally to kill and arrest educated Poles, they still attacked and killed Jews whenever they could.

Humiliation and torture

The Nazis' behavior reveals the intensity of their hatred of the Jews. The Nazis were not just interested in eliminating Jews who might be dangerous to them (as they were with the Poles). They felt it necessary to humiliate and torture Jews as much as possible.

Heinrich Himmler oversaw all the German security forces, including the Gestapo, the SS, the SD, and the Einsatzgruppen, *the specially trained strike forces attached to the SD.*

A synagogue burns. The local fire department prevented the fire from spreading to a nearby home, but made no attempt to intervene in the synagogue burning.

The Nazis reached the town of Bielsko on September 3, only two days after they invaded Poland. There, 2,000 Jews were forced into the courtyard of a Jewish school, beaten, and tortured. Some had boiling water poured on them while they hung by their hands. Others died when water from a hose was forced into their mouths until their stomachs burst. In the town of Mielec, 35 Jews were forced into a slaughterhouse, which was then set on fire, burning them alive. In Wloclawek, the Nazis interrupted prayers in a private house on Yom Kippur (the Day of Atonement, the most sacred Jewish holiday). They ordered the people to go outside and run; then they

ordered them to halt. Five or six of these Jews apparently did not hear this order—or simply did not halt quickly enough—and were shot dead. The next day, the Nazis burned down the town's two synagogues (Jewish houses of worship), something they would continue to do all over Poland. In the first six months of the German occupation, most Jewish synagogues in Poland were burned to the ground.

Often, the Nazis forced the Jews to watch as their sacred places of worship were destroyed. In one town, a young Jew reportedly ran into a burning synagogue to save the Torah scrolls (the first five books of the Bible, written on rolled-up

German soldiers amuse themselves while they force Jews to dig ditches in an empty lot in Kraków, Poland.

parchment or paper), the holiest object in the Jewish religion. The Germans shot him down as he came out, and he and the Torah he carried burned with the synagogue.

German soldiers routinely grabbed Jews on the streets and beat them. They cut off the beards of religious Jewish men, who wore the beards as a symbol of their faith. They forced Jews to crawl through the mud, to pull Germans around in carts, to give the stiff-armed Hitler salute.

The role of the army

The *Waffen*-SS units and *Einsatzgruppen* were so brutal that even German army generals were shocked by their actions. The generals became especially upset when regular army troops began taking part in these activities. The German officers seem to have viewed the murder and torture of civilians as criminal actions, not as part of the war effort. But, despite their verbal objections, the army generals did not demand that these actions be stopped. Instead, their main concern was to tighten the disciplinary reins on their own soldiers. The members of the *Waffen*-SS were supposed to follow army rules, meaning they would obey the orders of the army generals—not the SS leaders. More than anything, the generals wanted to maintain control over their troops. But some historians indicate that the military leaders were also watching their own backs, as they did not want the German army to be held responsible for the actions of the *Einsatzgruppen*.

Army higher-ups requested that these brutal "clearing" actions be delayed until after the military handed over control of a newly captured area to the German civilian authorities. That way, the *Einsatzgruppen* could commit their murders without directly involving the German army. On September 19, while the fighting in Poland was still going on, the army's request was denied by Reinhard Heydrich, the Nazi official who had created the *Einsatzgruppen*. Instead, Heydrich agreed only to keeping the military abreast of the *Einsatzgruppen's* future plans.

Heydrich's message

On September 21, Heydrich sent a secret message to the *Einsatzgruppen* commanders on "the Jewish question in the occupied territory." It described the actions to be taken against the Jews of Poland. Although the members of the SS, and especially the *Einsatzgruppen,* were directly in charge of carrying out his plan, Heydrich was not speaking just to them. His message also applied to the many different German authorities who had some role in the occupation of Poland. Heydrich sent copies of his key goals to the army, to what soon became the General Government, and to the government departments in charge of the German economy, food, and security.

Heydrich's first major point to the commanders was a reminder that the "final aim" of these actions was to be "kept *strictly secret.*" The "final aim," he said, "will require an extended period of time." However, the "stages leading to the fulfillment of this final aim" required immediate action.

This was the only time that the "final aim" was mentioned in Heydrich's message. Experts on the Holocaust (the period between 1939 and 1945 when the Nazi Party tried to physically eliminate the entire European Jewish population) strongly disagree about what Heydrich meant. Some believe the message proves that the Nazis had already decided to murder all the Jews of Poland. Proponents of this theory suggest that Heydrich's "final aim" later came to be called the "Final Solution." (See pp. 200–08.)

Reinhard Heydrich headed the SD and the Einsatzgruppen. *He would soon direct the execution of the Holocaust.*

Others think the Nazis wanted to force the Jews into a special "reservation," then perhaps send them into Soviet-held territory. They argue that the decision to kill the Jews came later.

Although there is evidence to support both sides of this argument, no clear proof of either theory exists. What is clear is that whenever the Nazis *did* make the decision to "solve" the "Jewish problem" by mass murder, Heydrich's plan helped make it possible.

Heydrich's plan: Placing Jews in ghettos

The first step in Heydrich's scheme was to remove as many Jews as possible from the sections of Poland that had become part of Germany. These Jews would be transferred into the General Government. Any remaining Jews were to be concentrated (gathered) in a few cities. Likewise, the Jews in the General Government would also be housed in as few points as possible. To make "later actions" easier, the concentration points were to be located at key railroad stops—or at least along railroad lines. Once again, the "later actions" were not described, but it is quite clear that the "concentration points" were not intended as a final destination for the Jews.

Regarding any town with less than 500 Jewish residents, Heydrich stated in his message that these Jews should be forced into the nearest "city of concentration." He gave the *Einsatzgruppen* commanders an excuse for these actions: "The reason to be given for the concentration of Jews into the cities" was that Jews had played an important role in guerrilla attacks (independent acts of warfare) on the Germans and in "plundering actions" (taking something wrongfully or by force).

This marked the beginning of the ghetto system. In the Middle Ages (500–1500), many European Jews were required to live in a special section of town and usually had to return there by nightfall. In some places, including parts of Germany, these ghettos lasted until the early nineteenth century. At the time of Heydrich's plan, however, there had been no ghetto in Europe for many decades. (The changes in the Jewish community in Germany are described in Chapter 1.) The Nazis were creating new ghettos to confine the Jews. Heydrich's message predicted that Jews would end up being barred completely from certain sections of town—or even from leaving the ghetto at all.

Heydrich's plan: The Jewish councils

The second section of Heydrich's message ordered the creation of a "Council of Jewish Elders" in each area, made up of "the remaining influential personalities and rabbis." Each of these councils would have 12 or 24 men, depending on the size of the town or city. The council in most ghettos became known as a *Judenrat* (pronounced YOO-den-rot), or "Jewish Council."

Heydrich emphasized that the *Judenrat* was *"fully responsible, in the literal sense of the word"* for ensuring that all

German orders were followed exactly and quickly. The events of the next few months made Heydrich's command clear. The members of the *Judenrat* would be held responsible—meaning they would pay with their lives and their families' lives—if the Jews of their area did not cooperate with the Germans.

In the small towns, the members of the *Judenrat* were to provide "in the shortest possible time" a census of the Jews in each area. Each report was to include certain statistical information, such as the numbers of Jews of each sex, their ages, and their occupations. The Germans would inform the *Judenrat* of departure dates, methods, and routes for the transfer of the Jews. The *Judenrat* "are then to be made personally responsible for the departure of the Jews from the countryside." The *Judenrat* had to provide food and other requirements for the trip to the ghetto. In the cities where ghettos were to be created, they were also responsible for housing the Jews being brought in from other areas.

An undated photo of Jews in a Polish ghetto. Heydrich's plan of restricting Jews to one designated area of a city harkened back to the Middle Ages.

Heydrich's plan: "Aryanization" of Jewish property

Heydrich's message then discussed the "Aryanization" of Jewish-owned businesses. "Aryanization" was the term the Nazis invented for seizing Jewish property and selling it to non-Jewish "Aryans." They used the word "Aryan" to describe white Europeans and especially Germans, whom they considered a superior race. (See "The Origins of Antisemitism" box on p.6.)

The *Einsatzgruppen* commanders were ordered to report to Heydrich continuously on the number of Jews in their areas, how many were being "evacuated" from the countryside, and how many were already in the cities. Heydrich wanted to see a survey of Jewish-owned businesses highlighting those that were important to the German economy and to war production. He also demanded an estimate of how quickly and easily each could be "Aryanized."

The beginning of the system of slave labor

Although Heydrich's message does not say so directly, it appears that the Nazis planned—at least temporarily—to use Jewish labor for the benefit of the German economy, especially for German military needs. That is probably the reason why he wanted to know the sex, ages, and occupations of the Jews. In addition, when Heydrich referred to preventing Jews from leaving the ghetto, he noted: "However, economic necessities are always to be considered in this connection."

The use of forced labor of Polish Jews began at the very beginning of the German occupation. Jews were grabbed off the street and forced to do things like clear rubble from the recent battles or fill in anti-tank ditches that the Poles had dug.

On October 26, 1939, five weeks after Heydrich's message, an official decree gave authority over Jewish forced labor to the top SS leader in each area of occupied Poland. Whenever any German agency needed some emergency work done, the SS (the Nazi Party's military wing) formed a "labor column" from Jews they arrested at random on the street.

Within a few months, the Germans had created labor camps that were more permanent. Soon, 30,000 Jews were digging a long anti-tank ditch near the new border with the Soviet Union. Forty-five thousand others held in 40 separate

camps were building a canal near Lublin. Another 25,000 worked on a project near Warsaw.

Jewish women forced to pull carts of quarried stones at the Plazow labor camp in Poland.

Before long, Jews were also being forced to work in factories. Many German companies—including some owned by the SS itself—built factories next to the work camps to "borrow" from the pool of labor. Some Nazi officials became rich by making deals with private companies. (Non-Jewish Poles were also sent to work camps.) Certain Jews were paid about 40 cents a day; most others were not paid at all. They labored under terrible conditions, without enough food, and the death rate was very high. Eventually, the work camps developed into a huge system of forced—or slave—labor. (The use of slave labor in Poland is discussed in Chapter 9, pp. 265-269.)

The first ghettos

At the same time as the forced-labor columns were being created, the Nazis moved ahead with Heydrich's plan to cre-

Slave Labor and Mass Murder

Historians agree that creating a system of slave labor was not the long-term Nazi goal for the Jews. Instead, slave labor began almost by accident and then grew. Some Nazi officials favored it because it made them rich and increased their influence. The army was interested in using the laborers for military production. But insufficient plans were made to accomplish this and other goals. For instance, the Germans made no real attempt to use workers according to their skills and physical abilities. Furthermore, the forced removal of Jews from western Poland to the General Government and from the countryside to city ghettos made no economic sense because it hindered production efforts. This supports the argument that slave labor was not the Nazis' real goal. But the clearest proof is what happened next.

Within two years, the Nazis began killing millions of Jews. (See Chapters 8 and 9.) From the beginning, the victims included many who could have worked. Those Jews who were not killed immediately were forced to work themselves to death—a program the Nazis called "destruction through work." Eventually the Nazis murdered almost all the Jews they could find, whether they worked or not. It seems clear that in the long run, the Nazis wanted to kill the Jews, not use them as slave laborers.

ate ghettos. They collected the lists of Jews from each *Judenrat.* Jews were distinguished by the yellow six-pointed star they were required to wear at all times, and they were not allowed to travel freely. (The six-pointed star or Star of David is a Jewish symbol.)

In late October 1939, less than two months after the German army had crossed the Polish border, the first ghetto was created in a town near Lódz as a kind of experiment. It took several months before the second ghetto was established. This one was set up in Lódz itself, the second-largest city in Poland before the war. Lódz was in Wartheland, an area of the country that had become part of Germany and was supposed to be free of all people of Jewish origin. However, hundreds of thousands of Jews were still living there.

From the time the Lódz ghetto was created, it took about a year for the Germans to complete the process of setting up ghettos throughout Poland. By April 1941, almost all Jews in both the General Government and the areas that became part of Germany were confined in ghettos. Later, after the German invasion of Russia in June 1941, another area (called Galicia) was added to the General Government. By the end of the year, this Jewish population had been transferred to ghettos as well.

Lódz was different from later ghettos in many ways: it was bigger, more industry-based, and completely cut off from

View of the gate at the Kraków, Poland, ghetto c. 1940.

the outside world. Unlike other ghettos, it was virtually impossible to smuggle food and weapons into Lódz; nor were its residents able to maintain contact with the Polish underground, a system of organizations that worked secretly to foil the Nazis' plans. Although these differences were indeed significant, the overall features of Lódz pretty well reflected the ghetto system throughout Poland.

The Lódz ghetto

The Nazis decided to situate the ghetto in a slum neighborhood of Lódz. Over 60,000 Jews, mostly very poor, already lived in the area. Early in February 1940, the 100,000 Jews who lived in other parts of Lódz were ordered to move into the ghetto. By the end of the month, all Poles and ethnic Germans were forced to leave it.

The Lódz ghetto was completely surrounded by barbed wire. Armed police prevented Jews from leaving. On March 6, several Jews found outside the ghetto were shot and killed. By May, the ghetto was considered "sealed": all non-Jews, except special police units, were barred from entering. Inside the ghetto, Jews were not allowed outdoors between 7:00 P.M. and 7:00 A.M.

The conditions at Lódz were dreadful. The buildings were mostly old, run-down, and poorly heated throughout the cold Polish winter. Few had indoor bathrooms or running water. There were about 32,000 apartments inside the ghetto, most of them consisting of only one room. On average, 4 people lived in every room. Over 160,000 people were jammed into an area of 1.5 square miles—about 30 city blocks. All food in the ghetto had to be supplied by the Germans, who never provided enough. Even so, many of the people were so poor they could not even buy what the Germans allowed. The combination of intense cold, poor sanitation, overcrowding, and an inadequate diet led to disease and death for many of the Jews of Lódz.

A plan for survival

Before World War II broke out, Lódz was the most important industrial city in Poland, rich in textile mills where cloth is made. A large part of the city's workforce was Jewish. The head of the Lódz *Judenrat,* Mordecai Rumkowski,

The picture shows a sign reading:

> WOHNGEBIET DER
> **JUDEN**
> BETRETEN
> VERBOTEN

A Jewish policeman and a German soldier direct pedestrian traffic across the main street of the Lódz ghetto before the wooden footbridge is built. The footbridge was used to get Jews from one side of the ghetto to the other while allowing the road below to remain open to traffic.

proposed that the ghetto could produce goods for the Germans if they provided workers with the necessary material. Rumkowski believed that making the Jews valuable to the Germans would protect them. In addition, because the Lódz ghetto was sealed off from the rest of the city, there was no other way for the people to get work.

The Nazis agreed. In addition to producing textiles, the ghetto became the largest armaments center in the area. At a time when Germany needed all the workers it could find, 80,000 Jews worked in 117 factories and workshops in the ghetto.

But wages were extremely low, and the Germans did not pay a fair price for the products they got from the Jews. In January 1941, a series of strikes and demonstrations broke out in the Lódz ghetto. The workers demanded higher wages and more food. Rumkowski, however, ordered the rebels to end these actions and refused to discuss their demands. He

Jüdische Soziale Selbsthilfe
KIELCE
Żydowska Samopomoc Społeczna

Dział dożyw. dzieci.

Leg. Nr _____

upoważnia do korzystania
z kuchni Ż. S. S.
ŚNIADANIA

Nazwisko i imię _____

*1600 śniadań
dziennie*

Adres _____

Miesiąc maj 1941 r.

| 31 | 30 | 29 |

A child's identification card that entitles him to receive rations from the soup kitchen in the Kielce ghetto. The Lódz Juderat issued similar cards to the inhabitants of the ghetto it served.

wanted nothing to interfere with producing goods for the Germans because he believed that the very survival of the people in the ghetto depended on it.

The *Judenrat*

In many ways, the Lódz *Judenrat* became the government of the ghetto, collecting taxes from the inhabitants, distributing food, making housing assignments, organizing streetcleaning, establishing a fire department, running a statistics office to keep records, and even controlling the Jewish police, which it used to enforce its decisions.

At the same time, the *Judenrat* was not like a real government at all. It had to carry out the orders of the Germans. In many places, early *Judenrat* leaders were arrested and shot if the Germans did not think they were cooperating fully. (The Germans allowed only men to be on a *Judenrat*.) In most

Favoritism and Corruption

One reason ghetto residents hated the *Judenrat*, the Jewish Council that was responsible for seeing that German orders were carried out in the ghetto, was because members often gave jobs and granted important favors to their relatives, friends, and supporters. Having an "in" with the *Judenrat* was called having "protection" or "Vitamin P." Besides family connections, one of the ways to get "Vitamin P" was to pay bribes.

At one point, almost 13,000 people worked for the various departments of the Lódz *Judenrat*. At that time, the entire population of the ghetto was around 100,000. The number of *Judenrat* employees was proportionally smaller in other ghettos, but still quite large: in Warsaw, which was much larger than Lódz, there were 6,000, in Lwów (Lvov) there were 4,000, in Bialystok there were 2,200, and in Vilna there were 1,500. Besides appointing people to special jobs, the *Judenrat* could dole out extra food rations or even spare a certain resident from heavy-labor details—things that often made the difference between life and death.

ghettos, the *Judenrat* became very unpopular. Although there were some important exceptions, the head of a *Judenrat* was often hated. Some of them, like Mordecai Rumkowski in Lódz, were viewed as dictators and traitors because they went along with the Germans' demands. Historians speculate that in some ghettos, the *Judenrat* was made up of people who were trying to protect their own lives and the lives of their families, no matter what the cost to others. But many others were simply trying to do their best to help their people.

Judenrat members faced very difficult choices as long as they believed that the people of the ghetto—or some of them—could be saved. Protecting the people meant cooperating with the Germans. But very soon, cooperating with the Germans meant handing over people for deportation (forcibly removing them) from the ghetto. These people were being sent to their deaths.

Cooperation or resistance?

In some ghettos, the *Judenrat* tried to find a middle road. They cooperated with the Germans on some things, such as the daily running of the ghetto, but they refused to help the Germans in deportation procedures. In some places, the *Judenrat* had contacts with anti-Nazi underground organizations outside the ghetto. This was especially true after Germany invaded the Soviet Union. In the part of Poland that had originally been taken over by the Soviet Union, guerrilla units (partisans, members of independent fighting units operating within enemy lines) connected to the Russian army were battling the Germans in the forests. In some ghettos, the *Judenrat* helped young Jews escape from the ghetto to join the partisans.

In many ghettos, though, organized resistance efforts were impossible to coordinate because the *Judenrat* opposed plans for armed rebellion against the Germans. The *Judenrat* and the Jewish underground (those who wanted to fight) clashed over the prospect of an uprising. The *Judenrat* thought members of the underground—usually young people—were hotheads who were putting everyone in danger. They thought that armed resistance to the Germans was suicide: the Germans would not just kill the underground fighters, but everyone in the entire ghetto.

Most of the people of the ghettos are thought to have agreed with the *Judenrat* on this point. Historically, the Nazis had always responded to attacks on them with mass killings. But when people came to realize that the Nazis intended to kill all the Jews even if they *did* cooperate, support for the Jewish underground grew.

The deportations

In Lódz, Rumkowski believed that the Jews would be protected by working for the Germans and cooperating with them. In some ways, Rumkowski's plan seemed to work. Because of its economic importance (and the fact that Nazi officials were getting rich from selling the ghetto's products), Lódz was the last ghetto that the Germans "liquidated" or eliminated.

Long before the Lódz ghetto was liquidated, though, its people were being murdered. In December 1941, Rumkowski

was told by the Nazis that 20,000 people would be deported from the ghetto. He was able to reduce that number to 10,000, and he convinced the Germans that the *Judenrat*—not the Germans—should choose them.

Rumkowski decided that the 2,000 people who had recently arrived in Lódz from nearby towns in Wartheland would be among the deportees. The rest of the 10,000 were people who had police records—and their families. Most of these were not hard-core criminals; they were ordinary people who had been caught stealing food or firewood. In other words, the very poorest people in the ghetto, along with their children, were being chosen for deportation.

It took almost two weeks for the 10,000 people to be deported from Lódz. No one knew where the Nazis were sending the trains packed with these people—or why. In fact, they were being sent to Chelmno, about 35 miles away,

Jewish deportees from the Lodz ghetto being taken to the Chelmno death camp in 1941.

Dates of Destruction

In most major towns, as in Lódz, deportations to death camps began long before the final liquidation of the ghetto. As the Germans intended, neither the *Judenrat* nor the rest of the Jews in the ghetto could be sure of their fates until the very end.

At the end of 1941, the Germans began deporting the Jews from the smaller ghettos of Wartheland to Chelmno. Essential workers remained until the next summer, when the ghettos were finally liquidated. Deportations to the Belzec death camp from the ghetto of Kraków (Cracow), the third largest city in Poland, began in March 1942, but the ghetto was not liquidated until a year later.

Over 300,000 people from the Warsaw ghetto, the largest and most important of all the ghettos, were sent to Treblinka and murdered between July and September 1942. However, the final liquidation of the Warsaw ghetto did not begin until April 1943. In Lwów (Lvov), which held the most Jews after Warsaw and Lódz, the first deportations from the ghetto occurred in March 1942, when 15,000 people were sent to Belzec. Fifty thousand more followed in August. In January 1943, the ghetto became a labor camp. Deportation from Vilna, one of the great centers of Jewish culture, began almost as soon as the ghetto was established in September 1941. The Vilna ghetto was liquidated in September 1943. Lódz lasted almost a year longer, until August 1944. (The death camps of Treblinka and Belzec are discussed in Chapter 8. The Warsaw Ghetto is discussed in Chapter 6.)

where they were immediately murdered. (What happened at Chelmno is described in Chapter 8, pp. 219-20.)

Then the deportations from the Lódz ghetto stopped for more than three weeks. But on February 22, 1942, the Nazis began deporting almost 1,000 people each day. There were no more "criminals" left to be chosen. Instead, as Rumkowski announced on March 2, "wholly innocent people have begun to be deported." From now on, he said, "only those people who work can remain." Those who could not find work

The Roma (Gypsies)

The only non-Jews in the Lódz ghetto were a group of 5,000 Roma (Gypsies), whom the Germans had transported into the city. A special section of the ghetto was set aside for them. It is not clear why the Nazis decided to send them to Lódz. All 5,000 were deported to Chelmno and killed in the first half of 1942.

The Roma are a nomadic (traveling) people originally from India, but some have lived throughout Europe for centuries. By the time of World War II, many Roma continued to wander from place to place, but some had settled in one community.

Nazi attitudes toward the Roma were very puzzling. The Nazis saw everything in terms of race and thought that the Aryan race was superior. But the Roma were also "Aryans." In fact, if the Nazis took their own theories seriously, the Roma were actually *more* Aryan than the Germans. Heinrich Himmler, head of the SS, the Gestapo, and the concentration camps decided that "pure" Roma were ex-amples of original Aryan tribes, who still lived like the ancestors of the Germans. On the other hand, Roma whose ancestors had inter-married with other ethnic groups—the majority of them had—were an example of racial mixing. Himmler thought this kind of racial mixing caused civilizations to collapse.

So Nazi policy at times was to kill all the "mixed-race" Roma, including people who were part Roma and part German. The "pure" Roma, however, were to be protected. Sometimes, however, the Nazis persecuted those Roma who had no permanent homes, while tolerating those who had settled down in one location. But in some countries under Nazi control or domination, *all* the Roma were hunted down and sent to death camps. Out of about 1,000,000 Roma in Nazi-controlled Europe, an estimated 200,000 were murdered. The Roma were also the victims of forced sterilization and horrible medical experiments. (See Chapter 9, pp. 271-73.)

"must leave the ghetto. The order must be carried out, there is no choice."

The deportations continued until early April. Almost 35,000 more people had been sent to their deaths. Early in May, another 10,000 were shipped out of the ghetto. This time it was Jews from Germany, Austria, and Czechoslovakia who had been sent to Lódz earlier.

Deporting the children

In the summer of 1942, the smaller ghettos of Wartheland were liquidated. Most of their people were sent to Chelmno to be killed. But 10,000 of them, young and rela-

Women work in the spinning workshop of a ghetto.

tively healthy, were taken to Lódz. The ghetto was becoming a giant labor camp.

Historical records indicate that one of the new arrivals had information about where the Lódz Jews were being sent—and what was happening to them. Their destination was Chelmno, and they were being killed by carbon monoxide gas in trucks. When Rumkowski was told, he supposedly said that he already knew. But choosing some people to die, he thought, was the only way to save the rest.

In September the Nazis ordered another deportation. This time they wanted the old and the sick. They also wanted 10,000 children under the age of ten. They threatened to deport the whole ghetto if the *Judenrat* did not supply the children.

Most of the people refused to hand over their children for the deportation. On September 5, 1942, the Jewish police began rounding up the children, along with the old and sick.

The Jewish Police

The Jewish police force was originally created by the Germans to carry out normal police work inside the ghetto. The officers were responsible for maintaining traffic control, preventing ordinary crime, and helping guard the ghetto gates. (These guards prevented people from leaving without permits. Unlike Lódz, most ghettos allowed some restricted travel outside the ghetto walls.) Armed German police watched the Jewish officers carefully, making sure they followed German orders and enforced the orders of the *Judenrat*, which were often unpopular.

Before long, the Jewish police were expected to hunt down food smugglers and arrest people who had not reported for forced labor. Ghetto residents came to view the Jewish force as the enemy—turncoats who used billy clubs and rubber hoses to help the Nazis in exchange for personal gain.

They had been promised that their own children and families would not be deported if they carried out this order. But the Jewish police did not catch enough people to satisfy the Nazis. The next day, German police units entered the ghetto. They continued their searches until September 12. Twenty thousand people were deported. The old, the sick, and 10,000 children were sent to die.

The end of the Lódz ghetto

The Lódz ghetto continued to exist, producing cloth and arms for the Germans, for almost two more years (until mid-1944), when there were less than 90,000 people left in captivity. There were more deportations and continued hunger and misery. The only hope was that Germany would soon be defeated in the war. Germany was at this point fighting the Soviet Union, the United States, and Great Britain.

The people of Lódz followed the news of the war as closely as they could. They knew the Russian army was pushing the Germans out of the Soviet Union and back into

Poland. There were celebrations throughout the ghetto on June 6, 1944 (D-Day), when the American and British armies landed on the beaches of Normandy along the coast of France.

In August 1944, with the Russian army only 75 miles away, the Germans announced that the entire Lódz ghetto, including the factories and workshops, was being moved. Rumkowski still urged the people of the ghetto to cooperate. The workers from each factory were ordered to report at a railroad siding together, but almost none did. Instead, they went into hiding. They were then hunted down, first by the Jewish police and later by the Germans. The roundup went on for weeks. Almost 80,000 people were captured and sent to Auschwitz, where almost all of them died in the gas chambers. Among them was Mordecai Rumkowski. (Auschwitz is described in Chapter 9.)

When the Russian army reached Lódz in January 1945, there were only 870 Jews left in the city. Over 170,000 had been killed. When Germany surrendered four months later, about 250,000 Polish Jews were still alive. (Most of them had been in Soviet territory.) The rest—3,000,000 Polish Jews—were dead.

6

The Warsaw Ghetto

Warsaw, the capital of Poland, had the largest Jewish population in all of Europe in the 1930s. Worldwide, only New York City had a larger Jewish population. There were about 375,000 Jews in Warsaw at the beginning of World War II—about 29 percent of the city's 1,290,000 people.

Before the German army invaded Poland in September 1939 (see Chapter 5), thousands of people, both Jews and non-Jews, fled from Warsaw. But over the next several months, thousands of others, mainly refugees from the areas of western Poland that were made part of Germany, moved in. The Germans expelled hundreds of thousands of people from these areas and forced them to move into what was left of Poland. About 90,000 Jews from other parts of Poland, most of them with virtually no possessions or money, crowded into Warsaw between the fall of 1939 and November 1940.

A Jewish businessman walks along a Warsaw street wearing the yellow star.

Separating the Jews

Step by step, the Nazis began to separate the Jews from the rest of the population and strip them of their most basic rights. Within just a few months, in fact, the party applied all the anti-Jewish orders that they had implemented over several years in Germany.

By November 1939, all Jews in Poland had to wear a six-pointed Jewish star (the Star of David) on their clothing at all times. Jews could not even change their address without permission. In December, they were ordered to register all their property with the Germans. In January 1940, an order barred Jews from traveling on railroads without special permits. Next, they were forbidden to enter restaurants and parks and excluded from many professions.

By March 1940, the Nazis had erected street signs around the main Jewish neighborhood of Warsaw. The signs warned that this was an "infected area." There was a typhus epidemic (a serious bacterial disease) in the city at that time. However, the epidemic was only an excuse for the Nazis to do what they had already planned.

The wall

Eleven miles of eight-foot-high brick walls were built around the "infected area," the main Jewish neighborhood. The Nazis made the Warsaw *Judenrat* (the council within the Jewish community that was responsible to the Nazis for the community) pay for this construction with money collected from the Jews. The walls had many gaps, and for a time people were allowed to pass from one part of Warsaw to another.

In August 1940, the Germans announced that a ghetto would be created. They began to force Jews to leave apartments in the "Polish" area of Warsaw. On October 12, 1940, loudspeakers throughout the city announced that all Jews must live in the ghetto by the end of the month. For the next few weeks, the city was in turmoil. Thousands of Jews from all over Warsaw searched for apartments inside the ghetto boundaries, while non-Jewish Poles were forced to move out.

The Jews brought their belongings into the ghetto on hand carts or on their backs. No one was sure of the final boundaries of the ghetto. Jewish property outside the ghetto was "confiscated"—stolen—by the Nazis. By the October 31 deadline, many Jewish people still had no place to live. The Germans then extended the deadline to November 15.

According to a German report written a year later, a quarter of a million people—113,000 non-Jewish Poles and 138,000 Jews—had to move when the ghetto was created. Poles were forced out of more than 11,000 apartments in the ghetto. These were usually small and often run-down, since the Poles who lived in the area were poor, as were many of the Jews. Jews had to leave nearly 14,000 apartments in other

parts of Warsaw. These were often larger and more modern, because wealthier Jews did not live in the neighborhood where the ghetto was located.

Although Jews had to live in the ghetto, they were unsure for a time whether they would be allowed to leave the restricted area to work, shop, or visit in the rest of the city. The answer came on November 16, 1940: the ghetto was sealed. Police were stationed at each of the 22 surrounding gates, preventing anyone from entering or leaving. The Jews who still had jobs outside the ghetto lost them. (Most Jews had already been fired on German orders.)

Around 450,000 Jews lived inside the ghetto walls by the end of 1940. That's about 200,000 people for every square mile, almost triple the number for the rest of Warsaw, which was itself a crowded city. In the ghetto, an average of nine people lived in every room.

Smugglers

Warsaw was divided in two. Outside the ghetto was the "Aryan side." The Germans used the word "Aryan" to describe white Europeans and especially Germans, whom they considered a superior race. (See "The Origins of Antisemitism" box on p. 6.) All connections between the ghetto and the "Aryan side" were supposed to be controlled by the Germans. But there were many secret contacts, especially through tunnels dug beneath the wall that ran down parts of the street.

Jews from the ghetto would sneak out each day to get food by selling or trading whatever possessions they had, especially old clothing. Then they smuggled the food back into the ghetto. Polish smugglers also went into the ghetto to buy and sell goods. Before long, people in the ghetto were making products such as hair brushes, woolen socks, pots, and spoons—all from material or scrap metal found in the ghetto or from materials brought in by smugglers.

The smugglers, especially the Jews, risked their lives each time they brought something in or took something out of the ghetto. A Jew caught outside the ghetto might be shot on sight. In October 1941, the Germans officially made smuggling an offense punishable by death. The majority of the smugglers were ordinary people who needed the food to

Opposite page:
A section of the 8-foot-high,
11-mile-long brick wall that
enclosed the Warsaw ghetto.

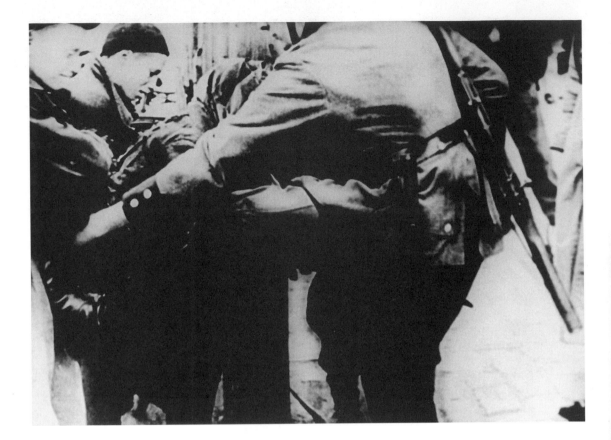

German soldiers search suspected smugglers at an entrance to the Warsaw ghetto. Smuggling was vital to survival in the ghetto

feed their families; many were children—it was easier for them to slip in and out of the ghetto without being caught. But some smugglers were professionals who made large profits and lived very well inside the ghetto. Some of them had been ordinary criminals—thieves and burglars—before the war. Whatever their motives, the smugglers became a very important part of the fight to survive in the ghetto.

Secret contacts

Some Jews continued to live on the "Aryan side" of Warsaw with false documents showing they were non-Jewish Poles. Some of them acted as links between the ghetto and the Polish underground—the huge secret network of anti-Nazi organizations that the Poles had created. The Polish underground had weapons, and it maintained secret radio contacts with the Polish government stationed in London. (The government officials had left Poland and settled in

Hunger

For most of the time that the Warsaw ghetto existed, hunger was the main problem plaguing its residents. Food in German-controlled Poland was rationed, so even people with money could legally buy only what the Germans allowed. Each person had ration coupons for different categories of food. Jews were not allowed to buy meat, poultry, fish, fruits, vegetables, eggs, or white flour. Their diet consisted mainly of potatoes and bread.

The official ration in the ghetto probably amounted to about 800 calories a day per person. This was half the ration for non-Jewish Poles and a third the ration for Germans in Poland. As the Nazis knew, people cannot survive for very long on 800 calories a day. (One peanut butter sandwich on white bread contains over 350 calories.) Hunger and malnutrition were everyone's reality. People ate potato peelings. Anyone who walked down a ghetto street with a package that might contain food was taking a risk. Packages were often grabbed from an owner's hands by people desperate for something to eat. Sometimes the "snatchers" ripped open the package and stuffed the contents into their mouths while they were still running.

For those who could not steal extra food or buy it from smugglers, death by starvation was certain. Over 43,000 people starved to death in 1941, almost one-tenth of the population. At a funeral for some children from a ghetto orphanage, the remaining children placed a wreath on their graves. It read: "To the Children Who Have Died from Hunger—From the Children Who Are Hungry."

Britain.) Through the underground, the people of the ghetto could contact Jewish organizations outside Poland.

Some members of the Polish underground did not cooperate very well with the Jews. Some were openly hostile to them. There was a long history of antisemitism (hate-filled prejudice against the Jews) in Poland. Relations between the Jews and the Polish underground—including the main underground military organization, the Home Army (the AK, from its Polish initials)—are still a subject of argument among historians.

Some members and leaders of the Home Army, however, tried their best to help the Jews. For example, the official newspaper of the Home Army carried regular reports on the Nazi actions toward the Jews. Its editor later helped establish contacts between the Warsaw military command of the Home Army and the Jewish underground inside the ghetto. Some non-Jewish Poles also acted as couriers, delivering messages between the Warsaw ghetto and Jews in the rest of Poland. Many Jews, especially young people who could more easily "pass" as non-Jewish Poles, acted as couriers as well.

The Jewish underground

People inside the ghetto also organized underground organizations. The political parties to which the Jews had belonged before the war tried to continue operations in secret. Most of these parties were involved in activities such as publishing newspapers and journals. They printed reports about what was happening in the ghetto and tried to convince their readers that something should be done about it.

Two of the parties, the Communists and the General Jewish Workers Union, known as the Bund, had direct connections with non-Jewish organizations of the Polish underground. The Bund, which had ties to the Polish Socialist Party, was much larger than the Communist Party in the ghetto. (Communism is a political and economic theory advocating the formation of a classless society through the communal, or group, ownership of all property. Socialism is a political and economic system based on government control of the production and distribution of goods. Socialists champion the removal of private property in a quest to attain a classless society.)

There were several different parties of Zionists, people who wanted to create a Jewish country in Palestine (most of which is now Israel), the ancestral homeland of the Jewish people. The Zionist groups in Warsaw kept in contact with Jewish organizations in other countries.

All of these parties had youth groups that were active in the underground. The youth groups were especially important in maintaining connections with Jews in the rest of Poland.

All underground activities were conducted in secret and were very dangerous. There was constant tension between the underground and the *Judenrat*—the Jewish Council, which was officially in charge of the ghetto. The underground thought the *Judenrat* was aiding the Nazi cause, and the *Judenrat* thought the underground was endangering the people of the ghetto. (See Chapter 5, pp. 126–27 and pp. 134–36 for more on the role of the *Judenrat*.)

A group portrait of the members of a Zionist youth organization in Kolbuszowa, Poland, 1940. Jewish groups were forced to act in secret during the German occupation of Poland.

News and disbelief

The underground's secret contacts allowed the Jews inside the ghetto to learn what was going on throughout the country. In December 1941, the Nazis began murdering thousands of Jews from western Poland by gassing them in sealed trucks at Chelmno. Chelmno was the first death camp, a guarded camp set up for the purpose of murdering hundreds of thousands of people. Two of the Jews who had been forced

The Secret Archives of the Warsaw Ghetto

Our knowledge of the Warsaw ghetto can be traced largely to the diaries of members of the underground. At the very beginning of the German occupation of Poland, a Jewish historian named Emmanuel Ringelblum began keeping careful notes on every aspect of Jewish life. He wanted future generations to understand the ghetto experience.

Soon Ringelblum recruited others to help him, and eventually dozens of people worked together to create a detailed written account of political and economic conditions, of religious and cultural life, even the jokes that people told. They recorded statistics, made copies of official announcements, wrote diaries and articles, and collected posters and photographs.

Ringelblum called the project *Oneg Shabbat* (Hebrew for "Sabbath Pleasures"), the name given to the Saturday afternoon gatherings that followed synagogue services. This written record was even more dangerous than other underground activities because there was so much material to hide. Eventually, the *Oneg Shabbat* archives were buried in crates in two separate locations in the ghetto. One was found after the war, but the other location is still unknown. Emmanuel Ringelblum and his family were shot in Warsaw in March 1944.

to bury the bodies of the victims at Chelmno escaped and reached Warsaw in January 1942. Through the Polish underground, their horrific news was passed on to London. (The victims of the Chelmno death camp came from the area around the city of Lódz, which is discussed in Chapter 5, pp. 130–42. Chelmno itself is discussed in Chapter 8, pp. 219–20.)

Information about what was happening at Chelmno was not widely known in the ghetto, but it may not have made any difference. Three months later, word reached the ghetto that Jews from the eastern Polish city of Lublin had been deported (forcibly removed from a city of residence) to an unknown destination. There were reports that they had been taken to a death camp at Belzec and killed. In Warsaw, the secret newspapers of the Jewish underground published warnings that the Nazis intended to kill all the Jews.

Most Warsaw Jews did not believe this news. They thought the stories must be exaggerated. Later, even with the emergence of eyewitness reports of the mass killings, some people still did not want to believe that the murders were part

A Jewish family in the Lublin ghetto. The killing of the Jews of Lublin was part of a secret Nazi plan.

of a plan. They thought one particular Nazi official must be to blame or that some SS soldiers had gone on a rampage. (The "SS" is an abbreviation for *Schutzstaffel,* the military unit of the Nazi Party.)

In fact, the killing of the Jews of Lublin was part of an official—though secret—Nazi policy. The mass murder of Jews had begun with the German invasion of Russia in June 1941. Sometime that year, the top Nazi leaders had decided to kill all the Jews of Europe. By January 1942, they had developed plans to carry out this decision. The words "killing" and "extermination" were never officially used; instead, the Nazis called it the "Final Solution" to the Jewish "problem." (See Chapter 7, pp. 200–11.)

Decades after the end of World War II, it is easy to say that the Jews of Warsaw were foolish to ignore the truth. But at the time, it was much harder to believe that the Nazis were organizing the murder of millions of people. In the entire history of civilization, nothing like this had ever happened before. The Jews—like people all over the world—could not accept that modern, civilized people would commit such a crime.

"The Bloody Night"

In early 1942, the Jews of Warsaw became the victims of a massacre. They called it "the Bloody Night." Of course, many thousands had already died of hunger and disease, and others had been shot when they were caught outside the ghetto. But until the Bloody Night, it was still possible to believe that the people of the ghetto—or at least those who could get enough food—would survive if they obeyed the Germans.

On Friday evening, April 18, 1942, truckloads of SS men and German soldiers rolled into the ghetto. The Germans went into apartments, dragged out about 60 men, shot them, and left them lying in the street. Fifty-two were dead, the rest injured.

The Nazis announced that the shootings had been a punishment because secret publications had appeared in the ghetto. They warned that if these publications did not stop, officials would take even harsher action next time. This led to a conflict between the Jewish underground and the *Judenrat.* To the *Judenrat,* the Nazi retaliation (repayment or punishment for some action) proved that underground activity risked the lives of *all* the people of the ghetto.

But members of the underground viewed the Bloody Night in a completely different light. The Jews who had been hunted down and shot by the Germans were not necessarily involved in creating and distributing secret publications. Rather, the Nazis had chosen men who were respected leaders of the ghetto—men from a variety of fields who held considerable influence over large numbers of people. The reason they had been killed, the underground thought, was to eliminate them from playing a role in future ghetto opposition to German actions. To the underground, this showed that the Germans were planning major new steps against the Jews. They were right.

"Resettlement"

On July 19, 1942, Heinrich Himmler, the head of all the Nazi security forces, including the SS, its military arm, ordered the "resettlement" of all Polish Jews by the end of the year. Like the term "Final Solution," the Nazis used words like "resettlement" to hide the truth. Jews were told they were being sent somewhere "in the east" where they could start new lives. This was a way of getting the Jews to cooperate, to avoid panic or resistance. In fact, "resettlement" was a part of the "Final Solution." The Nazis used the word in reference to moving the Jews to the places where they would be murdered.

The Nazis had built four death camps to kill the Jews of Poland. Chelmno had been operating since December 1941, Belzec since February 1942, and Sobibór since May 1942. The fourth camp was at Treblinka, about 50 miles from Warsaw. It was now ready to begin its work: killing the Jews of Warsaw. (See Chapters 8 and 9 for more about the death camps.)

On July 22, 1942, the Nazis informed the *Judenrat* that starting immediately, 6,000 people a day would be deported from the ghetto. Some of the *Judenrat* members were taken hostage. Posters appeared on the streets of the ghetto: "All Jewish persons living in Warsaw, regardless of age and sex, will be resettled in the East."

According to the posters, certain categories of people would be allowed to remain behind. People who worked for the *Judenrat,* the Jewish police, hospital and sanitary workers, and all their families would not be deported. Neither would people who worked for the private German companies that had been set up in the ghetto.

When all these categories were added up, people in the ghetto thought that "only" about 60,000 or 70,000 people were scheduled to be deported. It seemed as though the Nazis

Ghetto police escort Jews to the deportation trains for "resettlement."

intended to turn the Warsaw ghetto into a slave-labor camp, consisting only of workers and their families.

Thousands of Jews immediately tried to get jobs that were included in the special categories, especially jobs with the German companies. Some even supplied their own sewing machines, and many thousands were hired. Everyone wanted a stamped work permit that showed he or she was not subject to deportation.

The deportations

On the first day of the deportations, most of the arrests were made by the Jewish police, who became the most hated people in the ghetto. A few dozen SS men, plus German police and Ukrainian and Latvian auxiliary troops (extras) of the SS also participated. The first people taken were from the poorhouses. Starving, homeless people and beggars from the poorest section of the ghetto were another target. Jews from

Death of a Leader

On July 23, 1942, Adam Czerniaków, the head of the Warsaw *Judenrat,* committed suicide. In a letter to his wife, he wrote: "The SS wants me to kill children with my own hands. There is no other way out and I must die."

Czerniaków, like the leaders of every *Judenrat,* had faced an impossible situation. They could not carry out German orders while still protecting their people. Unlike some *Judenrat* leaders in other cities, he was an honest man, but this did not matter much. As historian Yehuda Bauer noted, although there is no doubt about "his personal courage, [Czerniaków] presided over a largely corrupt and inefficient administration."

Even the events surrounding his death are controversial. Although many people thought his suicide was an act of courage and honor, the Jewish underground blamed him for failing—even at the end—to call on the people of the ghetto to resist the Nazi murderers.

Germany—those who had been shipped to the ghetto two months earlier—were also among the first group of deportees. They were all taken to the *Umschlagplatz* ("transfer place"), a large square located near the ghetto railroad station. There they were loaded into sealed freight cars and taken to Treblinka to be killed.

The Germans were not satisfied with the speed of the deportation process. After the first few days, German police surrounded whole apartment houses and ordered everyone out. They checked everyone's papers and took anyone without a work permit to the *Umschlagplatz* to be deported. Then the Germans searched each building from cellar to attic to make sure no one was hiding.

If they did not find enough people to deport, the Germans simply added people who had work permits. They began to surround whole streets in the ghetto instead of just one building. By the middle of August, the Germans were ignoring permits entirely and taking people out of their workplaces instead of their homes.

The Orphans' March

On August 6, 1942, the Nazis raided every children's institution in the Warsaw ghetto, taking all the children away. One of these institutions was the orphanage run by Janusz Korczak, a famous educator. This is how historian Israel Gutman describes what happened when the Nazis arrived:

> Korczak lined his children up in rows of four. The orphans were clutching flasks of water and their favorite books and toys. They were in their best clothes. Korczak stood at the head of his 192 children, holding a child with each hand.... They marched through the ghetto to the *Umschlagplatz* where they joined thousands of people waiting without shade, water, or shelter, in the hot August sun. The children did not cry out. They walked quietly in forty-eight rows of four.

> One eyewitness, according to Gutman, viewed the children's procession as a silent protest against the murderous Nazis. Korczak and all the orphans were murdered at Treblinka.

Some people reported to the *Umschlagplatz* on their own. The Germans promised that anyone who showed up voluntarily would receive three kilograms (about 6.5 pounds) of bread and a kilogram (2.2 pounds) of jam. Many starving people could not resist this offer.

The deportations continued day after day. The entire operation involved around 50 SS men, 400 Ukrainian and Latvian SS auxiliaries, and the Jewish police. Although large numbers of SS and German army troops were stationed nearby, very few were needed.

Victims and survivors

The deportations began on July 22, 1942, and finally ended on September 9. Among the very last to be deported were members of the Jewish police and their families, despite Nazi promises that they would be safe. About 265,000 people were sent to Treblinka, where almost all—men, women, and

Jews selling off some of their possessions on the streets of the Kraków ghetto in order to obtain money for food in 1940.

children—were immediately murdered in the gas chambers. Approximately 12,000 people were sent to forced labor camps. Ten thousand others were murdered in the streets of Warsaw.

Eight thousand people managed to get to the "Aryan side" of Warsaw. Many were hidden by non-Jewish Poles who risked their lives working with the underground network. At the same time, the Jews were in constant danger of being turned over to the Germans by antisemitic Poles.

Of the 350,000 people who had been in the ghetto on July 22, less than 60,000 people were left by early September.

Around 35,000 of them—only a tenth of the original number in the ghetto—were allowed to stay behind. The rest were there illegally, hiding from the Germans.

The ghetto, which had been so overcrowded, was now mostly empty. The Germans divided it into four separate areas, with forbidden zones between them. No contact between the areas was allowed, and people were forbidden from venturing outdoors except between 5:00 and 7:30 in the morning and again from 4:00 to 8:00 in the evening.

Most of the old, the sick, and the children had been removed from the ghetto. Many of the people who remained had lost their entire families. Those left were mostly younger adults and (by ghetto standards) relatively healthy. At this point, they had an easier time obtaining food because they could barter (trade) or sell the possessions of those who had been deported. Consequently, the death rate in the ghetto went down.

The survivors of the ghetto understood that the Nazis would not stop their murderous plans until all the Jews were gone. Many of them felt guilty and angry with themselves for not trying to stop the deportations; they were, however, determined to resist the Nazis in the future. They had already taken the first steps.

The Jewish Fighting Organization

On the second day of the deportations, leaders of the different organizations of the Jewish underground met secretly to plan the next move. Some members of the political parties and youth groups wanted to begin armed resistance against the Germans. However, several of the most respected Jewish leaders were strongly opposed to this. They believed that fighting the German army was suicide. The Jews of the ghetto had no weapons and few had any military training. The ghetto was surrounded and cut off from help. Many Jewish leaders warned that the Germans would retaliate for the actions of a few rebels by killing thousands of people. These leaders often supported passive resistance (or nonviolent resistance), believing that remaining calm and not attacking the Germans was the best strategy for survival. They knew that some Jews would die no matter what course they took, but they clung to the hope that many—perhaps most—would live to see the end of this hellish ordeal.

A few days later, on July 28, 1942, several youth groups disregarded the advice of their elders and decided to form a military wing of the underground. They called it the Jewish Fighting Organization (usually referred to as the ZOB, from its Polish initials for *Zydowsk Organizacja Bojowa*). It had about 200 members in its early days. At the beginning, all of them were associated with youth groups that were connected to different political parties.

The ZOB was organized to maintain secrecy. Each member knew the identities of only a few others. Very few people knew about the overall structure of the ZOB—who made the decisions, how they were transmitted to others, and so on. Such guarded confidentiality would make it harder for an informer to destroy the organization. In addition to the threat of informers, there was the constant danger that a ZOB member would be arrested and tortured by the Nazis to reveal the organization's secrets.

The first actions of the ZOB

The ZOB began with no weapons at all. Early in August, in the middle of the deportations, the organization managed to obtain five pistols and half a dozen hand grenades. These weapons came from the military wing of the Polish Communist underground, not from the Home Army, Poland's main underground military organization. The ZOB was unable to get any weapons from the Home Army.

It would have been impossible to fight the SS men without more ammunition. The ZOB decided to take action where it could. A member of the ZOB shot and seriously wounded the commander of the Jewish Police. Many people in the ghetto believed that members of the Polish underground, not the ZOB, were responsible. The Jews had accepted the idea that their people, like many non-Jewish Poles, would not fight for their lives.

The ZOB suffered a major setback in early September 1942. Eighteen young people traveling with false identity papers were able to get out of Warsaw. They were trying to reach a forest in eastern Poland, where a Jewish partisan group was being formed. (Partisans were armed groups of anti-Nazi fighters who hid in mountain or forest areas and attacked German targets.) All but one of them was captured by the Germans, tortured, and executed. This led to the arrest in Warsaw of one of the ZOB's leaders, who had prepared their false papers. He was shot by the Germans, and another ZOB member was killed trying to rescue him. A third ZOB member was killed while she was trying to move the ZOB's weapons to a safer location. The weapons were captured by the Germans. The ZOB then faced the difficult job of finding new weapons.

Underground politics

There were several reasons why it was hard for the ZOB to get weapons from Poland's Home Army. Arms were valuable to the underground, and they did not want to waste them. Some Home Army leaders had no confidence that the Jews would actually use weapons against the Germans. The military situation in the ghetto was perceived as being hopeless. Messages sent by some Home Army leaders to London indicate that they thought the Jews were not capable of fighting. Their own prejudices against Jews made them believe that supplying weapons to the ghetto would be a waste.

In addition, the Home Army was very suspicious of the Polish Communists. The Communists were loyal to the Communist government of Russia, not to the Polish government in London. The Home Army wanted to preserve its strength and plan for a massive battle against the Germans when the Russian army arrived in Poland. The Communists wanted to move sooner to help the Russian army. Russia was losing millions of soldiers and civilians—far more than any other country—in the war against Adolf Hitler and his German forces. To the Russians, the Home Army's desire to save its forces until later meant that the Poles would wait while the Russians died. The ZOB sided with the Communists, not with the Home Army, on this point. Waiting to launch full-scale resistance to the Germans made no sense for the Jews because they realized they would all be dead before Germany could be defeated. To save as many Jewish lives as possible—or Jewish honor, if the lives would be lost anyway—the Jewish underground needed to fight as soon as possible, as hard as possible.

The Polish underground hoped that a great uprising would restore pride to the Poles and establish them as a powerful military force, independent of the Russian army—a force that would be able to safeguard Poland's interests against the Russians. (Russia wanted to claim the eastern parts of pre-war Poland as its own.)

The ZOB expands

When the deportations ended in September, several leaders of the Jewish underground who had been outside the ghetto returned to Warsaw. One of them was Mordecai Anielewicz, who had been in southwestern Poland organizing an armed resistance movement. He was only 22 years old, but he was widely respected for his bravery. He worked to strengthen the ZOB and became its commander.

Mordecai Anielewicz was one of the leaders of the ZOB, the Jewish Fighting Organization, one of the most important groups of the Jewish underground movement opposing the Nazis.

Most of the important political groups in the underground soon joined the ZOB. These included the Bund, most Zionist groups, and the Communists. The political parties that represented religious Jews did not join. Neither did one faction of the Zionist movement, a youth group called Betar that set up its own military organization, the Jewish Fighting Union (ZZW).

On October 29, 1942, the ZOB killed the deputy commander of the Jewish Police, then announced their responsibility for the action the next day in small printed notices posted in the ghetto. Soon after, they executed an official of the *Judenrat* who was known to have cooperated with the Nazis.

Telling the world

The underground also wanted to make sure the rest of the world knew what was happening to the Jews in Poland—especially in Warsaw. In the autumn of 1942, two leaders representing the entire Jewish underground met with Jan Karski, an officer in the Polish underground. Karski was about to be smuggled to London to report on what was going on in

Poland. One of the Jewish leaders at the meeting was Leon Feiner, a leader of the Bund, and the other was a Zionist leader who has never been positively identified. (At the time, Karski did not know the real names of the people he met, and they did not know his. In fact, the name "Karski," which he kept after the war, was originally one of the false names that he used to disguise himself from the Nazis.)

The Jewish leaders described the hunger and death in the ghetto. As they spoke, they paced the floor endlessly. "It was as though they were unable even to think of their dying people and remain seated," Karski wrote later.

The two leaders were afraid that the Polish government in England would not believe Karski's reports unless he had witnessed the Jews' plight firsthand. Karski was smuggled into the ghetto twice to see things for himself. On his first trip, Feiner went with him. They crawled through a tunnel dug connecting the "Aryan side" and the ghetto. The streets of the ghetto were littered with the naked bodies of people who had starved to death. "When a Jew dies," Feiner explained, "the family removes his clothing and throws his body in the street. Otherwise they would have to pay a burial tax to the Germans." People could not pay the tax, and they needed the dead person's clothing. Karski witnessed people in rags huddled against the buildings, staring into space, barely breathing as they waited to die. He saw two young Germans firing shots at Jews as a game. It was a "Jew hunt."

Later, disguised as a Ukrainian SS auxiliary policeman, Karski traveled to a camp that the Nazis used as a stop-off point for some of the Jews being sent to the Belzec death camp. He saw thousands of people sitting or lying in an open area, half-starved, and seemingly in a state of shock. The Jews were eventually forced into box cars, with the guards beating, bayonetting, and shooting those who moved too slowly. The dead and wounded were thrown into the cars on top of the others, who were now screaming. Finally, the doors of the box cars were sealed shut.

The message

When Karski reached London after a dangerous trip across Nazi-controlled Europe, he reported to the Polish government on what was going on at home. He also carried out

the mission given to him by the Jewish leaders: to repeat the message they had given him in Warsaw.

The Jewish underground sought help from the Allies, the countries fighting Nazi Germany, especially the United States and Great Britain. They wanted the Jewish communities of those countries to put pressure on their governments. Feiner had told Karski that unless something was done immediately, "our entire people will be destroyed. Perhaps a few may be saved, but three million Polish Jews are doomed." The Jewish and Polish undergrounds were not strong enough to fight the Nazis on their own, Feiner said. Only the Allies could save the Polish Jews. Feiner did not want a single leader of the Allied countries to "be able to say that they did not know that we were being murdered in Poland." He told Karski that the Jewish underground was "organizing a defense of the ghetto, not because we think it can be defended but to let the world see the hopelessness of our battle." Then, perhaps the world would act.

Jewish youth peer over the wall overlooking Mirowski Plac (Square) that divided the Warsaw ghetto into the small and large ghettos, 1941.

What the Jewish underground wanted from the Allies

The two Jewish underground leaders in Warsaw proposed a series of steps for the Allies to take. First, they wanted the Allies to announce publicly that ending the murder of the Jews was one of the goals of the war against Germany. Second, they wanted the Allies to tell the German people about the Nazi-organized killings through radio broadcasts and leaflets dropped from airplanes. This way, all Germans would have knowledge of the Holocaust, the Nazi Party's plan to physically eliminate the Jews of Europe.

The next request of the Jewish underground was that the Allies use the German people to put pressure on the Nazi government, thereby forcing them to stop the killings. According to Feiner, the German people as a group should be held responsible for the actions of Hitler's government. If nothing else worked, the Jewish leaders said, then selected German cities—those of special historical or cultural importance to Germany—should be bombed in retaliation. Lastly, German prisoners who remained loyal to Hitler after being told of the mass killings of the Jews should be executed.

Karski delivered the message to leaders of the British government and later to leaders of the American government and the American Jewish community. He met with U.S. president Franklin D. Roosevelt. Unable to return to Poland and rejoin the underground, Karski spoke at meetings in cities throughout the United States, telling the world about Poland and the murder of the Jews. He wrote a book, titled *Story of a Secret State*, that became a bestseller in America. But he was never sure that his message made a real difference.

Some of the Jewish underground's ideas had no chance of being carried out, as Karski knew. Although the Allies did warn that Germans would be held responsible after the war for crimes they committed, they would never execute German prisoners. If nothing else, it would only lead to the execution of British and American prisoners. In addition, the idea of "collective responsibility"—of punishing one German for crimes that a different German had committed or for intentionally bombing civilian targets—went against everything the Allies said they were fighting for.

When Karski warned the Jewish leaders in Warsaw that these ideas would only weaken their case with the British, one of the underground leaders is said to have replied: "We don't know what is realistic or not realistic. We are dying here! Say it!"

But it is not clear why the other ideas were rejected, most notably the point about the Allies announcing that saving the Jews from mass murder was one of the goals of the war. Some historians believe that the Allied leaders were afraid that such a statement might make the war less popular with their own people, who did not want to fight and die "for the Jews."

Appealing to the German people to stop the mass murders also never happened. Again, no one knows whether this would have had any effect. After all, Nazi Germany was a violent dictatorship, a police-state where no opposition was allowed. On the other hand, less than two years earlier, German public opinion had forced Hitler to stop the killing of mentally disabled and handicapped Germans by the Nazi government. (See Chapter 4, pp. 110–14.)

Historians are deeply divided about whether the Allies could have done more to save the Jews. In general, the Allied leaders believed that the best way to help the Jews was to win the war against Germany as quickly as possible. They opposed any action that they thought might interfere with this goal.

The January *Aktion*

While Jan Karski was telling the British and Americans about the desperate situation of the Warsaw ghetto, the ZOB figured out what to do next. The organization decided to hold a public demonstration in the ghetto to build popular support. Members posted notices around the ghetto:

> Jewish masses! The hour is near. You must be ready to resist. Do not go to the slaughter like sheep. Not a single Jew should go to the train. Those who cannot actively resist should resist passively by hiding. Our slogan should be: We should all be ready to die as human beings.

The demonstration was scheduled for January 22, 1943. But at 6:00 A.M. on January 18, armed German police and Ukrainian auxiliaries entered the ghetto to begin a new *aktion*

Ukrainian SS auxiliary soldiers searching for Jews in the Warsaw ghetto.

(operation)—more deportations. The ZOB still had very few weapons and little public support. The Germans had caught them by surprise; the ZOB had not prepared a full-scale military plan. But the organization was determined that this deportation would be different.

By this time, news of the total destruction of ghettos all over Poland had reached Warsaw. The Jews refused to leave the buildings and enter courtyards as ordered. Most people went to prepared hiding places. One of them, Mordecai Lensky, the ghetto's chief doctor, described what happened in the ghetto hospital. Thirty people crowded into a special room that had been hidden behind a closet. They listened fearfully while Ukrainian SS auxiliaries entered. The patients and some of the hospital staff had already been arrested. Only a thin wall separated the 30 hiding Jews from the Ukrainians:

When they saw there was no one in the place, the Ukrainians hurried to fill their pockets with whatever they could lay their hands on. They sought watches, ... jewelry, gold, and similar items. Approaching the closet door behind which the people were hidden, they extracted drawers and took various items away with them.

The people in hiding behind the closet door could hear the Ukrainians' voices and their every movement during their search. Fear penetrated deeply into the hearts of the ones hiding there, for there were some old people and little children in the place. The slightest movement, sneeze, or cough could have given them away.

Resistance

Although most of the Jews targeted for deportation tried to hide, the Germans were still able to grab many, especially from their workplaces. The Germans began to march a line of hundreds of these people toward the *Umschlagplatz*.

A dozen members of the ZOB, hiding pistols, joined the line. When a signal was given, each one attacked the nearest German guard. Several of the guards were killed, and their weapons were taken. Other SS men ran away.

German reinforcements arrived quickly; most of the ZOB members died in the gun battle. Their pistols and their few rounds of ammunition were no match for the heavily armed Germans. In the confusion, the line of people being brought to the *Umschlagplatz* scattered and hid in the ghetto.

Two other gun battles with the Germans took place a short while later. In one case, a group of German soldiers entered an apartment to search it for Jews. The ZOB was waiting and opened fire. One ZOB member was killed in the fight, but most were able to escape to another building.

As the roundup continued over the next few days, 200 German police and 800 SS auxiliaries were sent in—a much larger force than had been needed during the first deportation. It was considerably more difficult for them to find the Jews they wanted to deport. The Germans were much more cautious this time about searching cellars and attics. The operation continued for four days. All tolled, about 6,000 people were killed or deported. On the last day, taking revenge for the ZOB resistance measures, the Nazi forces shot 1,000 people on the streets of the Warsaw ghetto.

A new pride

Although most people in Warsaw, both Jews and Poles (including the Home Army), believed that the armed resistance of the Jews had stopped the Nazis from deporting everyone in the ghetto, this is probably not the case. The Nazis had not planned to deport everyone at that time. The best evidence indicates that they wanted to deport 8,000 people, leaving the rest for later, but the resistance they met made it much tougher for them to do this. It probably caused them to end the operation sooner and to deport about 2,000 fewer people than they had intended.

The Warsaw ghetto battle affected the public perception of the ZOB tremendously. The Polish underground praised the Jewish action as an extraordinary victory. Among other things, this enabled the ZOB to get more arms. The Germans, however, tried to keep the news of the resistance from spreading. German officers in Warsaw did not want their superiors in Berlin to know what had happened.

Many experts feel that the most important effect of the underground resistance was on the morale of the people of the ghetto. The Jewish underground, and especially the ZOB, were accepted as the real leaders of the ghetto. The authority of the *Judenrat* became weaker and was often ignored. The survivors of the ghetto felt a new pride.

The preparation

The Warsaw Jews soon focused on preparations for the next German attack. Cellars were dug and turned into bunkers (underground chambers) throughout the ghetto. The entrances to the bunkers were carefully hidden. Food and water supplies were prepared. A network of tunnels was dug to connect the bunkers to each other. Other tunnels were established underneath the ghetto walls to connect to the "Aryan side." Ladders were placed between roofs. People could travel from one building to the next either by going through the tunnels or over the roofs.

The ZOB organized 22 fighting squads, with a total of about 500 fighters. Each member was armed with a pistol and about a dozen rounds of ammunition plus four or five hand grenades, mostly homemade. The ZOB had about ten rifles all together and one or two submachine (lightweight automatic or semiautomatic) guns. In addition, they had around 2,000 "Molotov cocktails"—gasoline-filled bottles with a rag fuse. When the rag was lit and the bottle thrown at a target, it was supposed to explode on impact. This was the only weapon the ZOB could use against tanks or armored cars. The other Jewish military group, the ZZW, probably had another 250 fighters, who may have been somewhat better armed than the ZOB.

The uprising

At 3:00 on the morning of April 19, 1943, German troops surrounded the ghetto. It was Passover, the Jewish holiday that celebrates the Biblical story of Moses leading the Jews to freedom from their slavery in Egypt.

The Polish underground had learned that the Germans were planning another operation against the ghetto. This time the ZOB was ready. The streets were empty. People had hidden in the bunkers. Only the ZOB fighters remained, out of sight, in the nearby buildings and on the roofs. As the Germans moved inside the ghetto walls, they were met with bullets, grenades, and Molotov cocktails. Several Germans were killed or wounded. The Germans were not only surprised in a military sense, they were shocked. "The Jews have arms, the Jews have arms," one reportedly shouted as they took cover.

Battles raged in several sections of the ghetto. For the first time, the Germans were forced to turn back. "I did not have to give the order to retreat," the German commander said after the war, because the German soldiers "had simply run away." When the news of these events was telephoned to SS chief Heinrich Himmler in Berlin, he was furious. For SS troops to run from armed Jews was the worst disgrace Himmler could imagine. In addition, the Germans were afraid that the example of the ghetto might spread to the rest of Warsaw, causing rebellion among the Home Army as well. Himmler fired the commander of the operation and replaced him with SS General Jürgen Stroop, who was known for his ruthless treatment of civilians during the invasion of Russia. (See Chapter 7.)

SS general Jürgen Stroop among his troops during the Warsaw ghetto uprising in 1943.

The second battle

Three hours after their retreat, the German troops ventured back into the ghetto. This time, they used different tactics. They remained under cover and fired their rifles at long range against the Jewish fighters in the doorways and windows and on the roofs. The ZOB's pistols were useless in this kind of fighting, and they had few rifles. The underground fighters had to rely on getting close enough to their targets to hit them with hand grenades.

The Germans attacked one building at a time, forcing their way inside under heavy fire. The Jews, Stroop reported, "defended themselves everywhere, post by post, and at the last moment escaped through the attics or underground channels."

The first day of the Warsaw ghetto uprising ended with relatively few Jews, about 580, rounded up. Those who were caught were not taken to the *Umschlagplatz* but were shot on

Resistance in the Polish Ghettos

The ZOB was the best-known armed resistance movement in the Polish ghettos, and the Warsaw ghetto uprising was by far the largest battle. But armed resistance groups operated in at least 23 other ghettos in western and central Poland, and 60 more were set up in eastern Poland (an area the Nazis ran separately from the rest of the country). These groups faced many of the same problems that plagued the ZOB in Warsaw. It was very difficult to get weapons, and there were overwhelming German forces nearby. The underground was usually made up of people from many different political groups, each with their own ideas about how to handle the opposition measures. The *Judenrat* usually opposed armed resistance, and most of the population believed that their best hope of survival was to continue to work hard and wait for the Russian army. Most of the uprisings occurred when hope was gone. Still, there are many examples of poorly armed Jewish fighters battling the Germans. Among the most famous ghetto revolts were those in Bialystok in August 1943 and in Vilna in the next month. In addition, many thousands of Jews from the ghettos were able to escape and join partisan units.

the spot. The Jewish fighters took some casualties but probably not as many as the Germans.

As night fell, the Germans again left the ghetto. The Jewish fighters came out on the street, joined by the rest of the people of the ghetto. For one day at least, they had fought the Germans to a standstill.

Weeks of fighting

The next morning, April 20, 1943, the Germans entered the ghetto again. This time they brought artillery, tanks, and armored cars. There was heavy fighting, and at least one German armored car was destroyed by Molotov cocktails. The Germans, with their greater numbers and much heavier firepower, were always able to push the Jewish fighters back and capture a building, but then the fighting continued on the next street.

Jews captured during the Warsaw ghetto uprising of April and May 1943, led by the SS to the Umschlagplatz *for deportation.*

During the battle of the Warsaw ghetto, the Germans sent a force that averaged 2,100 soldiers into the ghetto each day. They were equipped with unlimited ammunition. Besides their rifles and many dozens of submachine guns, they had over 80 machine guns, a cannon, flamethrowers, and armored cars.

By the third day, the Germans who entered the ghetto fought in smaller formations, moving carefully under cover of heavy fire. They were no longer deporting helpless Jews. They were fighting a house-to-house battle.

The battle then shifted to the underground bunkers. The Germans used explosives to blow up the bunkers. They are believed to have fired smoke rockets and poisonous gas into them. They also burned down the buildings above the bunkers; the intense heat from the burned bricks above them and the lack of air to breathe forced many people out, where the Germans were waiting.

Many bunkers became useless, and the ZOB shifted people to other hiding places through the network of tunnels. Sometimes, when the heat or smoke made it impossible to stay underground, they came out shooting.

Block after block was burned down. The Jews hiding inside the houses were forced out. On April 22, German commander Stroop wrote that "whole Jewish families, swallowed by flames, jumped en masse from windows or let themselves down by knotted sheets." The German troops immediately shot those who climbed down and anyone who survived the jump.

Day after day, German troops searched for the hidden entrances to the bunkers. When they found one and tried to go in, they were met by small-arms fire. In return, they used explosives and smoke rockets. Sometimes, the ZOB traveled through the tunnels to get back to an area the Germans had cleared the day before.

A section of the Warsaw ghetto burns during the uprising of April and May 1943.

6: The Warsaw Ghetto **175**

By April 26, after one week of fighting, almost 30,000 Jews had been killed, according to Stroop's estimate. The ZOB fighters hid, came out briefly to attack Germans whenever they could, and then disappeared.

On May 8, almost three weeks after the Germans had entered the ghetto, the ZOB's command bunker at number 18 Mila Street was destroyed. Most of the ZOB fighters inside committed suicide rather than surrender.

On May 16, 1943, after 28 days of fighting, Stroop blew up the Great Synagogue of Warsaw to show that the battle was over. He reported that 56,000 Jews had been killed or captured during the operation, and the ghetto had been cleared of Jews. In fact, some fighting continued for at least two more weeks. A few ZOB fighters succeeded in hiding even longer. Armed clashes in the ruins of the ghetto reportedly took place as late as July.

The German army awarded General Stroop the Iron Cross First Class for commanding the operation. (He was hanged as a war criminal after the war.) The largest and most important Jewish community in Europe was gone. But, in the end, the Jews of Warsaw had met the expectations of the ZOB. They had not gone to the slaughter "like sheep." They knew their deaths were imminent, but they had fought "to die as human beings."

7

At the beginning of World War II (1939-45), the armies of Nazi Germany quickly won a series of overwhelming military victories. By the summer of 1940, they had conquered much of Europe. When France surrendered in June, only Great Britain remained at war with Germany. Britain refused to make peace with the Nazi government and prepared for a German invasion. Then, Adolf Hitler's air force, the *Luftwaffe,* was defeated by British fighter planes in the Battle of Britain (July-October 1940). In addition to British superiority in the air, the strength of the British navy helped keep the Germans in check. Hitler's forces were not able to cross the English Channel from France to invade Britain.

The war between Germany and Britain continued, but the bulk of the German army was not involved. German submarines attacked British ships, and there was fighting

Legend

- ■ ORIGINAL AXIS
- ◢ MILITARY CONQUEST
- ▦ DIPLOMATIC CONQUEST
- ▦ STILL FIGHTING AXIS

ATLANTIC OCEAN

NORWAY — OSLO
SWEDEN — STOCKHOLM
FINLAND — HELSINKI
ESTONIA
LATVIA
LITHUANIA
MOSCOW
U. S. S. R.

SCOTLAND
EIRE
WALES
ENGLAND — LONDON

DENMARK

NETH.
BEL.
BERLIN
GERMANY
WARSAW (POLAND)

FRANCE — PARIS
VICHY
SWITZ.
AUSTRIA
CZECHOSLOVAKIA
BUDAPEST
HUNGARY

PORTUGAL — LISBON
SPAIN — MADRID
CORSICA
ROME
ITALY
SARDINIA

BELGRADE
YUGOSLAVIA
BUCHAREST
RUMANIA
SOFIA
BULGARIA
BLACK SEA

GIBRALTAR
MEDITERRANEAN SEA
ALBANIA
GREECE
ATHENS
ANKARA
TURKEY

MOROCCO
TUNIS
TUNISIA
SICILY
CRETE

ALGERIA
TRIPOLI
LIBYA
TOBRUK
SALUM
SUEZ CANAL
EGYPT
ALEXANDRIA

0 — 300 MILES

in Africa between British and Italian forces. (Italy was Germany's ally throughout most of World War II.) Germany could not invade Britain, but the British could not invade Nazi-controlled Europe either. Hitler was finally able to turn his attention toward launching an attack on Russia.

Land, anticommunism, and racism

Hitler had always wanted Germany to conquer vast new territory. He felt that his nation's people needed this as *Lebensraum*—"room to live." This word implied that without this room, Germany could not survive. Germany was supposedly too small for the number of its people.

Hitler believed that this new land would have to come from eastern Europe. Germany would need to conquer White Russia (now the country of Belarus) and Ukraine. Both had long been part of the Russian empire, but at this time they belonged to the western part of the Soviet Union (short for the Union of Soviet Socialist Republics or USSR), the country that the Communists had set up in 1917 after overthrowing the Russian monarchy. (Communism is a political and economic theory advocating the formation of a classless society through the communal, or group, ownership of all property.)

In addition, the eastern half of Poland had become part of the Soviet Union in 1939. This was one of the terms of a deal Hitler had made with the Soviet government just before Germany invaded Poland and conquered the western half of the country. (See "The Nazi-Soviet Pact" box on p. 116.) The Soviets had also taken over the three small countries of Lithuania, Latvia, and Estonia, on the shores of the Baltic Sea. However, Hitler wanted these three Baltic states to be ruled by Germany as well.

All of the areas that Hitler sought to claim for Germany were part of the Communist-controlled Soviet Union. Going to war against the Soviet Union, then, would satisfy Hitler's hatred of Communists *and* his desire to make territorial gains.

Hitler's goals were heavily influenced by the Nazi Party's ideas about race. (See "The Origins of Antisemitism" box on p. 6.) The Nazis believed that Germans were members of a superior race and that this status gave them the right to rule over the "inferior" people of eastern Europe. Germany

Field Marshal Wilhelm Keitel, as chief of the high command of the German armed forces, was ultimately responsible for planning the invasion—and killing of the Jews—of the Soviet Union.

planned to take over the land in this region and populate it with Germans. The Poles, Russians, Ukrainians, White Russians, and others would then be allowed to serve the German overlords as sources of cheap labor. (See pp. 128–30.)

The western Soviet Union, including eastern Poland, was also the home of 5 million Jews. According to Nazi racial theories, the Jews were not even people: they were "subhuman." And Hitler believed that the Communist government of the Soviet Union played a key role in the Jews' supposed plot to rule the world. Jews and Communists were the same thing to the Nazis: an enemy that needed to be destroyed. For Hitler and the Nazis, the invasion of the Soviet Union would be a war to conquer land, to destroy communism, and to annihilate (wipe out completely) the Jews.

Plans for invasion and murder

In December 1940, Hitler ordered his generals to prepare a plan for the invasion of the Soviet Union. In March 1941, Field Marshal Wilhelm Keitel, chief of the high command of the armed forces, issued secret "orders for special areas" to the top German generals. Part of the order defined the role of Heinrich Himmler.

Himmler commanded most of the huge security forces of the Nazi police-state. He was the head of the SS, the Nazi Party's military-style organization composed of the most dedicated Nazis. (SS is an abbreviation for *Schutzstaffel*.) The SS ran the concentration camps, brutal prison camps where the Nazis sent their opponents without trial. One branch of the SS, called the SD (an abbreviation for *Sicherheitsdienst,* or Security Service), was involved in spying on Germans to find opponents of the Nazi government. It monitored affairs internally as well, spying on the rest of the Nazi Party to make sure the members remained loyal to Hitler. Himmler also controlled the *Geheime Staatspolizei,* or Gestapo (the secret police) and the regular German police. Many historians describe the SS as a "state within a state," an organization so powerful that

The RSHA: The Bureaucracy of Death

At the beginning of World War II in September 1939, the various branches of the SS, the Nazi Party's military arm, which also ran the concentration camps, and the government police became one giant organization called the Main Office for Reich Security, or RSHA from it German initials. (The Nazis called their government the Third Reich, or Third German empire.) The head of the RSHA was Reinhard Heydrich, the leader of the SD, the SS's spy ring, and second in command to Heinrich Himmler, who headed most of the Nazi security forces.

The RSHA had seven "bureaus" or offices. Bureau IV was the Gestapo (the secret police) and IVB was the branch of the Gestapo responsible for watching and controlling various religious groups. Section 4 of Bureau IVB, known as IVB-4, was the "Jewish Affairs Section." It was headed by Adolf Eichmann. Before the war, Eichmann was in charge of forcing Jews to leave Austria and Germany. Later, his job would be to round up Jews from all over Europe and send them to their deaths. Himmler, Heydrich, and Eichmann became the three men who, more than any other individuals, directed the Holocaust, the period between 1933 and 1945 when the Nazi Party tried to physically eliminate the entire European Jewish population.

it was like a government of its own. By the early 1940s, the SS—and especially the SD—had become the main organization in charge of the anti-Jewish policies of Nazi Germany.

According to Keitel's order, Himmler and the SS would be in charge of carrying out "special tasks" in the territory captured from the Soviet Union. The order stated that the "special tasks" were necessary because this war would be "the final struggle" between Nazism and communism. Himmler would have the authority to issue orders to the SS on his own, without permission from the army.

Genocide

Like so many of the Nazi plans that were put in writing, the language used in Keitel's part of the order was meant to hide its meaning from outsiders. The "special tasks," it soon became clear, included killing the Jews of the Soviet Union. Historians have found evidence suggesting that the "special tasks" part of Keitel's order was written by Hitler himself.

Jews had been persecuted in Nazi Germany for years. In the German-controlled part of Poland, thousands of Jews had been murdered and many more were facing starvation. (See Chapters 5 and 6.) But at the time of Keitel's order, the Nazis had not yet tried to plan the mass killings of all the Jews of a particular country. Keitel's order proved that the Nazis were not just planning to kill Jews, they were planning to kill the entire Jewish people. The complete destruction of an entire people or nation is called genocide. It was the beginning of the Holocaust.

Experts are not sure whether this decision applied only to the Jews of the Soviet Union, or whether it shows that Hitler and the Nazi government had already decided to murder all the Jews in Nazi-controlled Europe. Some scholars have argued that there must have been a later order, which has never been found, to extend the genocide to the rest of Europe. All disagreements about the existence and/or timing of the order aside, historians generally agree that the Nazis had decided by March 1941 to destroy at least the Jews of the Soviet Union. And by December of that year (at the latest), they had decided to kill all the Jews of Europe.

Hitler's speech to his generals

On March 30, Hitler made a secret speech to the top commanders assigned to the invasion of the Soviet Union. He spoke for two and a half hours. In a way, the speech was an explanation of Keitel's order. Hitler told the officers that in fighting the Russians, they had to forget their normal ideas of military honor. This was not going to be like a war between gallant knights, he said. This would be a clash of ideas and of races, "a war of destruction." Captured Communist officials, whether civilian or military, were not to be treated as prisoners of war: they were criminals, said Hitler, and should either be shot immediately or handed over to the SD. This order didn't just violate the generals' ideas about honor, it was also a military crime. Anticipating opposition from the German commanders, Hitler promised: "German soldiers guilty of breaking international law ... will be excused."

The generals, according to Keitel, sat silently through Hitler's speech, shocked by these ideas. "I do not expect my generals to understand me, but I shall expect them to obey my orders," Hitler said. And when the time came, the German generals did obey Hitler's orders. Many of them did much more.

Authorizing crimes

On May 13, 1941, Hitler issued a directive, thereby making the key points in his speech into official Nazi policy. It authorized members of the armed forces to shoot enemy civilians who resisted the Germans in any way. It allowed the army to punish a whole community if the people who had actually resisted could not be found. Most importantly, it stated that members of the armed forces would not be prosecuted for carrying out these actions, even if the actions were considered crimes according to military law. The German military was therefore given permission by Hitler to commit crimes without fear of punishment.

About three weeks later, on June 4, 1941, just before the invasion, German army headquarters issued a paper titled "Guidelines for the Conduct of the Troops in Russia." This was not a secret order but rather an "education" manual for the troops. According to the guidelines, the struggle against Bolshevism (the Russian Communist Party had originally been called the Bolshevik Party) "demands ruthless and energetic measures against Bolshevik agitators, guerillas, saboteurs, [and] Jews." (Agitators are people who attempt to stir up strong public feeling on a certain issue. Guerillas are members of fighting units who carry out independent acts of warfare. Saboteurs are people who engage in acts of sabotage, deliberate acts of destruction that hinder a nation's war effort.)

On June 6, the army high command issued the Commissar Order (*Kommissarbefehl*)—an order that became famous after the war when it was used as evidence at the trial of the top Nazis. (See Chapter 13.) Commissar means "commissioner" in Russian; the Communist government used this word for its officials, and it was also applied to the officer in each Soviet army unit who was in charge of making sure that the other officers and troops were informed of—and would carry out—the Communist Party's official position on each issue.

Copies of the Commissar Order were passed word of mouth by Germany's top field commanders. The Commissar Order declared that German officers were to make sure their troops understood that "consideration and respect for international law" with respect to commissars was "wrong." Commissars, including soldiers captured in battle, should be shot.

The army and genocide

Once the invasion of the Soviet Union began, the officers of the German army issued orders to their troops that made it clear that the German army was expected to participate in the murder of helpless civilians, including women and children. They emphasized to the soldiers that Jews—all Jews—were as dangerous an enemy as the Soviet army. For example, on September 12, 1941 (two and a half months after the invasion actually began), Keitel issued an order to the army again demanding "ruthless" measures "above all against the Jews, the main carriers of Bolshevism."

On October 10, Field Marshal Walter von Reichenau, the commander of the German Sixth Army operating in Ukraine, issued an order that met with Hitler's complete and undisputed approval. In fact, the Führer (the German word for leader) liked the order so much, it was used as a model for other generals. Reichenau's order to his soldiers was straightforward about the violence they were to inflict:

> The most essential goal of the war against the Jewish-Bolshevist system is the complete destruction of its means of power and the extermination of Asiatic [Soviet] influence from Europe. This creates tasks for the troops that are beyond the one-dimensional pattern of ordinary soldiering. In the Eastern region, the soldier is not just a fighter according to the rules of war.... The soldier must fully understand the necessity of a severe but just revenge against Jewish subhumanity.

Field Marshal Walter von Reichenau, commander of the German Sixth Army, handed down ruthless orders that his soldiers were eager to obey.

In addition, Reichenau said, the army needed to prevent any revolts in the countryside they had conquered, revolts which, "experience proves, [have] always been stirred up by Jews." (At that time there had been almost no resistance to the Nazis by the local people, Jewish or non-Jewish.) Reichenau's order told the troops that killing Jews was not only permissible, it was absolutely *necessary* in order to accomplish the goals of the war and to protect their own safety.

The *Einsatzgruppen*

The forces assigned to do most of the killing were called *Einsatzgruppen* ("special-action groups" or "special-duty groups"). Similar strike-forces had been used by the SD (the intelligence arm of the SS, the Nazi Party's military unit) to hunt down opponents of the Nazis when Germany took over Austria in March 1938. (See pp. 79 and 106.) During the invasion of Poland in 1939, the *Einsatzgruppen* followed closely behind the regular German army, arriving in a town immediately after the army entered it. Their job was to eliminate anyone who might lead opposition to the Nazis' plan to enslave the Polish people. The *Einsatzgruppen* killed Polish political leaders, members of the Polish nobility, professors, high school teachers, people with technical training, and many priests. They also arrested thousands of other Poles and sent them to concentration camps. (See Chapter 5, pp. 120–25.)

Each of the four *Einsatzgruppen* formed by Reinhard Heydrich, the leader of the SD, had between 500 and 900 members, for a total of about 3,000 men. Each group was assigned to specific geographic areas of the Russian invasion. The *Einsatzgruppen* were divided into smaller, special-duty units of about 100 to 150 men apiece, which were in turn subdivided.

The officers of the *Einsatzgruppen* came mainly from the *Waffen*-SS ("armed SS"; the SS units that were organized like regular army units), the SD, and the security police, with a few coming from the Gestapo. Later, Ukrainians and men from the three Baltic states would be used as auxiliaries, or extra fighters, to increase the size of the *Einsatzgruppen* when needed.

By choosing them from these organizations, Heydrich knew that both the officers and men of the new *Einsatzgruppen* were dedicated Nazis. They already believed that Jews and

Communists were one and the same and that both were dangerous enemies—enemies that had to be eliminated. Even so, during their special training for the invasion of the Soviet Union, they were bombarded by lectures about Nazi ideas, including the need to exterminate subhumans such as Jews. The members of the *Einsatzgruppen* were also given operational training in how to round up and kill large numbers of civilians. (Each *Einsatzgruppe* used the same procedures from the very beginning of the invasion, even though they operated many hundreds of miles apart.) By the time their training was over, the officers and men of the *Einsatzgruppen* had a thorough understanding of their job. Since it was possible to transfer out of the *Einsatzgruppen,* anyone who stayed in the units had decided that he would be willing to participate in mass murder.

While the *Einsatzgruppen* were being trained in Germany, Heydrich and the army worked out an agreement. Heydrich's Main Office for Reich Security or RSHA (see box

Jewish men digging their own graves before being executed by Waffen-SS *troops, in the Soviet Union, 1942. The officers of the* Einsatzgruppe *were selected from the* Waffen-SS.

Educated Men

The men chosen to command the *Einsatzgruppen* were dedicated Nazis, but they were not street thugs. Three of the four had Ph.D. degrees, meaning they had attained the highest level of education and were qualified to use the title "Doctor." This put them among a small group of the most educated people in pre-war Europe. The *Einsatzgruppe* commander who became the most notorious, Otto Ohlendorf, was both a lawyer and a research economist. Before and after the time that he commanded *Einsatzgruppe* D in the Soviet Union, Ohlendorf worked on economic studies. In between, however, he was directly responsible for the deaths of 90,000 people. He was hanged in 1951.

on p. 181) would have complete control over the *Einsatzgruppen,* which would be allowed to perform their "special tasks" in areas where military operations were still going on, not only in the rear of the combat zones. The *Einsatzgruppen* would be transported by cars and trucks, not on foot like infantrymen. They would not be fighting the Soviet army. Their job was to move fast so that they could capture and kill unarmed civilians before they could escape.

Invasion

On June 22, 1941, Germany launched its surprise attack on the Soviet Union. The Soviet army and government were completely unprepared. Germany's forces, led by tanks, pushed into Soviet territory with tremendous speed. Tens of thousands of Soviet troops were trapped and surrendered. The rest of the Soviet army retreated desperately toward the east, trying to prevent a total collapse. The German air force attacked the roads and railroads, cities and towns. The German blitzkrieg ("lightning war") caused chaos and panic, just as it had in Poland and in France. Civilians, including many Jews, found themselves trapped: there was no organized evacuation plan. Two-and-a-half-million Jews remained in areas that would soon be reached by the German army.

Historians indicate, however, that some of the people in the Soviet Union actually welcomed the Germans. This was especially true in Ukraine and the Baltic states. The Baltic states were independent countries that had been taken over by the Soviet Union only a year earlier. Many of their people thought the Germans would free them from Russian domination. The Communist government of the Soviet Union had treated them harshly, and the Soviet dictator, Joseph Stalin, was a brutal tyrant. Opponents of the Communists had been arrested and sent to Siberia. In Ukraine, many thousands of small farmers had been executed by Stalin's secret police during the 1930s, and hundreds of thousands—some claim millions—of people had died in famines that resulted from Soviet economic policies. It is not surprising that many people in these areas were relieved to see the Soviet army driven out and the Germans marching in.

Russia had a long history of violent antisemitism. Soviet dictator Joseph Stalin continued the tradition, outlawing Jewish cultural organizations and persecuting Jews and Christians who practiced religion. He also banned all news of what the Nazis were doing to the Jews of Poland.

Local antisemitism

Perhaps the darkest side of the German invasion of Russia was the spread of antisemitism that accompanied it. Many of the people who welcomed the German advance also agreed with the Nazis about the Jews. Like the Nazis, they had convinced themselves that the hated Communist government was run by Jews and that only the Jews benefited from it. (Although the Soviet government officially gave Jews equal rights with all other citizens, Stalin's government in fact banned all Jewish cultural organizations, persecuted people who tried to practice their religion, and was ruthlessly hostile to anyone who tried to maintain a Jewish identity.)

A long history of antisemitism existed among the people in these countries, and the arrival of the Germans only intensified the hatred. Jews were considered foreigners even though they had lived in these countries for hundreds of years. Especially in Ukraine, there were bloody pogroms (organized violence against Jews that was often supported by authorities) in the late nineteenth and early twentieth century. These pogroms were frequently organized by the government of the Russian czar (emperor), whom the Communists had overthrown in 1917. In 1919, during the war between the Communists and Ukrainian nationalists who wanted an independent Ukraine, the Ukrainian forces massacred tens of thousands of Jews.

Because of their desire to establish independent countries free of Russian domination, their hatred of the Communist dictatorship, and their antisemitism, it seemed likely that the people of these countries would be natural allies for the Germans. What they didn't understand was how the Nazis would treat *them*.

The Nazis encouraged the local people's antisemitism to help them destroy the Jews. Ukrainians and people from the Baltic states joined SS auxiliary units and other groups that aided the Germans. In addition, the Germans stirred up murderous anti-Jewish riots—new pogroms—whenever they could. But the Nazis' ideas about the superiority of the German "race" were so deeply ingrained and important to them that they did not try to shape the local people into a permanent allied force against the Soviet army. In fact, they did just the opposite.

The Germans never set up separate countries in the conquered area. Instead, each area was ruled directly by German officials, who treated the local population with contempt. German policy was simply to use these countries for the benefit of Germany. The Germans took everything of value and sent it home. The people were treated as semi-slaves. Before long, there were large partisan movements (independent, or guerilla, armies hiding in the countryside) that fought the Germans, often in cooperation with the Soviet army.

Lack of knowledge

More surprising than the fact that the non-Jewish population welcomed the Germans was the attitude of many Soviet Jews. Apparently, most Jews in the towns and smaller cities had no idea that the Nazis wanted to harm them. This made it easier for the Nazi troops to kill so many Jews in the first days of the invasion.

"The Jews are remarkably ill-informed about our attitude towards them," one German officer wrote in an intelligence report in July 1941. "They do not know how Jews are treated in Germany, or for that matter in Warsaw [the capital of Poland], which after all is not so far away." He noted that he had been asked whether Jews were treated differently than other German citizens at home. "Even if they do not think that under German administration they will have equal rights with the Russians, they believe, nevertheless, that we shall leave them in peace if they mind their own business and work diligently."

The amazement of the German officer is understandable. The Nazis had been in power in Germany for eight years by the time they invaded Russia. During that time, they had openly declared their hatred of the Jews and acted on that hatred by mistreating them in every way possible. The entire world knew that antisemitism was the cornerstone of the Nazi philosophy. But the Jews of small-town Russia were poor people, largely unaware of what was happening in the rest of the world.

Perhaps more astonishing, as the German officer indicated, was that the Russian Jews did not know what had been happening to the Jews in neighboring Poland for the past year and a half. Jews had been killed, their synagogues (houses of worship) burned, their property stolen. They had been forced into labor gangs and confined to walled-off areas of cities called ghettos, where they were starving to death. (See Chapters 5 and 6.) But the Soviet government, which controlled all the newspapers and radio broadcasts in the country, had been on friendly terms with Nazi Germany during this time because of the deal Hitler had made with the Soviets to divide Poland. Stalin had banned any news about Nazi atrocities against the Jews of Poland.

Between 1933 and 1939, however, the Soviet government had often publicized and denounced the Nazis' actions. A number of factors led many Jews to ignore these reports or question their truthfulness. For one thing, the Soviet government tended to spread stories about bad conditions in other countries to make their own government seem like a decent alternative. In addition, many Jews had favorable memories of the Germans: Germany had invaded and occupied parts of Russia between 1914 and 1918, during World War I. At that time, the German troops had been friendly and courteous to the Jewish population. Most Jews remembered the Germans as protectors against the hated government of the Russian czar. There had been no pogroms while the Germans had remained. Finally, the Jews and Germans were united by similarities in their languages. The German language was closely related to Yiddish, the everyday language of eastern European Jews. More than 20 years after the end of World War I, many Russian Jews still thought that the modern, western European Germans were not as anti-Jewish as their own neighbors, the so-called "backward" country people of the Soviet Union.

The shootings

Aided by the Jewish population's lack of knowledge, by the chaos of the Soviet army's retreat, and often by the anti-semitism of the local population, the Nazis were able to murder hundreds of thousands of Jews within the first few months of the Russian invasion. A subunit of an *Einsatzgruppe,* an *Einsatzkommando,* swept into one town or village after another, each time crushing another segment of the Jewish population.

In his post-World War II testimony, Otto Ohlendorf, commander of *Einsatzgruppe* D, described what happened in Russia. The Germans would "order the prominent Jewish citizens to call together all Jews for the purpose of resettlement." (Throughout Europe, the Germans told Jews that they were being "resettled" to some other area when they were really being sent to their deaths.) When the town's Jewish population had gathered in some central location such as a school or the grounds of a factory, "they were requested to hand over their valuables to the leaders of the unit." Then, the Germans marched them away, usually to a nearby forest. "The men, women, and children were led to a place of execution which in most cases was located next to an antitank ditch that had been made deeper." Everyone was told to remove their outer clothing. (In many of the *Einsatzgruppen aktions* [operations] the victims had to remove all their clothing.) "Then they were shot, kneeling or standing, and the corpses thrown into the ditch."

Ohlendorf testified that he never allowed shooting by individual men of *Einsatzgruppe* D. Instead, he "ordered that several of the men should shoot at the same time in order to avoid direct personal responsibility. The leaders of the unit or specially selected persons, however, had to fire the last bullet at those victims who were not immediately dead." The *Einsatzkommando* officer would climb into the ditch full of dead bodies and shoot people who were still moving.

Methods of murder

In other *Einsatzgruppen* operations, the victims were forced to lie down on their stomachs on the edge of a ditch. They were shot in the back of the neck with a rifle by an individual German standing directly over them. Then the body would be pushed into the ditch and the process would be repeated. Ohlendorf said that he disapproved of this method because "both for the victims and for those who carried out the executions, it was an immense burden to bear psychologically." The rifle was supposed to be placed very close to the victim's neck, and the blood and brains often splattered onto the Germans' uniforms. (Ohlendorf's background and tactics are discussed in boxes on pp. 188 and 194.)

In a report written in December 1941, an SS colonel in *Einsatzgruppe* A described how his unit killed Jews. His purpose was to impress his superiors with how hard his job was. Each operation took "thorough preparation," he said, and required considerable knowledge about local conditions. "The Jews had to be collected in one or more towns and a ditch had to be dug at the right site for the right number. The marching distance from the collecting points to the ditches averaged about five kilometers [three miles]. The Jews were brought in groups of five hundred, separated by at least two kilometers [1.2 miles] to the place of execution.... Vehicles [were] seldom available. Escapes, which were occasionally attempted, were stopped entirely by my men at the risk of their lives. For example, three men ... shot 38 escaping Jews and local Communist officials on a path in the woods, so that

Otto Ohlendorf, head of Einsatzgruppe *D*, testifying at the Nuremberg trial. Not a common thug, Ohlendorf held a doctorate in economics.

Explaining the Murder of Children

When Otto Ohlendorf, the commander of *Einsatzgruppe* D, testified in the Nuremberg trials after the war, he was asked why the lives of Jewish children were not spared. "The order was that the Jewish population should be totally exterminated," he answered. "According to orders, they were to be killed just like their parents." He defended the killings by saying that the Jews were a threat to the security of the German forces. But, the prosecutor demanded, how could children be a threat to the German army? It was not up to him to decide this, Ohlendorf explained, because "the order said that all Jews including the children were considered ... a danger for the security of this area."

The prosecutor tried again. "Will you agree that there was absolutely no basis for killing children except genocide and the killing of races?" "No," Ohlendorf said. If the children were allowed to grow up, he rationalized, then surely they would become the enemies of the Nazis, who had killed their parents. The only way to prevent this was to kill everyone.

no one got away." The colonel does not explain how his heavily armed soldiers were risking their lives by chasing down and shooting unarmed civilians.

The colonel's men had to travel from their base in the Lithuanian city of Kovno (Kaunas) to their *aktions*. The round trip was always between 90 and 120 miles. "Only careful planning enabled the Kommandos to carry out up to five operations a week" and still have time to keep up with their duties in Kovno. Things were easier in Kovno itself, the colonel admitted, because there were enough Lithuanian auxiliaries available. In comparison to the other operations, he said, Kovno was "a shooting paradise."

Kovno

Many of the Jews of Kovno were already dead when the SS colonel wrote this report. The murders began as soon as the Soviet army retreated from the city. Gangs of Lithuanian

German soldiers look on as a member of the Einsatzgruppe D *prepares to shoot a Ukrainian Jew kneeling on the edge of a mass grave filled with corpses.*

anti-Semites attacked and robbed Jews on June 23 and June 24, 1941. On June 25, they marched from house to house in the Jewish slum district of the city, killing every Jew they could find. It was a pogrom.

As they did in many places, the Germans in Kovno encouraged these actions and secretly helped organize the mobs. It was important, the commander of *Einsatzgruppe* A wrote, to make it seem that the local population had attacked "the Bolshevist and Jewish enemy on its own initiative and without instructions from the German authorities."

A thirteen-year-old Russian partisan, one of a large number of children who fought against the German army.

Ten thousand Jews were arrested and taken to Fort Number Seven, one of several old military posts surrounding the city. For several days, large groups were taken out and shot; sometimes the Lithuanians raped the women first. The bodies of the Jews, almost 7,000 of them, were buried in large pits.

The 30,000 surviving Jews of the area were forced to move to the slum district where the murder march had occurred. This became the ghetto, a closed-off district of the city where the Jews were confined. Throughout the summer of 1941, the Germans took hundreds of people from the

Jewish Partisans

Tens of thousands of Jews took part in the partisan movements that were organized to fight the Germans in the countryside. At first, however, even some of the partisan groups were antisemitic; they refused to allow Jews to join them or, in far worse cases, even killed them. This was less true of the groups that were controlled by the Soviet army. But, even then, partisan groups usually only accepted people who could supply their own weapons, which the Jews often could not do.

Some Jewish partisan units became famous. They were usually known by the names of their commanders—"Uncle Mischa" in western White Russia (Belarus) and "Abba Kovner" in Lithuania, to name just two. Kovner had been a commander of the armed resistance group in the Vilna ghetto (the FPO, the initials for United Partisan Organization in the Yiddish language). He escaped into the forest after the Germans put down a revolt in the Vilna ghetto in September 1943.

In addition to ordinary partisan groups, some Jews who escaped from the clutches of the *Einsatzgruppen* or from the ghettos tried to hide in the forests with their whole families. They established "family camps," which combined offensive partisan activities with defensive protection measures. Probably the largest of these was the camp commanded by the Belski brothers in western White Russia, which had 1,200 members. It was very difficult to protect this large number of people, including children, from German patrols.

Besides partisan groups, there were at least 60 armed resistance movements active in the ghettos located in the westernmost sections of the Soviet Union (those areas that had been part of Poland until 1939).

ghetto and shot them. In October, over 9,000 people, including thousands of children, were taken to Fort Number Nine and shot. The Germans called Fort Number Nine the *Schlachtfeld,* which means "slaughter ground." In the years that the Germans held Kovno, 100,000 people—70,000 of them Jews—were killed in the forts surrounding the city. This was the "shooting paradise" that the SS colonel described.

Minsk

The German army captured Minsk, the capital of White Russia (Belarus), on June 30, 1941, only eight days after the beginning of the invasion. The army placed most of the adult men of the city in a guarded camp. Then, *Einsatzgruppe* B arrived and picked out Jews, Communist officials, and "Asiatics.[Soviet people]" They were taken away and shot.

German police look through the clothing of people killed during a shooting action at Babi Yar, outside of Kiev, Ukraine.

By late July, all the remaining Jews of the Minsk area—between 80,000 and 100,000 people—were confined to a ghetto. The Germans ordered the creation of a Jewish Council (*Judenrat*) as they had done in the ghettos of Poland. Unlike most of the Jewish Councils in Poland, however, the Minsk *Judenrat* tried from the very beginning to help organize resistance to the Nazis. (The role of the Jewish Councils in Poland is discussed in Chapter 5, pp. 126–27 and pp. 134–36.) Some Jews from the Minsk ghetto were able to escape to join partisan units in the nearby forests, and others even formed their own units.

On November 7, and again on November 20, a total of nearly 20,000 people were taken from the Minsk ghetto and shot in the forest. They had been forced to dig pits for their own graves. In March 1942, the Germans murdered 5,000 people in retaliation for the *Judenrat's* failure to cooperate. Among the victims were the children of the ghetto orphanage, who were burned alive. After this, thousands of Jews

A Memorial to the Jews

During and after World War II, the Soviet government underscored the terrible suffering of the Soviet people at the hands of the Nazis and praised their heroism in defeating Germany. (At least 20 million Soviet citizens died in the war, far more than any other country.) But the government tried to downplay the fact that the Jews were the ones being targeted by the Nazis for extermination. Many observers consider this effort to ignore the Holocaust an example of Soviet antisemitism.

Fifteen years after the war, a tremendously popular young Russian poet, Yevgeny Yevtushenko, wrote a poem dealing with the issues of the Holocaust, Soviet silence, and antisemitism during World War II. The poem was called "Babi Yar":

> There is no gravestone at Baby Yar,
> Only coarse earth piled roughly over
>   the gash.
> I am afraid. Today I feel old,
> As old as the Jews....
>
> O my own people, my own
>   Russian folk,

> Believers in the brotherhood
>   of man!
> But dirty hands too often dare
>   to raise
> The banner of your pure and lofty
>   name....
>
> No drop of Jewish blood flows in
>   my veins,
> But every anti-Semite, with a bitter,
>   hard hate
> Hates me like a Jew.
> O know me truly Russian through
>   their hate!

The Soviet authorities attacked Yevtushenko for his poem, which gained worldwide attention. The government claimed he had smeared the Russian people and concentrated too much on the suffering of the Jews. In 1966, memorial plaques were placed at Babi Yar; in 1974, more than 30 years after the massacre, a monument was built at the site. But there was still no mention that almost all of the victims buried there were Jews. Recently, a new memorial was added describing the fate of the Jews.

---

tried to escape the ghetto to hide in the forests. In July 1942, another 30,000 people were shot. The last inhabitants of the ghetto were killed in October 1943.

Babi Yar

The worst massacre was at Kiev, the capital of Ukraine. The German army did not capture Kiev until September 19, after a battle that lasted 45 days. Within a few days, all Jews were ordered to report for "resettlement." They gathered together, carrying small bundles, and were led out of town past the Jewish cemetery to an area of sand dunes with a large ravine (a steep and narrow valley). The name of the place was Babi Yar.

As each small group reached Babi Yar, the people were ordered to strip, hand over their bundles, and march to the edge of the great ravine. Then they were machine-gunned. For two days, over and over, the machine gunners worked until the bodies filled the ravine. Thirty-three thousand died.

A system for genocide

The German tanks rolled through the Baltic states, White Russia, and Ukraine with stunning speed, then penetrated into Russia itself. Behind them, the *Einsatzgruppen* killed the Jews of town after town, 7,000 in Zhitomir, 4,000 in Vitebsk, 4,900 in Mogilev, 4,000 in Gomel.

The pattern was the same in every part of the Soviet Union captured by the Germans. The *Einsatzgruppen* would enter an area, round up as many Jews as they could, march them to an isolated area in the woods outside of their town, and shoot them. Then the *Einsatzgruppen* would move farther east, following the advance of the German army.

According to German statistics, 250,000 Jews were killed in the Baltic states and White Russia in the first three months of the invasion. Within five months, half a million Soviet Jews were dead. In January 1942, the commander of *Einsatzgruppe* A reported (or bragged) that "systematically, district by district, the Lithuanian sector was cleansed of Jews of both sexes. Altogether, 136,421 people were liquidated [killed] in a great number of individual operations." But these operations, even though some of them were very large, could not kill all the Jews. At this time, 2 million were still alive in Soviet territory conquered by the Germans. Millions more lived in other countries of Europe controlled by Germany. The Nazis had already decided that they should all die.

The "Final Solution"

During the first wave of mass shootings in the Soviet Union, Reinhard Heydrich, the man who had formed the *Einsatzgruppen,* was given new responsibilities. On July 31, 1941, a little over a month after the invasion of the Soviet Union

The First Massacres

The first wave of shootings by the *Einsatzgruppen* killed hundreds of thousands of people—and this only includes the casualties of *some* of the towns and cities they invaded. In many of these places, especially in the larger cities, the first massacres did not kill all the Jews. In cases such as these, a ghetto was usually set up to house the Jews until all of them could be killed, bringing the total number of deaths much higher than shown here:

Bakchiserai	1,099	Mariupol	9,000
Berdichev	35,000	Melitopol	2,000
Bobruisk	6,179	Minsk	21,000
Borisov	8,200	Mogilev	4,844
Chernigov	10,000	Piatigorsk	1,500
Dniepropetrovsk	31,000	Polotsk	8,000
Essentuki	1,500	Poltava	12,000
Gomel	4,000	Rostov	18,000
Kerch	7,000	Smolensk	3,000
Kharkov	20,000	Uman	30,000
Kiev	50,000	Vitebsk	4,090
Kislovodsk	2,000	Zhitimir	7,000

began, Heydrich received an order from Hermann Göring, the man in charge of Nazi policy toward the Jews. At that point, Göring was the most important Nazi leader after Hitler himself. (Soon, Himmler—the head of the SS, the Nazis' military arm, and Heydrich's boss—would take over Göring's job and become the second most powerful man in Germany.)

Back in 1939, Göring had put Heydrich in charge of forcing Jews to leave Germany and Austria. The Nazis called this process "emigration," although that term usually refers to people leaving their native land—voluntarily—to move to a new country. The German Jews had been *forced* to leave, sometimes as the price for being released from a concentration camp. This had been the Nazi "solution" to what they

considered the "Jewish problem." (See Chapter 3.) But now Germany controlled most of Europe. It was not possible to force the Jews from all these countries to move elsewhere, especially during wartime. So the Nazis decided on a different "solution."

Göring gave Heydrich authority "to carry out all necessary preparations ... for a total solution of the Jewish question in the German sphere of influence in Europe." (The German sphere of influence meant Germany itself, the countries that Germany had conquered in the war, and Germany's World War II allies.) After giving Heydrich the power to involve all agencies of the German government necessary to carry out his mission, Göring ordered Heydrich to "submit to me promptly an overall plan showing the preliminary ... measures for the execution of the intended 'Final Solution' of the Jewish question."

Reinhard Heydrich, head of the Main Office for Reich Security (RHSA) and the SD, the intelligence arm of the Nazis' military section, was chosen to carry out the "Final Solution."

There is no doubt about what Göring meant by the "Final Solution." He meant the physical destruction of the Jews. There is also no doubt that the decision was not Göring's alone. It had been discussed at the top levels of the Nazi Party and government. Victor Brack, one of Hitler's closest assistants, admitted after the war that several months before Göring's order to Heydrich, "it was no secret in higher Party circles that the Jews were to be exterminated." Although no written record of such an order survived the war, historians agree that the decision must have been made by Hitler, the Führer (leader) who made every important decision in Nazi Germany.

Heydrich: The executioner

Heydrich was chosen to carry out the "Final Solution" because he was the head of the Main Office for Reich Security or RSHA (see box on page 181), which controlled the *Einsatzgruppen* and the SD, the intelligence unit of the Nazi Party's military arm. This was not the first time that Heydrich had been put in charge of Nazi plans for the Jews. In addition to being in charge of the *Einsatzgruppen* during the invasion of

Russia and supervising the "emigration" of Jews from Germany, he had played a very important role in the relocation and then murder of Jews in Poland. As soon as the German army had conquered Poland in September 1939, Heydrich had issued an order to create ghettos. Jews were concentrated (gathered) in as few places as possible, with those from small towns forced into larger cities. Each ghetto was to be situated on a railroad line to make it easier for later actions, which Heydrich did not describe. Heydrich's order indicated that these were only the first steps in Nazi policy toward the Polish Jews. The "final aim," which was also left unexplained, would require an "extended period of time," and it was to be kept "strictly secret."

Heydrich began to plan the ways in which the "Final Solution" would be carried out. He met with Adolf Eichmann, head of the Jewish Affairs Section of the RSHA, who had been directly responsible for carrying out much of the "emigration" policy. At his trial in Israel in 1961 (see Chapter 13), Eichmann testified that Heydrich had said: "The Führer has ordered the physical extermination of the Jews." Heydrich sent Eichmann to the Polish city of Lublin to learn more about the methods being used to kill the Jews there.

Adolf Eichmann, head of the RSHA's Jewish Affairs Section, researched the fastest, most efficient and least bloody ways to kill millions of Jews.

Eichmann: The messenger

According to his testimony, Nazi officials at the Majdenek concentration camp in Lublin showed Eichmann how they had built airtight chambers disguised as farmers' cottages. The carbon monoxide exhaust gas from the motor of a captured Russian submarine could be pumped into the chamber to kill everyone inside. Eichmann later delivered a message from Heydrich to the SS commander in Lublin, General Odilo Globocnik. "It ordered Globocnik to start liquidating a quarter of a million Polish Jews," Eichmann testified.

Eichmann then went to Auschwitz, a concentration camp in southeastern Poland. Himmler had ordered that Auschwitz be changed into a death camp, a place designed

The Wannsee Villa, where details for the "Final Solution" were ironed out.

for the immediate killing of people, not for their imprisonment. Eichmann and the commander of Auschwitz discussed plans to make Auschwitz the main killing center for Jews from all over Europe. (See Chapter 9.)

Sometime later, probably in November 1941, Eichmann traveled to Minsk, in White Russia. This time he was sent by Heinrich Müller, who was then head of the Gestapo. There he watched as a group of Jews were forced to jump into a pit and were shot. "I saw a woman hold a child of a year or two into the air, pleading"; At his trial, Eichmann claimed he was terribly upset by this scene because he had children of his own. In fact, the purpose of Eichmann's trips was to figure out the best way—that is, the fastest, most efficient, and least bloody way—to kill millions of Jews.

The Wannsee Conference

In the winter of 1941, Heydrich called a conference at Wannsee, a lakeside suburb of Berlin. The conference was originally scheduled for December but was postponed, probably because the officials who were scheduled to attend the conference had to make plans to deal with an unexpected development. Japan, Germany's ally, had bombed Pearl Harbor in Hawaii and also attacked British-controlled areas in Asia, joining Germany in the war against Great Britain. Surprising almost everyone in Germany, Hitler then declared war on the United States. Germany was now at war with Great Britain, the Soviet Union, and the United States, the most powerful enemies possible. But this did not stop the Nazis from applying their resources—even resources needed to fight the war—to killing the Jews. It only delayed Heydrich's conference for a few weeks.

The conference was finally held on January 20, 1942. By this time, half a million Soviet Jews had already been killed. The Nazis had opened a death camp at Chelmno, in western Poland. There they were using gas vans to kill the Jews of the area. (See Chapter 8, p. 219.) Himmler had already given orders to make Auschwitz a huge death camp.

The purpose of the Wannsee Conference was not to decide what to do about the Jews; that decision had already been made. Instead, the conference was called to inform all the branches of the German government about the decision—and to make sure they were cooperating in carrying it out.

A total of 15 men were at the meeting, including Heydrich, Eichmann, and Müller, the head of the Gestapo. Among the others were high officials of the German Foreign Ministry and the ministries of the interior (police), justice, and economic planning. There was also a representative of the German governor-general of occupied Poland and two from the Ministry for the Occupied Eastern Territories, the agency in charge of captured Soviet territory. In addition, top officials were present from the head office of the Nazi Party and from the office of the Reich chancellor (the title of the head of the German government, roughly equivalent to prime minister, a position Hitler had held since 1933).

Heydrich's report

Heydrich reported on his previous attempts at solving "the Jewish problem" by forced emigration. But now, Heydrich stated, because of the war and "because of the possibilities in the east," Himmler had banned the emigration of Jews. Instead, Heydrich informed his listeners, "evacuation of the Jews to the east" was the current policy of Nazi Germany. He added that "practical experience is being gathered that is of major significance in view of the coming Final Solution to the Jewish Question." Heydrich was referring to the *Einsatzgruppen* operations in Russia and the experiments with gas vans at Chelmno.

The "Final Solution" meant sending Jews to the east "for labor utilization," said Heydrich. They would be separated by sex; those able to work would be put into large labor columns to build roads. Heydrich did not mention what would happen to those who were too old, young, or sick to work. But he made it clear that even those who could work would not live for long. He expected that "doubtless a large part will fall away through natural reduction."

Those who did not die from overwork, malnourishment, and disease were "the toughest element" of the Jews, according to Heydrich. If they were ever freed, they would be a seed from which the Jews might develop again. Therefore, they would "have to be dealt with appropriately."

Heydrich reported on the number of Jews in each country of Europe: the grand total was 11 million. Heydrich's figures included the Jews of Great Britain, which Germany was fighting, as well as countries that were not involved in the war, like Spain, Switzerland, and even Ireland. The aim of the "Final Solution," in other words, went even further than the "German sphere of influence in Europe." The goal was eventually to kill every Jew in all of Europe. The Nazis, according to their own figures, planned to kill 11 million people.

Discussing genocide

The 15 men at the conference discussed the problems involved in arresting and deporting the Jews of each country under German control. For example, the representative of the Foreign Ministry was worried that trying to deport the Jews of some German-occupied countries like Denmark might lead to opposition in those countries. (In fact, the Danish people succeeded in saving almost all Danish Jews, as described in Chapter 10.) In other countries, such as Romania, which was an ally of Germany and under strong German

Heydrich's Report to the Wannsee Conference

This table shows the number of Jews still alive in each country according to Reinhard Heydrich's report to the Wannsee Conference. The total is 10,803,500, but some of the figures Heydrich used were quite inaccurate.

For example, his estimate of 3 million Jews in Ukraine was almost double the actual number, and many of them had already been killed by this time. Similarly, there were less than half as many Jews in France as Heydrich thought.

Albania. 200	Latvia 3,500
Austria. 43,700	Lithuania. 34,000
Belgium 43,000	Netherlands 160,800
Bulgaria. 48,000	Norway. 1,300
Croatia 40,000	Poland (Bialystok District) . . . 400,000
Czech lands. . . . . 74,200 (Bohemia and Moravia)	Poland (Main Part). 2,284,000
Denmark. 5,600	Romania 342,000
Estonia . . . . "Free of Jews"	Serbia 10,000
France. 865,000	Slovakia 88,000
Germany. 131,800	Spain 6,000
Great Britain 330,000	Switzerland. 18,000
Greece 69,600	USSR (total) 5,000,000
Hungary 742,800	"Eastern Territories". 420,000
Ireland 4,000	Ukraine 2,994,684
Italy. 58,000	White Russia. 446,484

influence, the Nazis were afraid the government might protect Jews who could bribe government officials.

The conference members also discussed how to treat people who were half or a quarter Jewish, or who were married to non-Jews. They talked about certain exceptions, such as Jews who had won medals or had been seriously wounded fighting in the German army in World War I. These Jews would be sent to a special camp at Theresienstadt in Czechoslovakia, Heydrich said, rather than "resettled"—murdered. (In fact, most Jews sent to Theresienstadt were later sent to Auschwitz and killed. See Theresienstadt box on p. 294.) In addition, the Jews

Heinrich Müller, head of the Gestapo (the German secret police), helped plan the logistics of the "Final Solution" at the Wannsee Conference, then celebrated.

who were working at jobs necessary to the German war effort were not supposed to be deported until they could be replaced. This was a special concern of the army and of Hermann Göring, who was in charge of economic planning. This exception was usually ignored in practice—the men who ran Nazi Germany wanted to kill Jews even if it meant hurting their chances of winning the war.

Although the written record of the conference, prepared by Eichmann, does not describe it, Eichmann testified at his trial that the conference ended with discussions of exactly how to kill the Jews. The technical problems of mass shooting and poison gas were described and debated. Every person at the conference understood that "evacuation" meant killing. Each of them participated in planning the murders.

Soon, Eichmann would begin work on all these technical details: how to carry out the "Final Solution," how to round up the Jews in each country and provide the trains to send them east. The death camps in Poland were being readied for their first victims—readied to gas them and burn their bodies. But first, the men in charge of the "Final Solution" celebrated. When the Wannsee Conference ended and the others left, Heydrich, Müller, and Eichmann reportedly stayed behind. They sat around the fireplace, drinking brandy and singing songs.

A German eyewitness to genocide

The decision to kill the Jews of Europe was already being carried out in the Soviet Union. As the army and the *Einsatzgruppen* moved out of an area, it was handed over to German civilian administrators. They set up ghettos, where the remaining Jews were confined and forced to work for the Germans. Periodically, large groups of people—usually beginning with those too old, too young, or too sick to work—would be taken out of the ghetto and massacred. In the summer and fall of 1942, a second great wave of killings

Soviet POWs are forced to conceal the bodies of an Einsatzgruppe *action in Ukraine, 1943.*

swept through the occupied Soviet Union as most of the ghettos were eliminated completely.

In October, a German construction engineer named Hermann Friedrich Graebe was in Dubno, Ukraine, working as a civilian under contract to the army. He heard that the Jews of the Dubno ghetto were being killed in large pits near the construction project he was supervising. Graebe decided to see for himself and drove to the site. Truckloads of Jews were being unloaded near mounds of earth 6 feet high and 30 yards long. From behind the mounds, Graebe heard rifle shots. SS men and Ukrainian auxiliaries guarded the Jews as they undressed and put their clothes in piles. Graebe estimated that there were already 800 to 1,000 pairs of shoes. Groups of about 20 people at a time were ordered to go behind the mound. This is part of what Graebe saw:

> I walked around the mound, and found myself confronted by a tremendous grave. People were closely

wedged together and lying on top of each other so that only their heads were visible. Nearly all had blood running over their shoulders from their heads. Some of the people shot were still moving. Some were lifting their arms and turning their heads to show that they were still alive. The pit was already two-thirds full. I estimate that it already contained about a thousand people.

I looked for the man who did the shooting. He was an SS man, who sat at the edge of the narrow end of the pit, his feet dangling into the pit. He had a tommy gun on his knees and he was smoking a cigarette. The people, completely naked, went down some steps which were cut in the clay wall of the pit and clambered over the heads of the people lying there, to the place where the SS man directed them. They lay down in front of the dead or injured people; some caressed those who were still alive and spoke to them in a low voice. Then I heard a series of shots.

The Jews of Russia, the Jews of Europe

In the winter of 1942-43, the Soviet army began a series of great counteroffensives, large-scale military undertakings, against the Germans. In huge battles that destroyed whole army groups, the Germans were forced back and the Soviets recaptured the cities and towns that the German army had taken in 1941. It took almost two years to drive the Germans out of Soviet territory completely. Ninety percent of the Jews (about 228,000) in the three Baltic countries of Lithuania, Latvia, and Estonia had been killed; two-thirds of Ukrainian Jews (900,000) and about 60 percent (245,000) of those in White Russia (Belarus) were dead. Some 90 percent of the Jews of Russia itself survived, but only because the German army never reached them.

Most Russian Jews were shot to death. In some places, they were driven into the sea or a river and drowned. Some had been burned alive. On the personal orders of SS chief Heinrich Himmler, the Nazis also experimented with another method: Himmler wanted it used first on women and children, partly because he was afraid that shooting them was becoming too hard on the SS men. In addition, shooting was

Understanding the Holocaust

too slow and too public a process for the incredible number of people that Himmler intended to murder.

Specially constructed trucks were brought to Russia from Germany. They looked something like furniture vans. The women and children were forced inside and told they were being transported elsewhere. The motor was turned on, and the exhaust fumes were piped into the sealed truck. The women and children died in about 10 or 15 minutes.

This was the first time that gassing had been used as a method of killing the Jews. (The Nazis had used gas chambers to kill mentally and physically handicapped Germans in their so-called "euthanasia" ["mercy-killing"] program; see Chapter 4, pp. 108–14.) In December 1941, gas vans were used at Chelmno, located far away in western Poland. Soon, at Belzec, Sobibór, and Treblinka, exhaust fumes were being piped into sealed gas chambers instead of trucks; in this way, the Jews of Poland could be killed more quickly by fewer people. (These death camps are described in Chapter 8.) Before long, the Nazis were sending Jews from all over Europe to be murdered in the gas chambers of Auschwitz. Then, their bodies were burned in ovens specially installed for this purpose. (See Chapter 9.)

The genocide had begun in Russia with people being shot near their homes, then thrown into ditches to die. It ended under the high smokestacks of a modern factory of death.

Where to Learn More

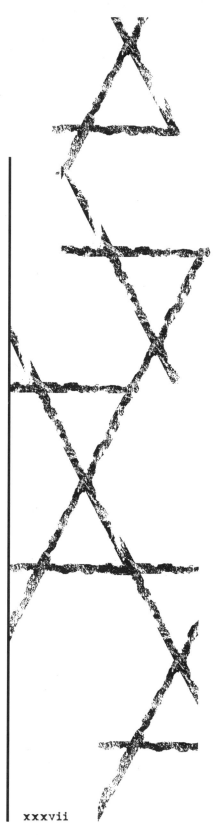

The following list focuses on works written for readers of middle school or high school age. Books aimed at adult readers have been included when they are especially important in providing information or analysis that would otherwise be unavailable, or because they have become classics. All books not specifically written for younger readers are noted as such.

General histories of the Holocaust:

Adler, David A. *We Remember the Holocaust.* New York: Henry Holt, 1995.

Altman, Linda Jacobs. *Forever Outsiders.* Vol. 1 of "Holocaust" series edited by Lisa Clyde Nielsen. Woodbridge, CT: Blackbirch Press, 1998.

Arad, Yithak. *The Pictorial History of the Holocaust.* New York: Macmillan, 1992.

Ayer, Eleanor H. *A Firestorm Unleased.* Vol. 4 of "Holocaust" series, edited by Lisa Clyde Nielsen. Woodbridge, CT: Blackbirch Press, 1998.

Ayer, Eleanor H. *Inferno.* Vol. 5 of "Holocaust" series, edited by Lisa Clyde Nielsen. Woodbridge, CT: Blackbirch Press, 1998.

Ayer, Eleanor H., and Stephen D. Chicoine. *From the Ashes*. Vol. 6 of "Holocaust" series, edited by Lisa Clyde Nielsen. Woodbridge, CT: Blackbirch Press, 1998.

Bachrach, Susan D. *Tell Them We Remember: The Story of the Holocaust*. Boston: Little, Brown, 1994.

Chaikin, Miriam. *A Nightmare in History: The Holocaust, 1933–1945*. New York: Clarion Books, 1987.

Herzstein, Robert E. *The Nazis*. Alexandria, VA: Time-Life Books, 1980.

Meltzer, Milton. *Never to Forget*. New York: Harper & Row, 1976.

Resnick, Abraham. *The Holocaust*. San Diego: Lucent Books, 1991.

Rogasky, Barbara. *Smoke and Ashes*. New York: Holiday House, 1988.

Rossel, Seymour. *The Holocaust: The Fire that Raged*. New York: Franklin Watts, 1989.

Sherrow, Victoria. *The Blaze Engulfs*. Vol. 3 of "Holocaust" series, edited by Lisa Clyde Nielsen. Woodbridge, CT: Blackbirch Press, 1998.

Sherrow, Victoria. *Smoke to Flame*. Vol. 2 of "Holocaust" series, edited by Lisa Clyde Nielsen. Woodbridge, CT: Blackbirch Press, 1998.

Shoenberner, Gerhard. *The Yellow Star: The Persecution of the Jews in Europe, 1933–45*. New York: Bantam Books, 1979.

Shulman, William L., compiler. *Resource Guide*. Vol. 8 of "Holocaust" series, edited by Lisa Clyde Nielsen. Woodbridge, CT: Blackbirch Press. 1998.

Shulman, William L., compiler. *Voices and Visions*. Vol. 7 of "Holocaust" series, edited by Lisa Clyde Nielsen. Woodbridge, CT: Blackbirch Press, 1998.

Strahinich, Helen. *The Holocaust: Understanding and Remembering*. Springfield, NJ: Enslow, 1996.

Wigoder, Geoffrey, ed. *The Holocaust: A Grolier Student Library*. 4 vols. Danbury, CT: Grolier Educational, 1997.

The following general overviews of the Holocaust are aimed at adult readers:

Bauer, Yehuda and Nili Keren. *A History of the Holocaust.* New York: Franklin Watts, 1982.

Dawidowicz, Lucy S. *The War Against the Jews, 1933–1945.* New York: Bantam Books, 1986.

Encyclopedia of the Third Reich. 2 vols. New York: Macmillan, 1991.

Gilbert, Martin. *The Holocaust: The History of the Jews of Europe During the Second World War.* New York: Henry Holt, 1986.

Gutman, Israel, ed. *The Encyclopedia of the Holocaust.* 4 vols. New York: Macmillan, 1990.

Hilberg, Raoul. *The Destruction of the European Jews.* New York: Holmes & Meier, 1985.

Levin, Nora. *The Holocaust: The Nazi Destruction of European Jewry, 1933–1945.* New York: Schocken, 1973.

Snyder, Louis L. *Encyclopedia of the Third Reich.* New York: McGraw-Hill, 1976.

Spiegelman, Art. *Maus: A Survivor's Tale.* Vol. 1, *Maus I: My Father Bleeds History.* New York: Pantheon, 1986. Vol. 2, *Maus II: And Here My Troubles Began.* New York: Pantheon, 1991. *Maus* is written in comic strip form, with the Jews depicted as mice and the Nazis as cats. Despite the format, it is a deadly serious, brilliantly imaginative work. *Maus I* tells the story of Spiegelman's father during the Holocaust; *Maus II* continues his story after the war has ended.

Yahil, Leni. *The Holocaust: The Fate of European Jewry, 1932–1945.* New York: Oxford University Press, 1991.

Zenter, Christian, and Friedemann Bedürftig, eds. *Encyclopedia of the Third Reich.* New York: Da Capo Press 1997.

Atlases:

Gilbert, Martin. *Atlas of the Holocaust.* New York: Macmillan, 1982. Martin, a leading Holocaust scholar, has written this atlas to describe the events of the Holocaust and show where they happened.

United States Holocaust Memorial Museum. *The Historical Atlas of the Holocaust.* New York: Macmillan, 1995. This atlas, also available as a CD-ROM, is aimed at general readers and has quickly become the standard work in the field of Holocaust studies.

German history, the early Nazi movement, the Nazi government, and policy towards the Jews before the Holocaust:

Allen, William Sheridan. *The Nazi Seizure of Power: The Experience of a Single German Town, 1930–1935.* New York: Franklin Watts, 1973. Allen's book is a classic study of the growth of Nazi influence and power. Although it is a work of adult social history, its detailed picture of what the Nazi "revolution" must have felt like to ordinary Germans will reward younger readers who have a strong interest in the subject.

Auerbacher, Inge. *I Am a Star: Child of the Holocaust.* Paramus, NJ: Prentice-Hall, 1986. *I Am a Star* is the memoir of a German Jewish girl who survived Thereisenstadt concentration camp.

Ayer, Eleanor. *Adolf Hitler.* San Diego: Lucent, 1996. Ayer's work describes the life and rise to power of German dictator Adolf Hitler.

Bauer, Yehuda. *Jews for Sale? Nazi-Jewish Negotiations, 1933–1945.* New Haven, CT: Yale University Press, 1994. Bauer's work, written for adults, is about the history of attempts to arrange Jewish emigration, including the role of the Zionist movement.

Berman, Russell A. *Paul von Hindenburg.* New York: Chelsea House, 1987. *Paul von Hindenburg* is a biography of Germany's World War I hero who became president and eventually appointed Hitler as chancellor.

Bosanquest, Mary. *The Life and Death of Dietrich Bonhoeffer.* New York: Harper & Row, 1968. Bosanquest's book describes the role of the Protestant Church during the Holocaust.

Bullock, Alan. *Hitler: A Study in Tyranny.* New York: Harper & Row, 1964. Bullock's biography on Hitler has heavily influenced most other studies.

Crisp, Peter. *The Rise of Fascism.* Charlottesville, VA: Book-wrights, 1991. *The Rise of Fascism* describes fascist movements, including Nazism, through the first half of the twentieth century.

Drucker, Olga Levy. *Kindertransport.* New York: Henry Holt, 1992. *Kindertransport* is the story of German Jewish children who were sent to England in order to escape Nazi persecution.

Eimerl, Sarel. *Hitler Over Europe: The Road to World War II.* Boston: Little, Brown, 1972. Eimerl's book focuses on German foreign policy before the war.

Friedlander, Saul. *Pius XII and the Third Reich.* New York: Knopf, 1966. Although *Pius XII and the Third Reich* is a difficult book for younger readers, it is an important study of the role of the Catholic Church, written by a foremost scholar.

Friedman, Ina R. *Fly Against the Wind: The Story of a Young Woman Who Defied the Nazis.* Bookline, MA: Lodgepole Press, 1995.

Fuller, Barbara. *Germany.* New York: Marshall Cavendish, 1996. Aimed at young readers, *Germany* includes the history, geography, government, and economic background of the country.

Gallo, Max. *The Night of the Long Knives.* New York: Harper & Row, 1972. *The Night of the Long Knives* is an examination of the SA purge and the murder of its leader, Ernst Röhm. Although aimed at an adult audience, it is worth the effort.

Goldston, Robert C. *The Life and Death of Nazi Germany.* New York: Bobbs-Merrill, 1967. Goldston's *The Life and Death of Nazi Germany* includes discussions of the Nazi government and political developments as well as material on foreign affairs.

Graff, Stewart. *The Story of World War II.* New York: E. P. Dutton, 1978.

Halperin, S. William. *Germany Tried Democracy: A Political History of the Reich from 1918 to 1933.* New York: Norton, 1965. Halperin's book was first published in 1946, soon after Germany's defeat in World War II. It remains one of the best works on the history of the Weimar Republic. Aimed at adults, it is detailed and sophisticated, but relatively clear and free from jargon.

Hartenian, Lawrence R. *Benito Mussolini*. New York: Chelsea House, 1988.

Heyes, Eileen. *Adolf Hitler*. Brookfield, CT: Millbrook Press, 1994. Heyes's *Adolf Hitler* provides readers with an insight into the life of Hitler, who rose from obscurity to become the leader of the Nazi Party.

Heyes, Eileen. *Children of the Swastika: The Hitler Youth*. Brookfield, CT: Millbrook Press, 1993. *Children of the Swastika* explores the phenomenon of the Hitler Youth, young people who blindly followed the Nazi policies.

Josephson, Judith P. *Jesse Owens: Track and Field Legend*. Springfield, NJ: Enslow Press, 1997. Josephson's recent biography that does a good job describing the 1936 Berlin Olympics.

Kluger, Ruth Peggy Mann, *Secret Ship*. New York: Doubleday, 1978. *Secret Ship* describes the illegal immigration to Palestine that occurred during the Nazi era.

Leeds, Christopher A. *Italy Under Mussolini*. New York: Wayland, Putnan, 1972. Leeds examines Italian Fascism, which was Hitler's early model for Nazism.

Marrin, Albert. *Hitler*. New York: Viking, 1987. Marrian's book, aimed at young people, focuses on Hitler's personal history and Nazism.

Nevelle, Peter. *Life in the Third Reich: World War II*. North Pomfret, VT: Batsford, 1992. Despite its title, *Life in the Third Reich* is not limited to the war years.

The New Order. Alexandria, VA: Time-Life Books, 1989. *The New Order* depicts Nazi Germany through contemporary photographs.

Niemark, Anne E. *Leo Baeck and the Holocaust*. New York: E.P. Dutton, 1986. Niemark's work is a biography of the leader of the German Jewish community, who eventually was sent to Theresienstadt concentration camp.

Read, Anthony. *Kristallnacht: The Nazi Night of Terror*. New York: Times Books/Random House, 1989. Read's book concentrates on *Kristallnacht,* the night in 1938 when the first public violence broke out against the Jews.

Rubinstein, William D. *The Myth of Rescue.* New York: Routledge, 1997. Rubinstein's book defends American immigration policy during the 1930s. It is a specialized book, aimed at adult readers.

Shirer, William L. *The Rise and Fall of Adolf Hitler.* New York: Random House, 1961. *The Rise and Fall of Adolf Hitler* is a biography aimed at younger readers by Shirer, the American journalist and historian whose *Rise and Fall of the Third Reich* (Simon and Schuster, 1960) is a standard general history for adults.

Skipper, G.C. *Goering and the Luftwaffe.* Danbury, CT: Children's Press, 1980. *Goering and the Luftwaffe* is a biography of Hermann Goering that focuses on his role as leader of the Nazi air force.

Snyder, Louis L. *Hitler's Elite.* New York: Hippocrene Books, 1989. Snyder's book describes the top Nazi leaders. Although it is aimed at general readers, it is not too difficult for young readers.

Snyder, Louis L. *World War II.* New York: Franklin Watts, 1981. Snyder's *World War II* is a military history for young readers.

Speer, Albert. *Inside the Third Reich.* New York: Macmillan, 1970. *Inside the Third Reich* is a fascinating look at the world of the top Nazis. Speer was Hitler's favorite architect, and more importantly, he ran Germany's arms program at the end of the war. The book is aimed at adult readers.

Spence, William. *Germany Then and Now.* New York: Franklin Watts, 1994. Spence's history of Germany is suited for younger readers.

Start, Clarissa. *God's Man: The Story of Pastor Niemöller.* Washburn, 1959. *God's Man* explores the role of former Nazi supporter and Protestant clergyman Martin Niemöller as well as the policies of the Protestant Church during the Nazi era.

Stein, R. Conrad. *Hitler Youth.* Danbury, CT: Children's Press, 1985. Stein's book, aimed at younger readers, discusses the Hitler Youth.

Stewart, Gail. *Hitler's Reich*. San Diego: Lucent Books, 1994. *Hitler's Reich* describes both Hitler's rise to power and what life was like in Nazi Germany.

Thalmann, Rita, and Emmanuel Feinermann. Crystal Night, 9-10 November, 1938. *New York: Putnam, 1974. The decisive turning-point in Nazi policy towards the Jews is described in this work for younger readers.*

Thomas, Gordon, and Max M. Witts. *Voyage of the Damned*. Stein & Day, 1974. *Voyage of the Damned* is about the voyage of the *St. Louis* and, although written for adults, is not too difficult for younger readers.

Toland, John. *Adolf Hitler*. New York: Doubleday, 1976. Although aimed at adult readers, Toland's *Adolf Hitler* contains plenty of valuable information.

Wepman, Dennis. *Adolf Hitler*. New York: Chelsea House, 1989. Wepman's biography includes material on Hitler's methods and rise to power.

Zassenhaus, Hiltgunt. *Walls: Resisting the Third Reich, One Woman's Story*. Boston: Beacon Press, 1974. Zassenhaus's first-person account tells of her attempts as a non-Jewish German woman to oppose the Nazis.

Zurndorfer, Hannele. *The Ninth of November*. Berrien Springs, MI: Quartet Books, 1983. *The Ninth of November* describes *Kristallnacht* from the perspective of one family.

The "Final Solution":

Auschwitz: A History in Photographs. Bloomington: Indiana University Press, 1993. Through photographs, this book tells the history of the death camp.

Breitman, Richard. *The Architect of Genocide: Himmler and the Final Solution*. New York: Knopf, 1991. Breitman's *The Architect of Genocide* describes how Heinrich Himmler, head of the SS, the Nazi military wing, supervised the plan to eliminate the Jews of Europe.

Browning, Christopher R. *Ordinary Men: Reserve Police Battalion 101 and the Final Solution in Poland*. New York: HarperCollins, 1992. *Ordinary Men* includes vivid descriptions of transports to the concentration camps and of shootings by the *Einsatzgruppen*.

Freidlander, Henry. *The Origins of Nazi Genocide*. Chapel Hill: University of North Carolina Press, 1995. *The Origins of Nazi Genocide* is an adult work that examines the euthanasia program.

Friedrich, Otto. *The Kingdom of Auschwitz*. New York: Harper Perennial, 1994. *The Kingdom of Auschwitz* is an adult work, but it is very short and insightful.

Gilbert, Martin. *Auschwitz and the Allies*. New York: Henry Holt, 1990. *Auschwitz and the Allies* is an adult book that gives a balanced opinion of America's policy on saving the Jews.

Goldhagen, Daniel J. *Hitler's Willing Executioners: Ordinary Germans and the Holocaust*. New York: Knopf, 1996. Although especially difficult for young people, *Hitler's Willing Executioners* describes the mass shootings by the *Einsatzgruppen*. Goldhagen's book is at the center of a major controversy about the role and motivation of "ordinary Germans" in Nazi genocide.

Hellman, Peter. *The Auschwitz Album: A Book Based Upon an Album Discovered by a Concentration Camp Survivor, Lili Meier*. New York: Random House, 1981. Hellman's work is a photographic record of the largest of the death camps.

Kogon, Eugen. *The Theory and Practice of Hell: The German Concentration Camps and the System Behind Them*. Los Angeles: Octagon, 1973. Originally written shortly after the war, *The Theory of Practice of Hell* is an adult book that has influenced many later studies.

Leitner, Isabella. *The Big Lie: A True Story*. New York: Scholastic, 1992. *The Big Lie* describes the author's experiences in Auschwitz.

Levi, Primo. *The Drowned and the Saved*. Tempe, AZ: Summit Books, 1988. This is a memoir of the Italian Jewish chemist who survived Auschwitz.

Levi, Primo. *Survival in Auschwitz*. New York: Macmillan, 1987. *Survival in Auschwitz* is Levi's adult work that chronicles his daily activities at the death camp.

Lifton, Robert Jay. *The Nazi Doctors: Medical Killing and the Psychology of Genocide*. New York: Basic Books, 1988. *The Nazi Doctors* is an adult work that discusses the role of the medical profession, including medical experimentation, in the Final Solution.

Millu, Liana. *Smoke Over Birkenau.* Philadelphia: Jewish Publication Society, 1991. *Smoke Over Birkenau* describes the lives of women prisoners at Auschwitz-Birkenau.

Reitlinger, Gerald. *The SS: Alibi of a Nation, 1922–45.* New York: Viking, 1957. Reitlinger's book looks at the SS, the military wing of the Nazi Party

Rubinstein, William D. *The Myth of Rescue.* New York: Routledge, 1997. *The Myth of Rescue* strongly defends Allied war policies, and argues that actions such as bombing Auschwitz were either impossible or useless. This book is probably too specialized for most young readers.

Stein, R. Conrad. *Invasion of Russia.* Danbury, CT: Children's Press, 1985. Despite its title, Stein's work is not limited to military events.

Steiner, Jean Francis. *Treblinka.* New York: Simon & Schuster, 1967. *Treblinka* is an adult work describing the Treblinka uprising.

Stern, Ellen Norman. *Elie Wiesel: Witness for Life.* New York: Ktav Publishing House, 1982. Stern's biography tells of the life of the Nobel Peace Prize-winning author, who survived Auschwitz and Buchenwald as a child.

Weisel, Elie. *The Night Trilogy: Night, Dawn, The Accident.* New York: Hill & Wang 1960, reprinted 1987. *The Night Trilogy* contains three autobiographical books, written for adults, about the Auschwitz and Buchenwald concentration camps.

Willenberg, Samuel. *Surviving Treblinka.* Maldin, MA: Basil Blackwell, 1989. Although *Surviving Treblinka* is aimed at general audiences, the story will also reward younger readers.

Wyman, David S. *The Abandonment of the Jews: America and the Holocaust, 1941–1945.* New York: Pantheon, 1984. Wyman's book is a powerful criticism of American policy toward the issue of saving Jews. It is a specialized book that may be difficult for young readers.

Zyskind, Sara. *Struggle.* Minneapolis, MN: Lerner Publications, 1989. *Struggle* is about Auschwitz.

Poland:

Bernheim, Mark. *Father of the Orphans: The Story of Janusz Korczak*. New York: E.P. Dutton, 1989. *Father of the Orphans* recounts the story of Janusz Korczak, director of the orphanage in the Warsaw ghetto. Korczak and his orphans were deported to the Treblinka death camp, where they were all murdered by the Nazis.

Drucker, Malka, and Michael Halperin. *Jacob's Rescue: A Holocaust Story*. New York: Bantam Skylark, 1993. *Jacob's Rescue* is the story of a Jewish child in Poland.

Gelman, Charles. *Do Not Go Gentle: A Memoir of Jewish Resistance in Poland, 1941–1945*. North Haven, CT: Archon Books, 1989. *Do Not Go Gentle* is the story of a teenage boy who fought as a partisan in Poland.

George, Willy. *In the Warsaw Ghetto, Summer 1941*. New York: Aperture Foundation 1993. *In the Warsaw Ghetto* includes photographs taken secretly by German troops.

Heller, Celia S. *On the Edge of Destruction: Jews of Poland Between the Two World Wars*. New York: Columbia University Press, 1977. Heller's adult work examines Polish Jewish history, sociology, religion, and ideology.

Hyams, Joe. *A Field of Buttercups*. Paramus, NJ: Prentice-Hall, 1968. *A Field of Buttercups* describes the life of Janusz Korczak, the famous Jewish doctor and educator who refused to abandon the children of his Warsaw orphanage.

Keller, Ulrich, ed. *The Warsaw Ghetto in Photographs*. Mineola, NY: Dover, 1984. *The Warsaw Ghetto in Photographs* is based on photographs taken by the Germans in 1941.

Landau, Elaine. *The Warsaw Ghetto Uprising*. New York: Macmillan, 1992. Landau's work concentrates on the story of the rebellion in the Warsaw ghetto.

Sender, Ruth Minsky. *The Cage*. New York: Macmillan, 1986. *The Cage* is an autobiography of Sender, a resident of the Lódz ghetto and a concentration camp survivor.

Sender, Ruth Minsky. *To Life*. New York: Macmillan, 1988. *To Life* picks up where Sender's first autobiography, *The Cage*, leaves off. It describes her liberation at the end of the war, and her search for her family.

Stewart, Gail B. *Life in the Warsaw Ghetto.* San Diego: Lucent Books, 1995. Stewart's book tells the story of the Warsaw ghetto, including the uprising that took place there.

Toll, Nelly S. *Behind the Secret Window: A Memoir of a Hidden Childhood During World War Two.* New York: Dial Books, 1993. *Behind the Secret Window* is the story of a child and her mother hidden by non-Jews in Lwów (Lvov), Poland.

Vishniac, Roman. *A Vanished World.* New York: Farrar, Strauss, & Giroux, 1983. *A Vanished World* uses photographs to describe the world of Poland's Jews before World War II.

Wood, Thomas E. *Karski: How One Man Tried to Stop the Holocaust.* New York: John Wiley, 1994. Wood's adult work discusses some complex political and diplomatic issues, but much of the book is a gripping story about Polish underground officer Jan Karski's attempt to save Poland's Jews.

Ziemian, Joseph. *The Cigarette Seller of Three Crosses Square.* Minneapolis, MN: Lerner Publications, 1975. Ziemian's book describes the life of Jewish children who lived on the "Aryan side" of Warsaw.

Zeinert, Karen. *The Warsaw Ghetto Uprising.* Brookfield, CT: Millbrook Press, 1993.

Other Countries:

Asscher-Pinkoff, Clara. *Star Children.* Detroit: Wayne State University Press, 1986. *Star Children* is the story of children in the Amsterdam ghetto.

Bitton-Jackson, Livia. *I Have Lived a Thousand Years: Growing Up in the Holocaust.* New York: Simon & Schuster, 1997. Bitton-Jackson's memoir discusses her life in Hungary during the Holocaust.

Frank, Anne. *The Diary of Anne Frank.* Edited by Otto Frank. New York: Doubleday, 1952. This first published version of Anne Frank's diary was edited by Frank's father, Otto. He removed some of Frank's criticisms of her mother, who had died at Auschwitz, as well as material that he believed was unsuitable for young people. *The Diary of Anne Frank: The Definitive Edition* (New York: Bantam

Books, 1997) has the sections removed by Otto Frank restored. *The Diary of Anne Frank: The Critical Edition* (New York: Doubleday, 1989) includes additional material about Frank's life before she began writing the diary.

Gies, Miep, and Alison L. Gold. *Anne Frank Remembered.* New York: Simon & Schuster, 1987. *Anne Frank Remembered* is directed at adult readers, but is not too difficult for younger audiences. Gies was the non-Jewish Dutch woman, an employee of Frank's father, who brought the family food in hiding and often spoke with Frank.

Gold, Alison L. *Memories of Anne Frank: Reflections of a Childhood Friend.* New York: Scholastic, 1997. *Memories of Anne Frank* is the story of Frank's closest friend, called "Hanneli," in Frank's diary.

Handler, Andrew, and Susan Meschel, eds. *Young People Speak.* New York: Franklin Watts, 1993. *Young People Speak* includes eleven authors remembering their childhoods in Hungary during the Holocaust.

Isaacman, Clara. *Clara's Story.* Philadelphia: Jewish Publication Society, 1984. Isaacman's work is the story of a child hiding in the Belgium port city of Antwerp.

Lindwe, Willy. *The Last Seven Months of Anne Frank.* New York: Pantheon, 1991. Lindwe's book describes Frank's time at Bergen-Belsen concentration camp, and is based on the recollections of fellow prisoners who survived.

Perl, Lila, and Marian Blumenthal Lazar. *Four Perfect Pebbles: A Holocaust Story.* New York: Greenwillow Books, 1996. *Four Perfect Pebbles* describes a child who survived the Westerbork transit camp in the Netherlands and then the Bergen-Belsen concentration camp.

Rol, Ruud van der, and Rian Verhoeven. *Anne Frank: Beyond the Diary.* New York: Viking, 1993. *Anne Frank: Beyond the Diary* describes the life of Frank and her family before they went into hiding.

Roth-Hano, Renée. *Touch Wood: A Girlhood in Occupied France.* Portland, OR: Four Winds Press, 1988. Although *Touch Wood* is a nonfiction work, it is written in the style of a novel. The work tells the story of Roth-Hano and her two sisters, who were French Jews hidden in a Catholic convent during Germany's occupation of France.

Siegal, Avanka. *Grace in the Wilderness: After the Liberation, 1945–1948*. New York: Farrar, Strauss, Giroux, 1985. *Grace in the Wilderness* describes Hungarian Jew Siegal's postwar experience.

Siegal, Avanka. *Upon the Head of the Goat: A Childhood in Hungary, 1939–1944*. New York: Farrar, Strauss, Giroux, 1981. Siegal's *Upon the Head of the Goat* is a prize-winning memoir about surviving the Bergen-Belsen concentration camp.

Resistance, survival, rescue, and justice:

Arendt, Hannah. *Eichmann in Jerusalem: A Report on the Banality of Evil*. New York: Penguin, 1977. Arendt's highly controversial work focuses on the "ordinariness" of Adolf Eichmann, the architect of the "Final Solution."

Ayer, Eleanor A. *The United States Holocaust Memorial Museum*. Parsippany, NJ: Silver Burdett Press, 1995. Ayer's book provides a detailed description of the museum and its exhibits.

Bauer, Yehuda. *They Chose Life: Jewish Resistance in The Holocaust*. New York: American Jewish Committee, 1973. Bauer, a major Holocaust scholar, aimed *They Chose Life* at middle-school age readers.

Berenbaum, Michael. *The World Must Know*. Boston: Little, Brown, 1993. *The World Must Know* uses the United States Holocaust Memorial Museum's collection to describe the history of the Holocaust.

Bierman, John. *Righteous Gentile: The Story of Raoul Wallenberg*. New York: Viking, 1981. Bierman's book looks at the life of Wallenberg, a young Swedish diplomat who saved at least 100,000 Hungarian Jews before he disappeared after World War II.

Block, Gay, and Malka Drucker. *Rescuers*. New York: Holmes and Meier, 1992. *Rescuers* includes the stories of four dozen different people, from all over Europe, who hid and saved Jews.

Gilbert, G.M. *Nuremberg Diary*. New York: New American Library, 1947, reprinted New York: Da Capo Press, 1995. *Nuremberg Diary*, originally published soon after the events, was written by Gilbert, the psychologist at the Nuremberg jail during the main trial. The author had complete freedom of access to the defendants and was able to engage in a series of remarkable conversations with them. The book is written for adults and includes some specialized psychological language, but large parts of it provide fascinating and understandable insights into the minds of the top Nazis.

Greenfield, Howard. *The Hidden Children.* New York: Ticknor & Fields, 1993. Greenfield's work describes the experiences of thirteen children hidden by strangers.

Haas, Gerda. *These I Do Remember: Fragments From the Holocaust.* Brooklyn, NY: Cumberland, 1982. *These I Do Remember* consists of excerpts of diaries, letters, and eyewitness accounts of the Holocaust from people all over Europe.

Hausner, Gideon. *Justice in Jerusalem.* New York: Harper & Row, 1966. *Justice in Jerusalem* describes the Adolf Eichmann trial from the viewpoint of the chief prosecutor.

Holliday, Laurel. *Children in the Holocaust and World War II.* New York: Pocket Books, 1995. Holliday's work includes excepts from twenty-two diaries kept by children during the Holocaust, some of whom were killed.

Keneally, Thomas. *Schindler's List.* New York: Simon & Schuster, 1982. Keneally's work, written for adults, is the book on which the award-winning film by Steven Spielberg is based.

Landau, Elaine. *Nazi War Criminals.* New York: Franklin Watts, 1990. *Nazi War Criminals* concerns the escape of wanted Nazis after the war, and the hunt for them.

Landau, Elaine. *We Survived the Holocaust.* New York: Franklin Watts, 1991. *We Survived the Holocaust* includes sixteen stories of survivors.

Linnea, Sharon. *Raoul Wallenberg: The Man Who Stopped Death.* Philadelphia: Jewish Publication Society, 1993. This is a biography of Wallenberg, who saved approximately 100,000 Hungarian Jews from death at the hands of the Nazis.

Meltzer, Milton. *Rescue: The Story of How Gentiles Saved Jews in the Holocaust.* New York: Harper & Row, 1988. Meltzer's book contains chapters on Oskar Schindler and the rescue of the Danish Jews.

Mochizuki, Ken. *Passage to Freedom: The Sugihara Story.* New York: Lee & Low Books, 1997. *Passage to Freedom* is the story of Chiune Sugihara, a Japanese diplomat in Kovno, Lithuania, who defied his government to issue thousands of transit visas to Jews fleeing the Nazis in the summer of 1940.

Morin, Isobel V. *Days of Judgment.* Brookfield, CT: Millbrook Press, 1995. *Days of Judgment* describes the trials of both Nazi and Japanese war criminals after World War II.

Rittner, Carol. *The Courage to Care.* New York: New York University Press, 1986. Rittner's work tells the stories of people who took chances by hiding Jews from the Nazis.

Roberts, Jack L. *Oskar Schindler.* San Diego: Lucent Books, 1996. Robert's biography is of the man who saved tens of thousands of Jews.

Rosenberg, Maxine B. *Hiding to Survive: Stories of Jewish Children Rescued from the Holocaust.* New York: Clarion, 1994. *Hiding to Survive* contains first-person accounts by fourteen Jewish survivors who, as children, were hidden and protected by non-Jews.

Stadtler, Ben. *The Holocaust: A History of Courage and Resistance.* West Orange, NJ: Behrman House, 1974. Stadtler's book discusses the Jewish underground that opposed the Nazis.

Taylor, Teleford. *The Anatomy of the Nuremberg Trials: A Personal Memoir.* New York: Knopf, 1992. Although aimed at adults, *The Anatomy of the Nuremberg Trials* provides a detailed account of the proceedings and the defendants as presented by Taylor, one of the prosecutors at the trials.

Weinberg, Jeshajahu, and Rina Elieli. *The Holocaust Museum in Washington.* New York: Rizzoli, 1995. *The Holocaust Museum in Washington* describes the way the United States Holocaust Memorial Museum was planned and designed to fulfill its purpose.

Fiction Works:

Boraks-Nemetz, Lillian. *The Old Brown Suitcase: A Teenager's Story of War and Peace.* Port Angeles, WA: Ben-Simon Publications, 1994. *The Old Brown Suitcase* tells the story of Slava and her family, who immigrate to Canada from Poland after World War II. As Slava adjusts to her new life, she struggles with her memories of her life in Warsaw before the war, in the ghetto, and in hiding.

Kerr, M. E. *Gentlehands.* New York: HarperCollins, 1978, reprinted Harper Keypoint, 1990. In *Gentlehands,* Buddy Boyle moves in with his grandfather against his parents' wishes, only to discover a terrible secret. Buddy's grandfather was a Nazi official, known as "Gentlehands" by his victims at Auschwitz because he toyed with the emotions of his victims before executing them.

Lowry, Lois. *Number the Stars.* New York: Houghton-Mifflin, 1989. *Number the Stars* is the story of a Danish family who risks their lives by taking in a young Jewish girl and pretending that she is part of their family.

Marvin, Isabel R. *Bridge to Freedom.* Philadelphia: Jewish Publication Society, 1991. *Bridge to Freedom* is the story about Rachel, a young Jewish girl escaping from the Nazis, and Kurt, a fifteen-year-old deserter from the German army. The two become allies as they try to make their way to Belgium and freedom.

Matas, Carol. *Daniel's Story.* New York: Scholastic, 1993. *Daniel's Story* is a fictionalized account based on actual events that children experienced during the Holocaust. It was published in conjunction with "Daniel's Story: Remember the Children," an exhibit at the United States Holocaust Memorial Museum.

Matas, Carol. *Lisa's War.* New York: Scholastic, 1987. *Lisa's War* is the story of thirteen-year-old Lisa, a Jewish girl living in Denmark. After the Germans invade her country and start deporting Jews, Lisa and her bother Stefan become involved in the Resistance.

Orlev, Uri. *The Man From the Other Side.* Translated from the Hebrew by Hillel Halkin. New York: Houghton Mifflin, 1989. In *The Man From the Other Side,* fourteen-year-old Marek, a Catholic, helps to hide a Jewish man from the

Warsaw ghetto. When the uprising occurs, Marek returns to the ghetto with the man to help in the fighting.

Provost, Gary, and Gail Levine-Provost. *David and Max.* Philadelphia: Jewish Publication Society, 1988. *David and Max,* winner of the 1994 National Jewish Book Award, tells the story of David, who spends the summer with his grandfather Max and learns about the horrors of the Holocaust.

Vos, Ida. *Hide and Seek.* Translated by Terese Edelstein and Inez Smidt. New York: Houghton Mifflin, 1981. In *Hide and Seek,* Rachel, a young Jewish girl, tells the story of her family's life in Holland during the German occupation.

Wolff, Virginia Euwer. *The Mozart Season.* New York: Henry Holt, 1991. In *The Mozart Season,* Allegra Shapiro, the youngest competitor in a violin competition, must not only struggle with her music, but also wrestle with her family history as she learns about her great-grandmother, who died in the Treblinka death camp.

Yolen, Jane. *Devil's Arithmetic.* New York: Viking Penguin, 1988. *Devil's Arithmetic* tells the story of Hannah, who is taken back in time during a Passover dinner to her grandfather's village in the 1940s. Soon after she arrives, Hannah and the rest of the Jews of the village are transported to a concentration camp, where every moment is a struggle to survive.

Holocaust Organizations:

There are hundreds of Holocaust organizations throughout the world. We have listed some of the more popular ones here.

ADL Braun Holocaust Institute
823 United Nations Plaza
New York, NY 10017
(212) 885-7804
Web: http://www.adl.org

El Paso Holocaust Museum and Study Center
401 Wallenberg Drive
El Paso, TX 79912
(915) 833-5656
Web: http://www.huntel.com/~hts/holocst.html

Holocaust Education and Memorial Centre of Toronto
4600 Bathurst Street
North York, Ontario
Canada M2R 3V2
(416) 631-5689
Web: http://www.feduja.org

Holocaust Museum Houston
5401 Caroline Street
Houston, TX 77004
(713) 942-8000
Web: http://www.hmh.org

Simon Wiesenthal Center/Museum of Tolerance
9760 West Pico Boulevard
Los Angeles, CA 90035
(310) 553-9036
Web: http://www.wiesenthal.com

Southern Institute for Education and Research
    at Tulane University
Tulane University
MR Box 1692
31 McAlister Drive
New Orleans, LA 70118
(504) 865-6100
Web: http://www.tulane.edu/~so-inst

Tampa Bay Holocaust Memorial Museum
    and Education Center
5001-11th Street
Madeira Beach, FL 33708
(813) 393-4678
Web: http://www.tampabayholocaust.org

United States Holocaust Memorial Museum
100 Raoul Wallenberg Pl., SW
Washington, D.C. 20024
(202) 488-0400
Web: http://www.ushmm.org

Yad Vashem
The Holocaust Martyrs' and Heroes' Remembrance Authority
PO Box 3477
Jerusalem, Israel 91034
972-2-6751611
Web: http://www.yad-vashem.org.il

Picture Credits

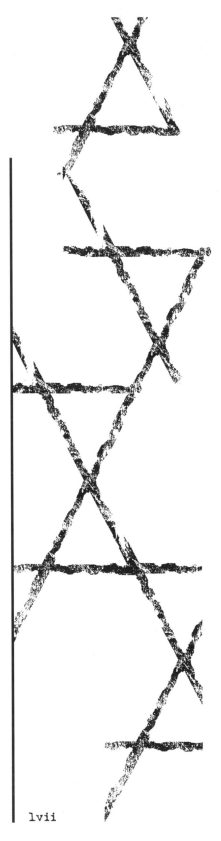

Photographs and illustrations appearing in *Understanding the Holocaust* were received from the following sources:

Cover photo courtesy of the USHMM Photo Archives.

Bildarchiv Preussischer Kulturbesitz. Reproduced by permission: pp. 3, 17, 29, 32, 42, 52, 54, 57, 104, 163, 175, 183, 185, 204, 307, 352, 388; **Foto Marburg/Art Resource. Reproduced by permission:** pp. 13, 15, 49, 101; **AP/Wide World Photos. Reproduced by permission:** pp. 20, 44, 79, 86, 93, 103, 105, 107, 109, 125, 153, 179, 193, 196, 280, 297, 361, 363, 380, 383, 399, 407; **Snark/Art Resource. Reproduced by permission:** pp. 28, 30, 99, 127, 172, 376; **USHMM Photo Archives:** pp. 56, 61, 65, 67, 69, 82, 83, 140, 144, 148, 156, 214, 215, 218, 223, 230, 248, 260, 261, 303, 329, 348, 357, 365, 367, 372, 397; **National Archives/USHMM Photo Archives:** pp. 63, 71, 76, 78, 168, 174, 319, 359, 366; **The Library of Congress/USHMM Photo Archives:** pp. 73, 195; **Photograph by Henry Grossman:** p. 85; **William Gallagher Collection/USHMM Photo Archives. Reproduced by permission:** p. 96; **Stadtarchive Nuerenberg/USHMM Photo Archives. Reproduced**

by permission: p. 112; Lena Fagen/USHMM Photo Archives. Reproduced by permission: p. 118; Trudy Isenberg/ USHMM Photo Archives: p. 122; Photograph by Raimund Tisch. USHMM Photo Archives: p. 129; Main Commission for the Investigation of Nazi War Crimes/USHMM Photo Archives. Reproduced by permission: pp. 131, 241, 243, 245, 266, 267, 268; Photograph by Paul Mix. USHMM Photo Archives: p. 133; Rafal Imbro Collection/USHMM Photo Archives. Reproduced by permission: p. 134; YIVO Institute for Jewish Research/USHMM Photo Archives: pp. 137, 270; Amalia Petranker Salsitz Collection/USHMM Photo Archives. Reproduced by permission: p. 151; National Archives in Krakow/USHMM Photo Archives. Reproduced by permission: pp. 159, 215; Irving Milchberg/USHMM Photo Archives: p. 165; Photograph by Heinrich Hoffmann. USHMM Photo Archives: p. 180; State Archives of the Russian Federation/USHMM Photo Archives. Reproduced by permission: p. 187; UPI/Corbis-Bettmann. Reproduced by permission: p. 189; Hessiches Hauptstaatsarchiv/ USHMM Photo Archives. Reproduced by permission: pp. 198, 209; The Library of Congress: pp. 203, 311, 317, 339; Bilderdienst Suddeutscher Verlag. Reproduced by permission: p. 208; Trudi Gidan Collection/USHMM Photo Archives. Reproduced by permission: pp. 217, 227, 304, 337; Photograph by Raimund Tisch. Professor Leopold Pfefferberg-Page Collection/USHMM Photo Archives. Reproduced by permission: p. 221; Photograph by Bernhard Walter. Yad Vashem Photo Archives/USHMM Photo Archives: pp. 225, 235, 252, 344; National Museum in Majdanek/USHMM Photo Archives. Reproduced by permission: p. 232; Photograph by Stanislaw Luczko. Main Commission for the Investigation of Nazi War Crimes/USHMM Photo Archives. Reproduced by permission: p. 249; Archiwum Akt Nowych/USHMM Photo Archives. Reproduced by permission: p. 255; Hadassah Rosensaft Collection/ USHMM Photo Archives. Reproduced by permission: p. 258; State Museum of Auschwitz-Birkenau/USHMM Photo Archives. Reproduced by permission: p. 265; Jerzy Ficowksi/USHMM Photo Archives: p. 272; Yad Vashem Photo Archives/USHMM Photo Archives. Reproduced by permission: p. 276; Central State Archive of Film, Photo and Phonographic Documents/ USHMM Photo Archives. Reproduced by permission: p. 277; Photograph by Fritz

Melbach. USHMM Photo Archives: p. 279; **Photograph by William Newhouse. USHMM Photo Archives**: p. 281; Government Press Office, Jerusalem/USHMM Photo Archives: p. 286; Frihedsmuseet/ USHMM Photo Archives. Reproduced by permission: p. 292; Toni Heller Collection/ USHMM Photo Archives. Reproduced by permission: p. 295; Henny Kalkstein Reemy Collection/USHMM Photo Archives. Reproduced by permission: p. 306; Photograph by R. Peron. Snark/Art Resource. Reproduced by permission: p. 314; French Embassy Press and Information Division: p. 316; Photograph by Alice Resch-Synnestvedt. USHMM Photo Archives: p. 321; Archive Photos/Popperfoto. Reproduced by Permission: p. 325; Corbis-Bettmann. Reproduced by permission: p. 330; Art Resource. Reproduced by permission: p. 335; Photograph by E.M. Robinson. Alice Lev Collection/USHMM Photo Archives. Reproduced by permission: p. 389; Janina Zimnowodzki/ USHMM Photo Archives: p. 391; Hulton-Getty/The Gamma Liaison Network. Reproduced by permission: p. 378; Archive Photos, Inc. Reproduced by permission: p. 401.

Index

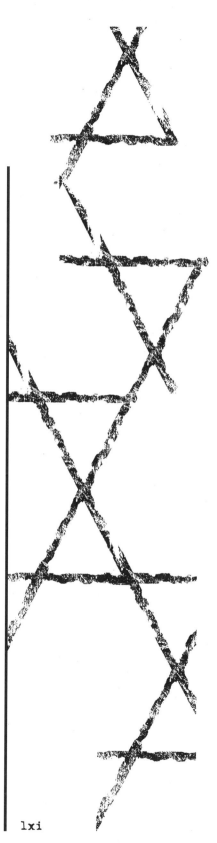

Italic indicates volume numbers;
(ill.) indicates illustrations.

A

Academy Awards
    See Oscar
Africa *1:* 55
fighting in World War II *1:* 179
Air Force, British
and immigration to Palestine *1:* 87
Air Force, German
    See *Luftwaffe*
AK
    See Home Army
Aktion Reinhard
    See Operation Reinhard
Aktions 1: 194
    of *Einsatzgruppen 1:* 192
Allied armies *2:* 350
Allies
    German attempts to split *2:* 346
    relations among *2:* 345-46
    World War I *1:* 13, 21
Alsace *1:* 20; *2:* 316
Altona
    gun battle in *1:* 48
American Jewish Joint Distribution Committee *2:* 345
Amsterdam *2:* 296, 408
    Jewish population of *2:* 296
    strike in (February 1941) *2:* 299, 301
Anielewicz, Mordechai *1:* 163, 163 (ill.)
Anne Frank House *2:* 408
Anscluss 1: 105 (ill.), 106
Anti-Christian ideas of Nazis *1:* 36, 96
Anti-Communism
    of Hitler *1:* 179
Anti-Jewish Boycott *1:* 61 (ill.), 64, 67 (ill.)
Anti-Jewish Laws *1:* 67, 74
    Catholic Church *2:* 392

France *2:* 332

Hungary *2:* 339-40

Anti-Nazi boycott *1:* 62

Antisemitic campaigns

Poland *2:* 396

Antisemitic laws *1:* 58

France *2:* 320, 326

Italy *2:* 336

Antisemitism *1:* 6

and Babi Yar monument *1:* 199

in Baltic States *1:* 189

in Eastern Europe *2:* 215

in France *2:* 311, 315 (ill.), 321

in Hungary *2:* 339-40

in Italy *2:* 335

in Lithuania *1:* 195

in Netherlands *2:* 295

in Poland *2:* 396

in Polish underground *1:* 149

in Ukraine *1:* 189

in United States *1:* 81

opposition to *2:* 302

Appeasement *1:* 108

Arabs *1:* 85

"Arbeit Macht Frei" *2:* 267, 267 (ill.)

Archives in Warsaw ghetto

See *Oneg Shabbath*

Argentina *2:* 369-70

Armistice *1:* 15

Franco-German (1940) *2:* 317

Arms production *1:* 102

Army, American *1:* 90; *2:* 281

and invasion of Italy *2:* 337

Army, British *2:* 280-81

and invasion of Italy *2:* 337

evacuation of army from France *2:* 316

Army, French

defeat by Germany *2:* 316

Jews in *2:* 316

Army, German *1:* 115

and genocide *1:* 185

and storm troopers *1:* 50, 92

attitude towards storm troopers *1:* 45

in France *2:* 323

in Netherlands *2:* 301

occupation of Italy by *2:* 337

role in attacks on Jews in Poland *1:* 123 (ill.), 124

shooting of hostages in France *2:* 323

Army, Polish *1:* 115

Army, Soviet *1:* 136

and counter-offensives against Germans *1:* 210

and Lodz ghetto *1:* 141-42

invasion of Poland *1:* 116

Arrow Cross Party *2:* 340, 343, 369

Aryans *1:* 6, 38, 72-73

Aryanization *1:* 79
    France *2:* 321
    Poland *1:* 128
Ashkenazic *1:* 2
Assimilation *1:* 4; *2:* 387
Atomic bomb *1:* 80
Au Revoir les Enfants 2: 406
Auschwitz *1:* 142, 203, 205, 211; *2:* 218, 243 (ill.), 248 (ill.),
    266 (ill.), 267 (ill.), 268 (ill.), 293-94, 309, 329 (ill.)
    as symbol of Holocaust *2:* 239
    concentration camp opened *2:* 240
    death march *2:* 278
    demolition of *2:* 276
    deportation of French Jews to *2:* 323-24
    deportations from Hungary to *2:* 344, 344 (ill.)
    deportations of Jews to *2:* 251
    diseases at *2:* 266
    Dutch Jews at *2:* 309
    escapes from *2:* 275
    first gassings at *2:* 246
    first prisoners *2:* 240
    food at *2:* 265
    general conditions *2:* 243
    knowledge of *2:* 346
    liberation of *2:* 277 (ill.)
    number of victims *2:* 282
    physical conditions of area *2:* 240
    proposal for bombing of *2:* 346
    sub-camps *2:* 273-74
    trial of personnel *2:* 368
    uprising of *Sonderkommando 2:* 274
Auschwitz II
    See Birkenau
Auschwitz III
    See Monowitz
Austria *1:* 14, 34, 74, 102
    Jewish emigration from *1:* 79
    Jewish refugees from *1:* 88; *2:* 313
    Jews of *1:* 74
    treatment of Jews in *1:* 106
    union with Germany *1:* 105 (ill.), 106
Austrian Empire *1:* 14
Austro-Hungarian Empire *2:* 338
Autobahns *1:* 102

B

Babi Yar *1:* 198 (ill.), 199-200
"Babi Yar" *1:* 199
Baltic States *1:* 200, 210
    annexation by Soviet Union *1:* 189
    attitude towards German invasion *1:* 189
    See also Estonia, Latvia, Lithuania
Bank accounts, Swiss *2:* 392-93
Barbie, Klaus *2:* 370, 377-78, 378 (ill.), 405
Battle of Britain *1:* 177

Bauer, Yehuda *1:* 157
Bavaria *1:* 7, 18, 26, 51, 62
Bavarian People's Party
    dissolution of *1:* 59
    Beer Hall Putsch *1:* 30-32
    defendants of *1:* 30 (ill.)
Belarussia *1:* 103, 179, 197, 200; *2:* 246
    Jewish partisans in *1:* 197
Belarussians *1:* 117
Belgium *2:* 297, 302, 304
    deportations to Auschwitz *2:* 250
    Jewish refugees from *2:* 316
Belski brothers *1:* 197
Belzec *1:* 138, 152, 155, 164, 211; *2:* 402
    discussion of *2:* 221
    physical description of *2:* 228
Ben-Gurion, David *1:* 85 (ill.); *2:* 370
Bergen-Belsen *2:* 258 (ill.), 280-81, 280 (ill.), 352 (ill.)
    trial of guards *2:* 353
Berlin, Germany *1:* 4, 68, 71
    deportations to Auschwitz *2:* 251
    Jewish population in *1:* 4
Biebow, Hans *2:* 369
Big business
    relationship to Nazi Party *1:* 53
The Big Lie *1:* 35, 47
Birkenau *2:* 245, 247, 248 (ill.), 249
Blackshirts
    in Italy *1:* 26; *2:* 334
Blitzkrieg *1:* 188
Block 10 (Auschwitz) *2:* 242, 263
Block 11 (Auschwitz) *2:* 242-44, 246
Blood libel *1:* 5; *2:* 396
"Bloody Night" *1:* 154-55
Blum, Léon *2:* 311-12, 311 (ill.)
Boehm, Alfred *2:* 236
Bohemia *1:* 107; *2:* 360
    See Czechoslovakia, Czech Republic
Bolivia *2:* 377
Bonhoeffer, Dietrich *1:* 99
Book burnings *1:* 47
Bordeaux, France *2:* 315
Bormann, Martin *2:* 357
Bosnia *2:* 400
Bosnian Muslims *2:* 399 (ill.), 400
Brack, Victor *1:* 202
Brand, Joel *2:* 345
Bradley, Omar *2:* 281 (ill.)
Brand mission *2:* 345
Brando, Marlon *2:* 406
Brandt, Karl *1:* 110 (ill.)
Breslau, Poland *1:* 4
Britain *1:* 165
Browning, Christopher R. *2:* 222-23
Brownshirts *2:* 334
Brundage, Avery *1:* 72

Buchenwald *1:* 114; *2:* 214 (ill.), 281 (ill.), 400
Budapest, Hungary *2:* 340, 342, 348
    Jews in *2:* 339
Bund *1:* 163-64; *2:* 387
   in Warsaw ghetto *1:* 150
Bunker 1 (Birkenau) *2:* 247
Bunker 2 (Birkenau) *2:* 247
Bunkers, underground
    Warsaw ghetto *1:* 170-71

C

Canada *2:* 259
"Canada" *2:* 259, 268
Carbon monoxide *1:* 111; *2:* 246
Catholic Church *1:* 10, 97
    anti-Jewish teachings *2:* 398
    antisemitism in early *1:* 5
    changes in liturgy *2:* 398
    France *2:* 311, 378, 391
    hiding of Jews by *2:* 338
    Netherlands *2:* 302
    Center Party *1:* 19
    dissolution of *1:* 59
Chamberlain, Neville *1:* 108, 109 (ill.)
Charlemagne *1:* 95
Chelmno *1:* 137-38, 140, 151, 155, 205, 211; *2:* 219
    deportation of Roma to *1:* 139
Children
    at Auschwitz *2:* 243 (ill.), 329 (ill.)
    deportation from Lódz ghetto *1:* 140
    in Warsaw ghetto *1:* 148-49, 158
Children, French Jewish
    deportation to Auschwitz *2:* 323
Children's homes
    raids on by SS in France *2:* 329
Children's Memorial Garden (Yad Vashem) *2:* 408
Chirac, Jacques *2:* 333, 390
Christianity *1:* 5, 96
Churches *1:* 96
    Danish *2:* 293
    Hungarian *2:* 341
Churches, Protestant *1:* 98
    Netherlands *2:* 302
Civil rights of Jews
    in France *2:* 311
Clauberg, Claus *2:* 264
Clergymen *1:* 91
Clift, Montgomery *2:* 406
Coal *1:* 9
Cold War *2:* 364
Collaboration *2:* 318, 327
Collaborators *2:* 329, 332
    in France *2:* 318, 319 (ill.)
    trials and executions of *2:* 332
Cologne, Germany *1:* 4, 9

Commissar Order *1:* 184; *2:* 358
Communist Party *1:* 12, 90
    arrest of leaders *1:* 54
    banning of *1:* 58
    in France *2:* 311
Communists *2:* 246
    Jewish *1:* 150, 163
    Polish *1:* 162
    Soviet *1:* 179
Concentration camps *1:* 55, 74, 77; *2:* 217, 230 (ill.), 260 (ill.)
    and euthanasia program *1:* 113
    as punishment for opposing antisemitism *2:* 302
    educated Poles sent to *1:* 121, 186
    general conditions *2:* 240
Concordat *1:* 97
Confessing Church *1:* 98-99
Conservative parties *1:* 53
    deal with Hitler *1:* 51
Copenhagen, Denmark *2:* 288, 291-92
Coughlin, Charles *1:* 81
Council for Assistance and Rescue
    See *Vaadah*
Cracow (Poland) ghetto
    See Kraków (Poland) ghetto
Crematoria *2:* 258 (ill.)
    at Auschwitz *2:* 246, 250, 256
    in euthanasia program *1:* 111
Crimes against humanity *2:* 355
Crimes against peace *2:* 355
Criminals
    in concentration camps *2:* 240
Croatia, Yugoslavia *2:* 400
Crystal Night
    See *Kristallnacht*
Cuba *1:* 83
Czar, Russian *1:* 11-12
    and pogroms *1:* 190
Czechoslovakia *1:* 34, 74, 106, 207; *2:* 216, 219, 293, 360
    Hungarian seizure of territory from *2:* 341
    Jewish refugees from *2:* 313
Czech Republic *2:* 360
Czerniaków, Adam *1:* 157

D

Dachau *1:* 56 (ill.), 90, 91 (ill.); *2:* 218 (ill.), 242, 270
Daladier, Edouard *1:* 109 (ill.)
The Damned 2: 406
Day of Atonement
    SeeYom Kippur
D-Day *2:* 308, 330 (ill.), 331
    effect in Lodz ghetto *1:* 142
Death camps *1:* 155; *2:* 216, 235 (ill.)
    and Dutch Jews *2:* 301
    arrival at *2:* 225 (ill.)
    knowledge of *2:* 326

Death march *2:* 279 (ill.)
    Auschwitz *2:* 278
    Hungary *2:* 348
De Gaulle, Charles *2:* 317, 317 (ill.), 331
Demanjuk, John *2:* 379-80, 380 (ill.)
Denazification *2:* 353-54
Denmark *1:* 206; *2:* 288, 291, 293-94
Department stores *1:* 34, 62
Deportations *1:* 156 (ill.); *2:* 223 (ill.), 227 (ill.)
    from Hungary *2:* 342, 344, 347
    from Netherlands *2:* 300 (ill.), 303
    from Polish ghettos *1:* 136, 139, 141; *2:* 217 (ill.)
    from Warsaw ghetto *1:* 156, 158
The Deputy *2:* 401
Der Stürmer *2:* 359, 359 (ill.)
De Sica, Vittorio *2:* 406
"Destruction through work" *2:* 265-66, 273
Detention camps
    in France *2:* 321, 330
The Diary of Anne Frank *2:* 404
    See Frank, Anne *2:* 309
Discrimination against Jews
    in nineteenth century *1:* 2
Displaced persons *2:* 389
Dmytryk, Edward *2:* 406
Doctors
    at Auschwitz *2:* 253, 263
    Jewish *1:* 68
Dönitz, Karl *2:* 359
Drancy transit camp *2:* 322-24, 331, 379, 392
Drexler, Anton *1:* 28
Dreyfus, Alfred *2:* 312
The Drowned and the Saved *2:* 401
Dutch
    See Netherlands *2:* 295

E

Eastern Europe
    antisemitism in *2:* 215
East Germany *2:* 364
Ebert, Friedrich *1:* 17
Economy
    in German *1:* 40
Eichmann, Adolf *1:* 181, 203 (ill.), 204-05; *2:* 343 (ill.), 376
    and Brand mission *2:* 347
    and forced emigration *1:* 181, 203; *2:* 371
    and genocide *1:* 203
    in Hungary *2:* 343, 348
    trial of *2:* 369, 376 (ill.)
Eichmann trial *2:* 369-77, 372 (ill.)
    effect on Israel *2:* 390
Einsatzgruppe A *1:* 193, 195, 200
Einsatzgruppe B *1:* 197
Einsatzgruppe D *1:* 188, 194, 195 (ill.); *2:* 351

Einsatzgruppen 1: 120, 128, 186, 200
    at Nuremberg trials *2:* 367
    composition of *1:* 186
    in Poland *1:* 120, 186
    in Soviet Union *1:* 187 (ill), 192
    leadership of *1:* 188
    mass shootings by *1:* 120, 186, 195 (ill.), 208, 209 (ill.)
    training of *1:* 186
Einstein, Albert *1:* 80, 80 (ill.)
Eisenhower, Dwight *2:* 281 (ill.)
Elections
    1924 *1:* 41
    1928 *1:* 40-41
    1930 *1:* 44
    1932 *1:* 46, 48-50
    1933 *1:* 52
    state *1:* 50
Emergency decree *1:* 54
Emigration
    forced *1:* 201, 205
    Jewish *1:* 68, 79
Enabling Act *1:* 57
England
    expulsion of Jews *1:* 5
Erenhalt, Sara *2:* 279
Essen, Germany *1:* 23
Estonia *1:* 36, 179, 210
"Ethnic cleansing" *2:* 400
Ethnic Germans *1:* 118, 132
Euthanasia program *1:* 108; *2:* 220
    and concentration camps *1:* 113
    authorization of *1:* 112 (ill.)
    protests against *1:* 111
    starvation in *1:* 113
    use of crematoria in *1:* 111
    use of gas chambers in *1:* 111
Evian Conference *1:* 81-82, 82 (ill)
Extreme nationalists *1:* 26, 36

F

Family camps
Auschwitz *2:* 269
    in Soviet Union *1:* 197
Fareynegte Partizaner Organizatsye
    See FPO
Fascism *1:* 26; *2:* 334, 336
Fascist Party *1:* 25; *2:* 334
Fascists
    arrests of Jews by *2:* 338
    in France *2:* 311
    in Italy *1:* 26; *2:* 334
    in Spain *2:* 336
    lack of antisemitism *2:* 335
Federal Republic of Germany
    See West Germany

Feiner, Leon *1:* 164-65
"Final Solution" *1:* 154, 200; *2:* 216, 246, 371
     conflict with German war effort *1:* 208; *2:* 224
     in France *2:* 323, 325
     knowledge of *2:* 383
Fischer, Ludwig *2:* 368
Flick Case *2:* 365
Forced emigration *1:* 205
Forced labor
     Hungary *2:* 341
Ford, Henry *1:* 11, 81
Fort Number Nine (Kovno) *1:* 197
Fort Number Seven (Kovno) *1:* 196
FPO *1:* 197
France *1:* 12, 14-15, 21-22; *2:* 220, 297, 311, 313, 316, 319-20, 322, 326,
     330, 390-91
     attitude of population during occupation *2:* 318
     defeat by Germany *2:* 316
     deportations to Auschwitz *2:* 250
     expulsion of Jews *1:* 5
     immigration to *1:* 85
     Jewish immigrants in *1:* 85
     Jewish victims of Holocaust in *2:* 333
     Jews in Italian-occupied areas of *2:* 336
     surrender of *1:* 177
     trials of collaborators *2:* 369
Frank, Anne *2:* 404 (ill.)
     arrest of *2:* 308
     death of *2:* 309
     diary of *2:* 309
     family of *2:* 307
     hiding of *2:* 307 (ill.)
Frankfurt, Germany *1:* 4, 9-10
Frank, Hans *1:* 118 (ill.), 119; *2:* 359
     trial of *2:* 357
Frank, Margot *2:* 307
Frank, Otto *2:* 307, 309
Free Corps *1:* 16, 17 (ill.), 26, 29, 51; *2:* 242
Free French Party *2:* 317, 331
Freikorps
     See Free Corps
French police *2:* 323, 391
     apology for role in Holocaust *2:* 327
     arrests of Jews by *2:* 337
Frick, Wilhelm *1:* 44 (ill.); *2:* 358
Friedrich, Otto *2:* 239, 253
Fritzsche, Hans *2:* 361
Führer *1:* 28, 94
Funk, Walther *2:* 360

G

Galicia *1:* 131; *2:* 223
Gas chambers *2:* 220, 232 (ill.)
     at Auschwitz *2:* 246, 249 (ill.), 250, 256
     at Majdanek *1:* 203

description of *2:* 230
    in concentration camps *1:* 114
    use in euthanasia program *1:* 111
Gas vans *1:* 205, 211
Gendarmes
    See French police
General Government (Poland) *1:* 118, 125-26, 130-31; *2:* 215
Genocide
    plan for Soviet Union *1:* 182
Gerlier, Pierre *2:* 392
German Communist Party *1:* 18-19
German Democratic Republic
    See East Germany
German Empire
    control of Alsace and Lorraine *2:* 316
Germanic tribes *1:* 25
German Labor Front *1:* 58, 89
German Revolution (1918) *1:* 14
Germans
    knowledge of "Final Solution" *2:* 384
    postwar attitudes towards Holocaust *2:* 382
German Volk *1:* 25
German Workers' Party *1:* 28
Germany
    creation of *2:* 382
    division and occupation of *2:* 350, 364
    effects of Holocaust on *2:* 382
    Jewish refugees from *2:* 313
    unification of *1:* 7
Gestapo *1:* 55, 75, 77, 90, 120, 180, 186, 204; *2:* 243-44, 275, 305
    and immigration to Palestine *1:* 87
    at Nuremberg *2:* 362
Ghettos *1:* 140 (ill.), *2:* 216
    deportations from *1:* 136-37, 139, 141
    in Hungary *2:* 343
    in nineteen century Germany *1:* 2, 3 (ill.)
    in Poland *1:* 125, 127 (ill.), 128, 130, 133, 135-36, 141
    in Soviet Union *1:* 208-09
    liquidation of *1:* 138, 140-42
Gilbert, Martin *2:* 282
Glickman, Marty *1:* 72
Globocnik, Odilo *1:* 203; *2:* 375
Goebbels, Josef *1:* 47, 64, 65 (ill.), 75
    and "destruction through work" *2:* 267
    death of *2:* 351
Goeth, Amon *2:* 368, 402
Gold *2:* 394
Goldhagen, Daniel *2:* 386
Göring, Hermann *1:* 53, 55, 62-63, 77, 79 (ill.), 208; *2:* 357 (ill.)
    and genocide *1:* 201
    trial of *2:* 358
Graebe, Hermann Friedrich *1:* 209
Grass, Günter *2:* 401
Great Britain *1:* 12-14, 20
    immigration to *1:* 85
Great Depression *1:* 41, 101

Great Synagogue (Warsaw)
    destruction of *1:* 176
Greece *2:* 220
    deportations to Auschwitz *2:* 251
Grossen-Wannsee Conference
    See Wannsee Conference
Grynszpan, Hershel *1:* 75, 75 (ill.)
Gurs transit camp *2:* 321 (ill.)
Gutman, Israel *1:* 158
Gypsies
    See Roma

H

Hadamar *1:* 113
Hall of Remembrance (Yad Vashem) *2:* 408
Hamburg, Germany *1:* 4, 9, 83
    gun battle in *1:* 48
    Jewish population in *1:* 4
Havana, Cuba *1:* 83
Hebrew *1:* 6
Heine, Heinrich *1:* 2
Hershy, John *2:* 402
Hess, Rudolf *2:* 257 (ill.)
    trial of *2:* 360
Heydrich, Reinhard *1:* 79, 120, 124-29, 125 (ill.), 181, 200, 202 (ill.), 205, 208; *2:* 216, 219, 360
    and creation of ghettos *1:* 124-25
    and creation of *Judenrat 1:* 126
    and forced emigration *1:* 201
    as head of Nazi Jewish policy *1:* 202
    as head of RSHA *1:* 181
Hiding of Jews
    by Catholic Church *2:* 391 (ill.), 392
    in France *2:* 329
    in Netherlands *2:* 304, 306, 306 (ill.)
High Command (German Army) *2:* 362-63
    at Nuremberg trials *2:* 368
Himmler, Heinrich *1:* 77, 90, 120, 121 (ill.), 155, 181, 205; *2:* 224
    and demolition of gas chambers *2:* 276
    and gas vans *1:* 210
    and invasion of Soviet Union *1:* 180
    and medical experiments *2:* 264
    and Roma (Gypsies) *1:* 139
    and secret contacts with Allies *2:* 347
    and Warsaw ghetto uprising *1:* 171
    death of *2:* 351
    opposition to deportation of Hungarian Jews *2:* 348
    plan for treatment of Poles *1:* 119
    stopping of Hungarian deportations by *2:* 347
    visit to Auschwitz *2:* 244, 245 (ill.)
    visits Treblinka *2:* 232
Hindenburg, Paul von *1:* 45-46, 48, 49 (ill.), 50, 58, 67, 94
    attitude towards Hitler *1:* 45
Hitler, Adolf *1:* 28 (ill.), 109 (ill.), 183 (ill.); *2:* 335 (ill.)
    and "Final Solution" *2:* 224

and genocide *1:* 202-03; *2:* 375

and sterilization of handicapped *1:* 108

background *1:* 27

becomes chancellor *1:* 52, 52 (ill.)

death of *2:* 351

goals of *1:* 60

hatred of France *2:* 311

in Munich *1:* 19

in presidential election (1932) *1:* 46

service in World War I *1:* 27

speaking ability of *1:* 27-28

trial of *1:* 31

Hitler's Willing Executioners" *2:* 386

Hitler-Stalin Pact

See Nazi-Soviet Pact

Hitler Youth *1:* 99-100, 99 (ill.); *2:* 360

Hochuth, Rolf *2:* 401

Holland *2:* 220, 295

deportations to Auschwitz *2:* 250

Holocaust

evidence of *2:* 385

knowledge of *2:* 347

special nature of *2:* 381

survivors of *2:* 389 (ill.), 390, 397 (ill.)

Holocaust 2: 384

Holocaust denial *2:* 382, 385

Holocaust Remembrance Day *2:* 390

Home Army *1:* 149, 161

antisemitism in *1:* 162

relations with Jews *1:* 150

relationship to ZOB *1:* 162

Homosexuals *2:* 260

Horthy, Miklós *2:* 339-40, 339 (ill.), 343

Höss, Rudolf *2:* 240, 242, 246, 256, 278, 282

testimony at Nuremberg *2:* 242

trial of *2:* 242, 368

Hostages

shootings of by SS *2:* 322, 331

Hotel Terminus 2: 405

Hungary *2:* 338, 342-44, 349

at Auschwitz *2:* 258

deportations to Auschwitz *2:* 251

Jews in *2:* 339-40

trials of war criminals *2:* 369

Hunger

in Warsaw ghetto *1:* 149

Hydrogen cyanide

See Zyklon B

Hyper-inflation *1:* 21, 30

I

If This is a Man 2: 401

I.G. Farben *2:* 244-45, 273-74

trial of *2:* 365, 366 (ill.)

Indo-European languages *1:* 6

Indo-Europeans *1:* 38
Industrial Revolution
    in Germany *1:* 9
Industrialists *1:* 95
Inflation *1:* 21, 30
Inside the Third Reich 2: 361
International Military Tribunal *2:* 353
International Red Cross *2:* 270-71
International War Crimes Tribunal *2:* 400
Internet
    use by Holocaust deniers *2:* 385
The Investigation 2: 401
Ireland *1:* 206
Israel *1:* 84; *2:* 370, 375, 380
    founding of *2:* 387
Israelites *2:* 313, 333
Istanbul *2:* 347
Italians
    rescues of Jews by *2:* 338
Italy *1:* 179; *2:* 334
    deportations of Jews from *2:* 337 (ill.), 338
    deportations to Auschwitz *2:* 251
    Jewish victims in *2:* 338
    Jews in parts of France controlled by *2:* 336
    occupation of southeastern France by *2:* 330
    protection of Jews by *2:* 336

J

Jackson, Robert *2:* 356
Japan *1:* 205
Jehovah's Witnesses *2:* 260
Jerusalem *2:* 390, 407
Jewish Coordinating Council *2:* 299
Jewish Council
    See *Joodse Raad*
    See *Judenrat*
Jewish Fighting Organization
    See ZOB
Jewish Fighting Union
    See ZZW
Jewish General Workers Union
    See Bund
Jewish immigration
    to France *2:* 313
    to United States *1:* 80
Jewish Police *1:* 133 (ill.), 134, 142; *2:* 227 (ill.)
    in Warsaw ghetto *1:* 156, 158, 161, 163
Jewish star
    See Star of David
Jewish War Veterans of America *1:* 62
Jews, German *1:* 2; *2:* 388 (ill.)
    in World War I *1:* 13
Jews, Italian *2:* 335
Jews, Soviet
    and ignorance of Nazi antisemitism *1:* 191

Jodl, Alfred *2:* 358
John Paul II, Pope *2:* 398
Joodse Raad 2: 298-301
Judenrat 1: 126-27, 130, 132, 140-41, 155
     in Minsk *1:* 198
     in Warsaw *1:* 145, 151
     relations with Jewish underground *1:* 154
Judgment at Nuremberg 2: 406
Junkers *1:* 8-10, 45, 92
     and anti-Catholicism *1:* 10

K

Kaiser *1:* 14-15, 24, 30, 38, 95
Kállay, Miklós *2:* 342-43
Kaltenbrunner, Ernst *2:* 358
Kapos 2: 240-41
Karski, Jan *1:* 163-64; *2:* 408
Keitel, Wilhelm *1:* 180-81, 185; *2:* 357 (ill.), 358
Kessel, Sim *2:* 253
Kielce ghetto
     ration card from *1:* 134 (ill.)
Kielce, Poland
     pogram in *2:* 396
Kiev, Ukraine *1:* 199, 201
Knudsen, Jorgen *2:* 291
Kolomyja, Ukraine *2:* 223, 225
Kommissarbefehl
     See Commissar Order
Korczak, Janusz *1:* 158
Kosinski, Jerszy *2:* 401
Kovner, Abba *1:* 197
Kovno (Kaunas), Lithuania *1:* 194-95
Kovno ghetto *1:* 196
Kraków (Poland) ghetto *1:* 131 (ill.), 159 (ill.); *2:* 402
     liquidation of *1:* 138
Kremer, Johann *2:* 264
Kristallnacht, 1: 75, 76 (ill.), 87
Krupp von Bohlen, Gustav *2:* 362
Krupp Works *1:* 101 (ill.); *2:* 362

L

Labor camps *1:* 128
     in Netherlands *2:* 302-03
Labor unions
     Nazi takeover of *1:* 58
Landsberg prison *1:* 32 (ill.)
Lanzmann, Claude *2:* 405
Latvia *1:* 179, 210; *2:* 224
Latvian SS auxiliaries *1:* 156, 158
Laval, Pierre *2:* 319, 323, 325, 325 (ill.), 327
     trial and execution of *2:* 332
Lebensraum 1: 102, 117, 179
Legal profession
     Jews in *1:* 62

Leipzig, Germany *1:* 4, 9, 77

Lensky, Mordechai. *1:* 168

Levin, Nora *2:* 316

Levi, Primo *2:* 278, 400-01

Ley, Robert *2:* 362

Lichtenberg, Bernard *1:* 97

Lidice, Czechoslovakia *2:* 219

Liebehenschel, Arthur *2:* 368

Liebknecht, Karl *1:* 14, 16

Lifton, Robert Jay *2:* 263

Lindberg, Charles *1:* 81

Lithuania *1:* 179, 200, 210; *2:* 224
    Jewish partisans in *1:* 197

Lithuanians
    and killings of Jews *1:* 196

"Little red house" *2:* 247

"Little white house" *2:* 247

Lódz ghetto *1:* 130, 133, 133 (ill.), 136, 137 (ill.), 139, 141-42; *2:* 369
    deportation of children from *1:* 140
    deportations to Auschwitz *2:* 217 (ill.), 251

Lódz, Poland *1:* 117-18, 132; *2:* 219, 369

Lubbe, Martinus van der *1:* 52

Lublin (Poland) ghetto *1:* 118, 129, 138, 152, 153 (ill.), 203; *2:* 221

Ludendorff, Erich *1:* 29, 31

Luftwaffe *1:* 55, 115, 177; *2:* 296

Lüger, Karl *1:* 27

Luther, Martin *1:* 5

Luxemburg, Rosa *1:* 16

Lvov (Lwów) ghetto

Lvov (Lwów), Poland *1:* 135; *2:* 221

liquidation of *1:* 138

Lyons, France *2:* 377, 405

M

Madagascar *1:* 119

Madagascar Plan *1:* 119

Main Office for Reich Security *1:* 181; *2:* 343, 358, 370

Majdanek *1:* 203; *2:* 218
    trial of staff *2:* 351

Malle, Louis *2:* 406

Marx, Karl *1:* 2

Mass shootings *2:* 213

Master race *1:* 60

Mauthausen *2:* 280, 303 (ill.)

Medical experiments *2:* 242, 362-63, 370
    on Roma (Gypsies) *1:* 139

Mein Kampf *1:* 31, 33, 108

Mendelssohn-Bartholy, Felix *1:* 2

Mengele, Josef *2:* 264, 265 (ill.), 269, 370

Mercy killing
    See euthanasia program

Middle Ages
    antisemitism in *1:* 5
    persecution of Jews in *1:* 5

Milice *2:* 329, 378, 406
    execution of members of *2:* 332
Minsk, Belarussia *1:* 197-98, 201, 204; *2:* 376
Minsk ghetto *1:* 198
Mitterand, Francois *2:* 332
Monowitz *2:* 245, 273, 365
Moravia, Czechoslovakia *1:* 107; *2:* 360
Moscow, Russia *1:* 36
Moulin, Jean *2:* 378
Müller, Heinrich *1:* 204, 205, 208, 208 (ill.); *2:* 351
Munich Conference *1:* 108, 109 (ill.)
Munich, Germany *1:* 18, 26-27, 74
Mussolini, Benito *1:* 25, 109 (ill.); *2:* 334, 335 (ill.), 336
    and antisemitism *2:* 336
    and protection of Jews in Italian-occupied France *2:* 337
    as head of German puppet government *2:* 338
    overthrow of *2:* 337
Mythology *1:* 25

N

Nacht und Nebel
    See Night and Fog
National Socialism *1:* 37
National Socialist German Workers' Party
    See Nazi Party
Nationalist Party *1:* 53
    dissolution of *1:* 58
Navy, British *1:* 14, 21, 177
    and immigration to Palestine *1:* 87
Navy, French *2:* 320
Navy, German *1:* 14, 20; *2:* 292, 359
Nazi flag *1:* 38
    banning of *2:* 382
Nazi Party
    banned in West Germany *2:* 382
    in late 1920s *1:* 40
    officials *1:* 44 (ill.)
    possibility of split in *1:* 50
    program of *1:* 34, 53
    votes for (1928) *1:* 40
Nazis
    Dutch *2:* 295
    origins of *1:* 28
Nazi-Soviet Pact *1:* 116, 179
Neo-Nazis *2:* 386
Netherlands *2:* 294, 296-97, 304
    deportations to Auschwitz *2:* 250
    German invasion of *2:* 296
    hiding of Jews in *2:* 305-06
    Jewish population of *2:* 296
    Jewish refugees from *2:* 316
    trials of war criminals from *2:* 369
Neurath, Constantin Von *2:* 360
Newspapers *1:* 89

Nazi *1:* 62
        secret *1:* 150, 152, 154
Nice, France *2:* 330
        SS attempts to capture Jews in *2:* 331
Niemöller, Martin *1:* 98
Night 2: 400
Night and Fog 2: 405
"Night and Fog" decree *2:* 358
"Night of Broken Glass"
        See *Kristallnacht*
"The Night of the Long Knives" *1:* 70, 92-93
        Jews and *1:* 96
Nobel Prize *2:* 400-02
Normandy
        American and British landings in *2:* 331
        effect in Lodz ghetto *1:* 142
        invasion of *2:* 308
Norway *2:* 290
        deportations to Auschwitz *2:* 251
Nuremberg, Germany *2:* 354, 383 (ill.)
Nuremberg laws *1:* 69 (ill.), 70
Nuremberg synagogue *2:* 359
Nuremberg trials *2:* 353, 356-57, 357 (ill.), 362-68, 363 (ill),
        364 (ill.), 367 (ill.)

O

Ohlendorf, Otto *1:* 188, 192-93, 193 (ill.); *2:* 367
        postwar testimony *1:* 194; *2:* 367
Olympic Games (1936) *1:* 71, 71 (ill.), 73
Oneg Shabbath 1: 152
One-party state
        law establishing *1:* 59
"Operation Reinhard" *2:* 215
Operations
        See *Aktions*
Ophuls, Marcel *2:* 405
Orphanages
        in Warsaw ghetto *1:* 149, 158
Oscar *2:* 402, 405-06
Oswiecim
        See Auschwitz
O the Chimneys 2: 402
Owens, Jesse *1:* 72, 73 (ill.)

P

The Painted Bird 2: 401
Pakula, Alan J. *2:* 406
Palestine *1:* 83-84, 86 (ill.)
        German Jewish immigration to *1:* 85
        Poland Jewish immigration to *1:* 87
Papen, Franz von
        trial of *2:* 361
Papon, Maurice *2:* 379, 390
Paraguay *2:* 370

Paris, France *1:* 75; *2:* 316, 322
    arrests of foreign Jews in *2:* 323
    liberation of *2:* 331
    resistance uprising in *2:* 331
Partisans *1:* 136
    Jewish *1:* 161, 173, 197
    Soviet Union *1:* 190, 196 (ill.)
Passover *1:* 171
Passports
    of Jews *1:* 88
Patton, George *2:* 281 (ill.)
Pearl Harbor, Hawaii *1:* 205
People's Front
    See Popular Front
Pétain, Henri Phillippe *2:* 316-18, 316 (ill.)
    meeting with Hitler *2:* 319
    trial and imprisonment of *2:* 332
Picasso, Pablo *1:* 106
Piper, Franciszek *2:* 251, 283
Pius XI, Pope *1:* 97
Pius XII, Pope *2:* 401
Plazów labor camp *1:* 129 (ill.); *2:* 369, 402
Pogroms *1:* 6
    in Hungary *2:* 339
    in Kielce *2:* 396
    in Kovno *1:* 194
    in Soviet Union *1:* 190
    in Ukraine *1:* 189
Pohl, Oswald *2:* 365
Poland *1:* 20, 102, 107; *2:* 216
    destruction of *1:* 117
    division of *1:* 117 (ill.)
    German conquest of *1:* 107 (ill.), 115
    Jewish immigration from *1:* 87
    Jewish population of *1:* 115
    postwar *2:* 394, 397
    war crimes trials in *2:* 368
Poles
    gassing of at Auschwitz *2:* 246
    murder of by *Einsatzgruppen 1:* 120
Police State
    beginnings of *1:* 54
    revocation of citizenship of some Jews *2:* 313
Political prisoners *2:* 260
Pope Pius XI
    See Pius XI
Pope Pius XII
    See Pius XII
Popular Front *2:* 311-13, 316
Portugal, Spain *2:* 315
    role of diplomats in Hungary *2:* 348
Prague, Czechoslovakia *1:* 107
Prisoners of war
French *2:* 318
    gassing of *2:* 246

Soviet *2:* 218, 239, 247
    Ukrainian *2:* 220
Propaganda *1:* 47, 64
Protection of German Blood and German Honor Law *1:* 70
Protests
    against euthanasia program *1:* 111
    against anti-Jewish legislation *1:* 63
Protocols of the Elders of Zion 1: 11
Prussia *1:* 7, 48, 55, 92, 95
Pulitzer Prize *2:* 404
Pyranees Mountains
    smuggling of Jews across *2:* 305

Q

Quarantine barracks
    at Auschwitz *2:* 261

R

Race and Resettlement Main Office of SS
    See RuSHA
Racial antisemitism *1:* 6
Racial laws
    See antisemitic laws
Racial theories *1:* 103
    and euthanasia program *1:* 108
Racism, Nazi
    and attitude to Eastern Europe *1:* 179
    and invasion of Soviet Union *1:* 179
    and treatment of conquered Soviet territory *1:* 190
Raeder, Erich *2:* 360
Railroads *1:* 9
Rathenau, Emil *1:* 10
Rathenau, Walter *1:* 14
Rath, Ernst vom *1:* 75
Red Cross
    See International Red Cross
Refugees *1:* 68
    Evian Conference *1:* 82
    Jewish *2:* 292 (ill.), 313, 321, 328
Reich *1:* 94
Reich Central Office for Jewish Emigration *1:* 79
Reich Citizenship Law
    See Nuremberg Laws
Reichenau, Walter von *1:* 185-86, 185 (ill.)
Reichstag *1:* 40, 43-45
Reichstag fire *1:* 52, 54 (ill.), 55
Religion *1:* 5
    Pre-Christian *1:* 25
    Protestant *1:* 5
Religious prejudice *1:* 5
Reparations *2:* 382
Reserve Police
    in Germany *2:* 222
"Resettlement" *1:* 155, 156 (ill.), 192; *2:* 214, 215 (ill.)

Resistance *2:* 331
    in France *2:* 318, 322, 329
    Jewish *1:* 136, 140 (ill.), 173, 160, 197; *2:* 318
Resnais, Alain *2:* 405
Rhineland *1:* 20, 105
    German troops entering *1:* 103
Ribbentrop, Joachim von *2:* 357 (ill.), 358, 360
Ribbentrop-Molotov Pact
    See Nazi-Soviet Pact
Righteous Among the Nations (Yad Vashem) *2:* 315, 408
Ringelblum, Emmanuel *1:* 152
Riots, anti-Jewish
    in Soviet Union *1:* 190
Robota, Róza *2:* 275-76, 276 (ill.)
Röhm, Ernst *1:* 51, 92, 93 (ill.), 95
Roma *1:* 139; *2:* 219, 239, 267, 271-73, 272 (ill.)
    and "destruction through work" *2:* 267
    medical experiments on *2:* 265
Romania *1:* 87, 206; *2:* 251
    Hungarian seizure of territory from *2:* 341
Roosevelt, Franklin D. *1:* 81-82, 101, 166
Rosenberg, Alfred *1:* 36, 96, 96 (ill.)
    trial of *2:* 358
Rotterdam, Holland
    German bombing of *2:* 296, 297 (ill.)
RSHA *1:* 181, 202; *2:* 370
    agreement with German army *1:* 187
Ruhr, Germany *1:* 22-23, 30
Rumkowski, Mordechai *1:* 132-33, 135-38, 140
RuSHA *2:* 366
Russia *1:* 12, 97
    German invasion of *2:* 246
    See also Soviet Union
Russian army *2:* 233, 235, 276
Russian Empire *1:* 179
Russian revolution *1:* 11-12, 36
Rwanda, Africa *2:* 400

S

SA *1:* 29, 29 (ill.), 51, 61, 61 (ill.), 67 (ill.), 68, 75, 90, 92; *2:* 362
    appointed as police officers *1:* 55
    ban on *1:* 47
    growth of *1:* 43
Sachsenhausen *2:* 240, 242
Sachs, Nelly *2:* 402
Saliège, Jules-Gérard *2:* 333, 391
Sauckel, Fritz *2:* 358
Saxony *1:* 7
Schacht, Hjalmar *2:* 361
Schindler, Oskar *2:* 402-03, 403 (ill.), 408
Schindler's List *2:* 402
Schirach, Baldur von *2:* 360
Schlondorff, Volker *2:* 401
Schools
    expulsion of Jews from *1:* 78 (ill); *2:* 300

Schumann, Horst *2:* 264
Scientists
        German *2:* 354
SD *1:* 120, 180, 186
        at Nuremberg trial *2:* 362
Secret police, German
        See Gestapo
Secret police, Soviet *1:* 189
Security Service
        See SD
"Selections"
        at Auschwitz *2:* 252, 252 (ill.), 269
Semites *1:* 6
Semitic languages *1:* 6
Sephardic Jews *1:* 2
Serbia *2:* 400
Serbs *2:* 400
        Massacre by Hungarians *2:* 342
Seyss-Inquart, Artur *2:* 297-98
        trial of *2:* 359
Shaw, Irwin *2:* 406
Shoah *2:* 405
Shootings
        of Jews *1:* 192
Sicherheitsdienst
        See SD
Simon, Adina *2:* 305
Simon, Joachim "Shushu" *2:* 305
Skinheads *2:* 386
Slave labor *1:* 128, 129 (ill.); *2:* 218, 358, 360, 364-65
        at Auschwitz *2:* 273-74
        lack of postwar compensation for *2:* 382
        payment to SS for *2:* 274
        relationship to extermination *1:* 130
Slovakia *1:* 107; *2:* 250, 345
Smugglers
        in Warsaw ghetto *1:* 147-48, 148 (ill.)
Sobibór *1:* 155, 211; *2:* 221
        Dutch Jews at *2:* 309
        physical description of *2:* 228
        uprising *2:* 235
Social Democratic Party *1:* 14-17
        banning of *1:* 58
        votes for (1928) *1:* 40
Socialism *1:* 14
Socialist Party
        in France *2:* 311
Socialists
        Jewish *2:* 387
Sonderkommando *1:* 186; *2:* 256-57, 268, 274
Sophie's Choice *2:* 406
The Sorrow and the Pity *2:* 405
Soup kitchen
        in Germany *1:* 42 (ill.)
Sousa Mendes, Aristides de *2:* 315
South America *2:* 370

Soviet Union *1:* 103, 179
    invasion of *1:* 188
    Jews of *1:* 180
    policy towards Jews *1:* 189
    treaty with Germany *1:* 116
    western conflict with *2:* 364
Spain *1:* 2, 105, 206
    apology for expulsion of Jews *2:* 398
    expulsion of Jews *1:* 5
    role of diplomats in Hungary *2:* 348
    smuggling of Jews to *2:* 305
Spandau Prison, *2:* 361, 361 (ill.)
Spanish Civil War *1:* 105; *2:* 336
    German veterans of *1:* 104
Spartacus League *1:* 14
"Special-action groups"
    See *Einsatzgruppen*
"Special-duty groups"
    See *Einsatzgruppen*
Speer, Albert *2:* 360
Spielberg, Steven *2:* 402
SS *1:* 74, 77, 90, 92, 186; *2:* 216, 224, 240, 241 (ill.), 244
    as "state within a state" *1:* 180
    at Nuremberg trial *2:* 362
    ban on *1:* 47
    in France *2:* 323, 325, 329-31
    in Hungary *2:* 343
    origins of *1:* 39
SS-owned companies *2:* 274
SS *St. Louis 1:* 83, 83 (ill)
Stalin, Joseph *1:* 189, 189 (ill.), 191
Star of David *1:* 144, 144 (ill.); *2:* 291
    in Belgium *2:* 302
    in France *2:* 322
    in Netherlands *2:* 300, 302
Starvation
    in euthanasia program *1:* 113
    in Warsaw ghetto *1:* 149, 164
States, German *1:* 7 (ill.), 58, 165
Steel *1:* 9
Steel production
    in Germany *1:* 40
Sterilization
    of mentally and physically handicapped *1:* 108
    of Roma (Gypsies) *1:* 139
Stoller, Sam *1:* 72
Storm troopers *1:* 16, 29-31, 33, 36, 46, 50-51, 61, 68, 76, 90; *2:* 242, 334
    ban on *1:* 47
    growth of *1:* 40, 43
Strasser, Gregor *1:* 44 (ill.)
Streep, Meryl *2:* 406
Streicher, Julius
    trial of *2:* 359
Stroop, Jürgen *1:* 171-72, 172 (ill.), 175-76; *2:* 369
Styron, William *2:* 406
Sudetenland *1:* 106

Supreme National Court (Poland) *2:* 368, 403
Swastika *1:* 38-39
Sweden *2:* 292, 304, 348
Swiss banks
        Nazi gold in *2:* 394
Switzerland *1:* 88, 206; *2:* 304, 392, 394
        and Jewish refugees *1:* 87
        role of diplomats in Hungary *2:* 348
Synagogues *1:* 74-76
        burning of *1:* 122 (ill.), 123
Szálasi, Ferenc *2:* 369

T

T-4 Program *1:* 110
        authorization of *1:* 112 (ill.)
Tattoos
        at Auschwitz *2:* 261, 261 (ill.)
Terezin
        See Theresienstadt
Theresienstadt *1:* 207; *2:* 269-70, 270 (ill.), 293-94
Third Reich *1:* 95
Thyssen, Fritz *1:* 53
Tiger Hill 1: 87
Times of London 1: 11
The Tin Drum 2: 401
Torah *1:* 123
Torture *2:* 244, 275
        of Jews *1:* 121
Toulouse, France *2:* 333, 392
Touvier, Paul *2:* 378, 390
Tracey, Spencer *2:* 406
Transports
        to Auschwitz *2:* 247
        to death camps *2:* 222
Transylvania, Romania
        Hungarian annexation of *2:* 341
Treaty of Versailles *1:* 26, 33, 102, 105
        areas Germany lost as result of *1:* 20 (ill.)
Treblinka *1:* 138, 155, 157-58, 211; *2:* 221, 368, 380
        physical description of *2:* 228
        uprising *2:* 235, 237
The "Tube" *2:* 229
Tunnels
        in Warsaw ghetto *1:* 170
Turkey *1:* 14
Turks
        attacks on in Germany *2:* 386
Twins *2:* 269
        medical experiments on *2:* 265
Typhus *1:* 145; *2:* 272, 266, 309

U

Ukraine *1:* 103, 199; *2:* 246
        attitude towards German invasion *1:* 189

communist persecution in *1:* 189
pogroms in *1:* 189
Ukrainian guards *2:* 221 (ill.), 222, 229, 237
Ukrainians *1:* 117; *2:* 220
in SS auxiliary units *1:* 156, 158, 168, 168 (ill.), 190, 209
Umschlagplatz 1: 157, 169
"Uncle Mischa" *1:* 197
Underground, Jewish
in Poland *1:* 121, 132
in Polish ghettos *1:* 136
in Warsaw ghetto *1:* 150-51, 160
relations with *Judenrat 1:* 154
Underground, Polish *1:* 148, 152, 171
relations with Jews *1:* 149
Underground, Polish Communist *1:* 161
Unemployment *1:* 100
in Germany *1:* 43
Union of Soviet Socialist Republics
See Soviet Union
United States *1:* 13, 62
and denazification *2:* 354
and war crimes trials *2:* 353
antisemitism in *1:* 81
depression in *1:* 41
German declaration of war against *1:* 205
immigration to *1:* 80-81, 85
United States Coast Guard *1:* 84
United States Holocaust Memorial Museum *2:* 407 (ill.), 408
University of Delft *2:* 298
University of Leiden *2:* 298
University of Michigan *2:* 348
Uris, Leon *2:* 402
USSR
See Soviet Union

V

Vaadah 2: 345
Van der Lubbe, Martinus *1:* 52
Vatican
role of diplomats in Hungary *2:* 348
Vel' d' Hiv', Paris *2:* 324
Vélodrome d'Hiver *2:* 324
Vichy, France *2:* 317, 319-20, 323, 325-26, 328
anti-Jewish policies *2:* 320
antisemitic laws *2:* 320
knowledge of Holocaust *2:* 326
Vienna, Austria *1:* 27
Hitler entering *1:* 105 (ill.)
Vilna (Poland) ghetto *1:* 135, 173, 197
liquidation of *1:* 138
Visconti, Luchino *2:* 406
Visser, Lodewijk *2:* 299
Volk *1:* 25
Volksdeutche *1:* 118

W

Waffen-SS *1:* 121, 124, 186, 187 (ill.)
The Wall 2: 402
Wallenberg, Raoul *2:* 347-49, 348 (ill.), 408
Walter, Bruno *1:* 80
Wannsee Conference *1:* 204, 204 (ill.), 205, 208; *2:* 216, 370
War crimes. *2:* 355
War crimes tribunal
     in Bosnia *2:* 400
     in Rwanda *2:* 400
War Guilt Clause *1:* 21
Warsaw ghetto *1:* 146 (ill), 165 (ill.); *2:* 402
     creation of *1:* 145
     population of *1:* 147
Warsaw ghetto uprising *1:* 171, 174 (ill.), 175 (ill.); *2:* 369
     creation of *1:* 145
     German forces in *1:* 174
     Jewish deaths during *1:* 176
Warsaw, Poland *1:* 129, 135; *2:* 221, 228, 394, 395 (ill.)
     Jewish population of *1:* 143
     surrender of *1:* 107 (ill.), 115
Washington, D.C. *2:* 408
Weimar Republic *1:* 19, 24, 27, 30
Weiss, Peter *2:* 401
Weizäcker, Ernst von *2:* 385
Weizäcker, Richard von *2:* 384
Wels, Otto *1:* 57 (ill.)
Westerbork transit camp *2:* 295 (ill.), 301, 304 (ill.), 309
Western front *1:* 12
Westerweel, Joop *2:* 305
West Germany *2:* 364
     banning of Nazi Party and insignia *2:* 382
     war crimes trials in *2:* 369
White Russia
     See Belarussia
Wiesel, Elie *2:* 400, 401 (ill.)
Willenberg, Samuel *2:* 236-37
World Jewish Congress *2:* 394
World War I *1:* 13 (ill.), 16, 30, 67; *2:* 316
     and German treatment of Russian Jews *1:* 191
     and Hungary *2:* 338
Hitler's service in *1:* 27
Jewish veterans of German army in *1:* 207
     military cemetery *1:* 15 (ill.)
World War II
     countries captured by Germany during *1:* 179 (ill.)
     early German victories *1:* 177
Soviet counter-offensives *1:* 210

Y

Yad Vashem *2:* 390, 407-08
Yellow star
     See Star of David
Yevtushenko, Yevgeny *1:* 199

Yiddish *1:* 2, 192; *2:* 313, 394
Yom Kippur *1:* 122
The Young Lions 2: 406
Youth groups
    in Warsaw ghetto *1:* 151, 161
Yugoslavia *2:* 400
    German invasion of *2:* 341
    Hungarian seizure of territory from *2:* 341
    massacres by Hungarians in *2:* 342

Z

Zionism *1:* 84; *2:* 387
Zionists *1:* 151 (ill.), 163; *2:* 375
    and the Gestapo *1:* 87
    in Warsaw ghetto *1:* 150
ZOB *1:* 161-63, 167, 170, 176; *2:* 402
    first gun battle with Germans *1:* 169
    formation of *1:* 161
    organization of *1:* 161
    weapons of *1:* 171
Zyklon B *2:* 246, 248, 254 (ill.), 263
ZZW *1:* 163, 171